G.I.

THE AMERICAN SOLDIER IN WORLD WAR II

BY LEE KENNETT

WARNER BOOKS

A Warner Communications Company

Grateful acknowledgment is made for permission to quote from or reproduce the following material: letters written by Sanford Africk, from *Jewish Youth at War: Letters from American Soldiers*, (New York, 1945), by permission of Shirley H. Hirschel; lines from "So Sorry," by Corporal John Alexander, from *Reveille: War Poems by Members of our Armed Forces*, selected by Daniel Henderson, John Kiernan, and Grantland Rice, (New York, 1943), by permission of Oak Tree Publications, Inc.; John J. Roche, "First Squad, First Platoon," by permission of John J. Roche; postcard written by Frank P. Dunlap, by permission of Frank P. Dunlap.

WARNER BOOKS EDITION

Copyright © 1987 by Lee Kennett

This Warner Books Edition is published by arrangement with Charles Scribner's Sons, New York.

Cover illustration by Peter Caras

Warner Books, Inc.
666 Fifth Avenue
New York, N.Y. 10103

A Warner Communications Company

Printed in the United States of America

First Warner Books Printing: January, 1989

10 9 8 7 6 5 4 3 2

For Allison

Contents

Preface   ix

1 The Draft   3

2 Greetings . . .   24

3 The World of the Training Camps   42

4 The View from the Barracks   66

5 The Compleat Soldier   91

6 Aboard and Abroad   110

7 The Challenge of Combat   127

8 The Variables of Battle   149

9 Their Luck Ran Out   172

10 The Liberators   191

11 The Conquerors   211

12 Reunion   228

Notes   243

Bibliography   251

Index   257

Preface

THIS BOOK is the story of a collective experience. It recounts an episode in the lives of several million American men whom fate—and its agent, the Selective Service System—called forth to fight in the greatest war in modern times. For many, answering that call took them on the most extraordinary adventure of their lives, and I have tried to recapture something of that adventure.

For each man who served, the adventure was different; in a sense there were as many versions of World War II as there were G.I.s. What is offered here is a distillation of sorts, and as such it cannot always correspond to what the individual G.I. saw or felt forty years ago or remembers today. Then there is another caveat: The experience related here is purely vicarious, for my military service was in a later war and not in the U.S. Army. But then it is the task of the historian to write about events he never witnessed and men he never met, and while the hazards of such work are obvious, I believe that I have captured the essence of the G.I. story.

Much of the story I drew from the men themselves, from reminiscences they shared, from their letters and memoirs, and even from their responses to the many opinion surveys the Army conducted during the war. I have tried to fill out the story of the G.I.

with testimony from those who led him, from those who opposed him in battle or fought beside him as allies, and from those who knew him as liberator or conqueror. Finally, I have reviewed the considerable literature on the American soldier from the pens of historians who have preceded me.

Long before I had assembled the elements of my story, I knew it was one that I wanted to tell not to other historians, but to people who read history simply because they find it pleasurable and enlightening. Walter Prescott Webb said that writing destined for such a readership should be "unfootnoted and interesting." The most casual glance at the pages that follow will show that this work meets the first of Webb's criteria (and I have done what I could to meet the second). Many of the sources are identified in the text, but where it seemed appropriate I have indicated the source for quotations by means of end notes keyed to page numbers. Finally, I have added a select bibliography containing books cited in the text and others that proved especially useful to me.

Many people helped me in the course of my work, including first of all the considerable number of ex-servicemen whom I have interviewed or simply talked with over the past few years. I also owe a debt to many of my students who over the past three years conducted interviews with World War II veterans as part of their class assignment and at the same time helped their professor strengthen his grasp of his subject. Then there were people at various institutions who gave very generously of their time and expertise: at the National Archives, John Taylor, Tim Nenninger, and Will Mahoney; at the Army's Military History Institute at Carlisle Barracks, Pennsylvania, David Keough, John Slonaker, Richard Sommers, and Dennis Vetock; at the George C. Marshall Research Library, Archivist John Jacob and Larry Bland, editor of *The Papers of George Catlett Marshall*; at the Army's Command and General Staff College, Fort Leavenworth, Kansas, Colonel Louis D. F. Frasché, who heads the Combat Studies Institute, and Dr. Roger Spiller of the Institute's staff; at the American Battle Monuments Commission, Colonel William E. Ryan, Jr.; at the MacArthur Memorial, Archivist Edward J. Boone, Jr.; and at the North Carolina State Archives, Archivist Suellen Hoy. In

Paris, Chantal Tourtier-Bonazzi of the Archives Nationales was extremely helpful; and in Freiburg, I was grateful for the help of Horst Boog, Wissenschaftlicher Direktor of the Militärgeschichtliches Forschungsamt, and of Bruen Meyer, archivist at the Bundesarchiv-Militärarchiv. I also used with profit the resources of a number of other archives and libraries, including the libraries of Duke University, the University of Virginia, and the University of Georgia; the Bibliothèque Nationale in Paris; the archival and library holdings of the Service Historique de l'Armée, in Vincennes; the British Library; and the Public Record Office, Kew. For the illustrations I am indebted to the Department of Defense Still Media Records Center and to Virginia Horrell of the Center's staff.

I consulted a number of fellow historians in the course of my work, always with benefit. Especially helpful were Martin Blumenson, Georges Clause, Harold Deutsch, Edward Drea, Colonel John Elting, Dale Floyd, Jean-Pierre Husson, Jay Luvaas, Klaus-Jürgen Müller, Claude Sturgill, and Major Dean Williams. Equally helpful were a number of people who at various times supplied me with information or assisted me in other ways, among them William R. "Buck" Johnson, Everett Lee, John J. Roche, Charles Sylvester, Richard Unda, Major General Carl D. Wallace, and Hosea Williams. I owe a special word of thanks to three former G.I.s who read the text and gave me the benefit of their insights: Melvin Herndon, Phil Pollock, and Harold Leinbaugh. Kathy Coley and Donna Marshall prepared the typescript with competence and unfailing good humor. Finally, Laurie Schieffelin, my editor at Scribners, gave me the benefit of her good judgment and her keen sense of style.

G.I.

THE AMERICAN SOLDIER IN WORLD WAR II

⋆ 1 ⋆

The Draft

IT WAS one of the most tumultuous sessions of Congress in living memory. The late-summer heat of Washington helped to make tempers short, and the calamitous news from abroad contributed to the mood of crisis, but it was the Burke-Wadsworth bill that turned the halls of Congress into a battleground. That it aroused strong passions is not surprising: It called for peacetime military conscription, something unprecedented in the nation's history. The bill went into the congressional hoppers in the third week of June 1940, the same week that France collapsed; committee hearings went on while the Luftwaffe and the Royal Air Force met in the opening skirmishes of the Battle of Britain. The proposal came before the Senate at the end of August, and the House took it up in the first days of September, just as the German bomber offensive against England intensified; a partisan of the Burke-Wadsworth bill recalled: "Every time they bombed London we gained a vote or two in the House or Senate."

Even so, the partisans of the nation's first peacetime draft did not have an easy time of it. While Claude Pepper of Florida championed the bill in the Senate, a group of women calling themselves the Congress of American Mothers hanged him in effigy on the Capitol grounds. Six women wearing widow's veils took up silent vigil in the Senate gallery, then moved to the House when the debate shifted there. On September 3 a member of the Peace Mobilization Society was dragged from the House gallery shouting "American conscription is American fascism." On September 5 the agitation in the gallery was overshadowed by the spectacle on the floor of the House, where two representatives engaged in a fistfight, the most violent episode the aged Doorkeeper could remember in fifty years of service; outside, a thousand demonstrators sang "Ain't Gonna Study War No More." After the measure passed both houses in final form, the protesters continued their efforts in front of the White House, but on September 16, President Roosevelt signed Burke-Wadsworth into law as the Selective Training and Service Act of 1940.

So it was that Selective Service—"the draft"—became an element in the nation's life and ultimately the determining element in the lives of countless Americans. By the end of the war Selective Service had held the names, and in a sense the fate, of some fifty million American males between the ages of eighteen and sixty-four. The system probed the fitness of over twenty million, and fed eleven million into the armed services, an operation that has been described as the largest personnel inventory in the nation's history. The great mass of men mobilized went into the United States Army. When the Army reached its peak strength of 8,300,000 in 1945, over seven million of that number had been supplied through Selective Service. The G.I. Army was an amalgam of sorts, made by adding the selectees to the Regulars—the career Army, which numbered 137,000 in 1939—and the National Guard and Reserves. The Regulars and the Guardsmen contributed an invaluable knowhow, especially in the first year or two; but the draftee was the basic metal in the alloy, the one that determined its characteristics and above all its temper.

But none of this could be foreseen in 1940. In fact, despite its novelty and the sound and fury that had attended its birth, the draft had only a minimal effect at first. The War Department, which had been studying conscription schemes for years, had hoped for a system that would give it the cream of the nation's young manhood—physically and mentally sound specimens in their late teens and early twenties—and let it keep them long enough to teach them the soldier's trade. But political leaders did not want to provoke American mothers by taking their male offspring while they were legally still minors, nor did they feel they could keep young men under the colors very long in a nation that was, after all, at peace. So Congress limited the term of service to one year and authorized the Army to take a maximum of 900,000 men from those aged twenty-one to thirty-five; this would only be a modest spoonful, dipped from a manpower pool estimated at some seventeen million.

By the end of 1940 "the draft" had entered the nation's everyday vocabulary—much to the chagrin of the newly created Selective Service System, which disliked the term and carefully avoided using it (Selective Service officials claimed it had been imposed by newspapers because it was easier to fit into their headlines than Selective Service). And the draft entered America's folklore as well, with a connotation more humorous than sinister. A new comic strip, *Draftie*, appeared to chronicle the military adventures of its hero, and a Detroit dance instructor introduced an energetic step called the Draftaway, in which the dance partners become airborne simultaneously; and for weeks people told the story of the young couple who named their firstborn Weatherstrip because he kept his father out of the draft.

Yet there was some concern over how the nation's young men would take to the new military obligation. That summer, poet and Librarian of Congress Archibald MacLeish told an audience that America's youth was morally unprepared for military service. Too much reading of Hemingway, Dos Passos, and other novelists had "immunized" them to moral or ethical appeals. Writing in *Harper's Magazine*, Mortimer J. Adler warned: "Whether they go to war or not, irreparable harm has been done to the young men of this generation"; the culprits in this case being cynical college professors. Fortunately, it was possible in 1940 to probe the feelings of those young men directly through the medium of the poll. George Gallup's Institute of Public Opinion had been carrying out its surveys since 1935 and was still perfecting its techniques. It had never done opinion sampling among those under twenty-one, but when the draft issue surfaced and the *Reader's Digest* suggested a poll of the young, Gallup's organization undertook the job. It polled Americans between the ages of sixteen and twenty-four, with some questions directed at both sexes, others asked only of males. *Reader's Digest* published the results in its October 1940 issue, and they probably afford us our best clue to the attitudes of the young men who would fight World War II.

Despite Dos Passos and a decade of depression, the findings were heartening: "American youth is tough-fibered, loyal and hopeful, the young people believe this is a good country, worth working and fighting for. They have faith in the future. They are not radical—in fact they are surprisingly conservative in their views." The pollsters asked boys and young men if they objected personally to a year of military service, and 76 percent said they did not. Many added, "If I'm likely to fight, I'd rather know how." The unemployed had slightly less objection than those who were working or in college; schooled by the Great Depression, the men in the latter groups hoped to cling to an occupational niche or to finish carving one for themselves. The fundamental acceptance of compulsory military service by this "slice" of the nation's manhood (something over ten million) closely approximated its acceptance by the general population, which Gallup's poll sounded several times on the issue.

The *Reader's Digest* article appeared in time to reassure Selective Service officials, who were preparing the first step—a nationwide registration set for October 16. The government was anxious for the registration to be as complete as possible. President Roosevelt issued a proclamation for the occasion, and so did state governors. Radio and press joined in the publicity campaign, and even bars and nightclubs put up good-humored reminders about "R-Day." So intense was the buildup that one registrant recalled: "It had me feeling like I was going into the Army." Here and there, ill-informed young men did think just that—a man who showed up to register in Davidson County, Tennessee, brought along his rifle.

To the relief of Selective Service officials, the registration was massive and smoothly executed. Though there had been some concern over calls for noncompliance by pacifist organizations, only a handful of young men refused to register as a testament of their beliefs, the most publicized of them being eight students at Union Theological Seminary. The only other identifiable groups to boycott the registration were certain Indian tribes. The Seminoles withdrew into the Everglades, and a spokesman explained that they were still technically at war with the United States. A small faction among the Hopis also failed to appear. An Indian Bureau official reported that their failure had nothing to do with pacifism but was merely a refusal to obey any law of the government of the United States. These episodes could not detract from the fundamental success of the operation. There would be five more registrations into 1942, when the process became a continuous one as American males reached their eighteenth birthdays. But the registration of October 16, 1940, was the important one. By that evening Selective Service had the names and addresses of sixteen million men, and it would soon have much more information on them when they filled out its eight-page questionnaire (DDS Form 40). And by law each registrant now carried in his pocket DDS Form 2, his registration card.

The only real difficulty in registration was presented by the questionnaire. The generation of 1940 was not used to filling out complicated forms (only three Americans out of a hundred filed federal income tax returns). A fair proportion of young men had to get help with DDS Form 40; even so, they had difficulty supplying Selective Service with the information it needed, both in the initial registration and subsequently. Asked if he had ever been an inmate in an institution, a registrant would scrupulously report his hospitalization for an appendectomy; on occasion he would confess to a crime he had not committed:

Have you ever been convicted of treason? Yes.
Give particulars: Automobile accident.

The penalties for violating the Selective Service Act were severe —up to five years' imprisonment and a ten-thousand-dollar fine— and the government set out to enforce the act scrupulously. In November the Union Theological Seminary students were sentenced to a year in federal prison. (According to a nationwide poll, the public approved of the convictions; a quarter of those polled did not think the sentence was severe enough.) The following April, when professional baseball player "Cy" Moore punched a Selective Service official during an argument over his draft status, he was immediately bound over on federal charges. In the course of the war a half-million violations of the Selective Service Act were turned over to the Federal Bureau of Investigation, but the immense majority of those cases involved registrants who simply neglected to keep Selective Service informed of their whereabouts, and did not result in prosecution. Open, intentional resistance was exceedingly rare. Never at any time were there more than ten thousand persons imprisoned for refusing military service, less than 0.04 percent of all registrants.

The first selectees were designated for induction into the Army in November 1940 (the Navy, Marines, and Coast Guard preferred to recruit, supplying all their manpower needs by that means until the end of 1942). The new soldiers were for the most part healthy, unattached, often unemployed young men, and many were not disturbed at the prospect of military service. Journalists had begun praising the "New Army," ultramodern and mechanized, a place where soldier-technicians did interesting things with sophisticated weapons and machines. One panegyrist wrote: "Nowhere in the world will you find less bloodthirstiness than you will in the Army. All that tough stuff belongs in the movies and in novels. If you enter into the thing in the right spirit, it can be lots of fun."

Some young men had acted even before the Burke-Wadsworth bill became law. Cartoonist Bill Mauldin joined the National Guard that summer, impressed by the arguments of a buddy: "When we get into a mess there'll be a draft and they'll catch you anyway. In the National Guard you'll be among friends, you'll stay out of the infantry, and you'll solve your civilian unemployment problem." Other young men simply asked their local draft boards to send them, either to "get it over with" or to try the challenge of twelve months in uniform. In some states these volunteers were numerous enough to fill the first month's quotas. Others waited. "My feelings were mixed," one young man remembered. "In many ways I would hate giving up my own life, and yet the idea intrigued me. I wanted it and I didn't want it, and all the time I knew that it didn't matter what I wanted because the whole thing had been decided for me. For the first time in my adult life I had no choice to make."

At first the monthly draft calls were small, taking an average of ten men from each of the 6,500 local Selective Service Boards— draft boards in the universal parlance—and each board had a pool of something over three thousand registrants. Through a complicated lottery system pioneered in World War I, the men were called as their numbers came up. The nationwide call for December 1941 was for only twenty thousand; the Army had almost reached its quota of nine hundred thousand. Then came Pearl Harbor. Almost overnight the Selective Service System became a looming presence. General Lewis B. Hershey, who was to preside over the system for three decades, emerged as a familiar figure; colorful and outspoken, he was much quoted in the press.

With the coming of war, military manpower needs shot up astronomically. Those already in uniform were now to be retained for the duration of the war plus six months, and to join them came a flood of selectees; the December 1942 call was for nearly half a million. From 1942 onward a man's chances of being drafted no longer hinged on his number so much as they did on whether he could be spared from civilian life and whether or not he met the induction standards of the armed forces. (After 1942 the Navy and Marines also drew their men from Selective Service.) While the services had the final say in whom they took, Selective Service chose the young men from the pool of registrants and sent them for induction. The awesome power of deciding who went to war and who stayed home resided essentially in the local draft boards. Selectees could appeal board actions to higher boards, or even to the President, but in three cases out of four the decision of the local board was confirmed.

The boards were modeled on similar institutions used with success in the First World War. The board members, usually five in number, tended to be locally prominent, most often business and professional men in their forties and fifties. Veterans were often appointed, since they would not be asking young men to do anything they had not done themselves (World War I hero Sergeant Alvin York was the chairman of the local board in Fentress County, Tennessee). Board members were federal officials with letters of appointment from the President, but they served without pay. While they were well supplied with guidelines and instructions from the system's national headquarters, their decisions were emphatically their own. In a very real sense the fate of a young man of draft age was in the hands of his neighbors, men who often knew him or at least knew members of his family. And as the boards determined who should go, and when, they also determined in considerable degree the composition of the wartime Army.

The system had one disadvantage in that the government could not reach into the pool and pick up individuals it might have special need of. At one point the Pentagon had a list of persons it wanted put in uniform so it could use them as cryptanalysts. Though General Hershey's relations with the Army were close and cordial, he flatly refused to intervene with local boards. Nor was the Army more successful in preventing certain men from being drafted, notably the young physicists it had working as civilians on its super-secret Manhattan Project. Though the state Selective Service director involved was treated to a tour of a physics lab, the boards sent the young men off for induction just the same.

The government staunchly defended the system from first to last, believing a man would accept service more readily if the selection were made in his community. However, the arrangement also assured that most of the anger and resentment the draft created was not directed at Washington, but remained within the community. As General Hershey put it, the local boards had to "do the unpleasant thing." Service on a draft board often meant the loss of friendships and also of business; in small, inbred localities the bitterness could linger a long time. Boards were sometimes openly accused of favoritism and quite frequently suspected of it —though they were rarely found guilty of it. They could not defend their actions in individual cases because a selectee's dossier was confidential. A board member recalled with considerable bitterness: "We had a fellow turned down as a psychopath and he wouldn't tell anyone why he was turned down. He and his father spread the word around that if you had a few dollars and knew the right people, it was easy to stay out." When the war intensified and the communities began to suffer casualties, the boards did not have an easy time of it. General Hershey remembered: "There was a lot of boards telling me it was certainly tough last week, we had three boys, they found out they had been killed." Gallup Polls indicated that the vast majority of the population felt the draft boards did a good job. Today most veterans say the same thing, but here there has been a mellowing of attitudes. A poll in the Ninth Division at the end of 1941 revealed half the selectees felt their boards had selected the wrong man.

The boards were constituted with little concern for what is today called minority representation. Virtually no blacks served on southern boards despite discreet suggestions from Washington. A postwar report on Selective Service in South Carolina acknowledged: "We did not put any Negroes on the Local Boards or Appeal Boards, the reason for which was explained to their satisfaction." Yet blacks enjoyed a special protection under the Selective Service Act: Their proportion of each month's call could not exceed their percentage of the population—10.6 percent. In fact, the percentage of blacks in the Army never reached 10.6 percent, chiefly because Army leadership held to the traditional notion that they were of limited usefulness, especially in combat. The Army took only sparingly of the manpower Selective Service made available in its periodic "black calls."

Among other ethnic groups there were occasional complaints that they were being made to carry more than their share. The government picked up rumblings of discontent among Polish-Americans in the Chicago area, though the lists of draft board members contained many Polish names. The Cherokee Indians of

North Carolina petitioned for a draft board of their own. A historian of the Mexican-American contribution to the war wrote that in the Southwest "the boards were loaded with Spanish names in their files, and very few were ever exempted, reclassified or found too essential to be drafted." In sum, the system was one in which "mainstream" America saw to it that ethnic America assumed its share of the burden and in some instances what seemed distinctly more than its share. And local boards did not overlook what might be called Marginal America: The community's freeloaders and troublemakers, the youths who were "a bit wild," could easily be spared, and the rigor and discipline of military life might straighten them out. This view was also shared by judges and local law enforcement officials. It was not shared by the Army, as we will see.

Selective Service regulations made specific allowance for conscientious objectors, and there were provisions for such persons to take noncombat roles in the service or undertake some sort of alternative work. But a young man who presented himself as a conscientious objector was generally not well viewed by his local board. In Illinois, where 70 percent of board members were veterans, the boards were described as "inwardly resentful" of the conscientious objector's unwillingness to defend his country. When a member of a board in the Bronx was asked if his board had had any persons ask for the status of conscientious objector, he answered, "We've had some, but we've always talked them out of it." Local boards were particularly hostile to Jehovah's Witnesses, refusing to recognize that each Witness was a minister in his faith and entitled to deferment as such. Over their protests the boards sent them for induction, where they refused to take the inductee's oath. Of the fourteen thousand persons imprisoned for resisting the draft in the course of the war, four thousand were Jehovah's Witnesses.

Selective Service regulations also provided deferment for dependency—the III classification—and here local boards were very generous in granting deferment, at least in the first part of the war. The boards respected marriage and family, and their inclination was to send the bachelors and the unattached first. But there were subtle distinctions in family status, for the boards felt that a young man who married after Selective Service was voted might well have taken a wife just to escape the draft (marriage rates did in fact go up in the fall of 1940). In such cases boards were less inclined to grant deferments, but even within the recently married group there could be fine nuances. A New York board member explained that when the board knew a recently married registrant had been "keeping company" with his wife for a considerable time, it was more inclined to grant a deferment. Asked what a considerable time would be, he replied "at least a year."

The state of a man's marriage could be of considerable interest to his board. In North Carolina, the State Director's office suggested local board members keep several questions in mind when classifying or reviewing married registrants: "What is the attitude of the registrant in regard to his family? Is the registrant a wastrel, or is he inclined to save his money with the idea of establishing a home? Are they pooling their incomes and saving the surplus, or does each go his or her separate way?" Should the board learn that a man had quit his job and was living on his wife's earnings, it would reclassify him I-A—the final way station on the road to induction—and send him off with the next month's quota. General Hershey explained their reasoning: "They think she [the wife] and society, and perhaps even the man, would be better off to put him to work, and they do."

Fatherhood enhanced a man's chances for deferment even more, but here again there were distinctions. The "Pre–Pearl Harbor Father" was a category apart. Children conceived after that fateful date still counted, but not as much. (Boards sometimes called in medical help to confirm pregnancy, establish dates of conception, or in some cases rule on paternity.) The boards also tended to be suspicious of adoptions arranged after the war started.

It is clear, then, that a local board's action frequently rested on rather intimate knowledge of a registrant's activities and personal life, knowledge board members often possessed simply because they lived in the same community. But the boards also received a wide variety of confidences and revelations, often from correspondents who signed themselves "True American" or "Anonymous Citizen." Some of this correspondence found its way to national headquarters, where it was filed under the ironic label "Fan Mail." A twelve-foot stack of this fan mail has been preserved in the National Archives, and it makes enthralling reading: A woman writes to draw the draft board's attention to her shiftless son-in-law, who would probably benefit from military discipline; a man in Dallas sends in the names and addresses of "three cowardly cousins"; a correspondent in Brooklyn wonders if Selective Service has overlooked a certain pair of brothers, adding, "This particular case is arousing plenty of curiousity, suspision to the people living on 59 Street." There is a request scrawled on ruled paper from a nickel tablet: "Please locate Enoch Calhoun and put him in the service. He has diserted his family and took another woman with him."

The other aspect of a man's life that interested his draft board was what he did for a living. From 1943 on the most important deferment category was Class II, reserved for those whose civilian work was essential to the community or to the war effort. A physician or dentist could usually count on deferment if there was a need for his services in the community, though occasionally black doctors and dentists claimed that white draft boards were less understanding in their cases. Professional associations were eager to share with draft boards their own view of priorities. The American Medical Association—"the damn doctors," in General Hershey's language—urged deferment or direct commission for their members, but it also wanted the boards to give "less consideration" to osteopaths, chiropractors, and chiropodists. Selective Service officials complained that the American Chemical Society and the Manufacturing Chemists' Association were working for "a virtual blanket deferment of chemists and chemical engineers and for their classification by a government agency other than the System."

Workers in defense plants could usually count on deferments from the draft, though many under twenty-six were reclassified I-A late in the war. Organized labor had little leverage with the system, for it rarely had a representative on a local board. The boards took a dim view of strikes, particularly in defense plants. The draft could be used for strikebreaking, and when the workers at North American Aviation walked off the job in the summer of 1941, the government urged the reclassification of the strikers. The boards scarcely needed encouragement; the Illinois Selective Service Director reported that he had been telling his local boards to draft strikers for "months."

By general acknowledgment, the group most widely deferred was farmers and farm laborers. A Selective Service study completed in 1942 showed that while men in agriculture made up 23 percent of the country's male work force, they were only 15 percent of those inducted. By 1944 young farm laborers were the only large reservoir of manpower the Army had not tapped. But should a farmhand quit work and drift about, his board would soon have him on his way to an induction station.

If the man working in agriculture was among the last to go, the man who made his living as an actor was among the first. Local boards seem to have felt this was the most expendable of professions; according to the 1940 census there were 6,931 working actors in the country, and by mid-1942 3,503 of them were in the U.S. Army—a far higher proportion than for any other profession. Among others drafted early and massively were professional athletes. A surprising number of them had various disabilities. People would not believe that a man might be an excellent baseball or football player, yet have a physical defect that barred him from service, even though newspapers dwelt extensively on Joe DiMaggio's eyesight and Hank Greenberg's flat feet. Selective Service received pictures of athletes clipped from those same papers, along with the angry question: "Why isn't this man in uniform?" Periodically, revelations would stoke the public's anger, as when the players on a championship football team proved to be mostly IV-F (unfit for military service). Ultimately the Army gave in: "The War Department adopted a policy waiving defects that would not be aggravated by military service, thus taking the boxer out of the ring and the ball player off the diamond, regardless of his potential value to the service, to satisfy public opinion."

There was popular interest, and to a degree public concern, regarding the draft status of famous musicians and Hollywood stars. Actor Jimmy Stewart won public approval when he fattened himself to meet Army weight requirements; fellow actor Lew Ayres did not when he chose the path of the conscientious objector. Benny Goodman's fans understood when they learned that he had been classified IV-F because a portion of his spine was missing. Frank Sinatra also received a deferment on medical grounds, a decision that triggered a stern memo from Army Chief of Staff George C. Marshall:

> . . . I noticed that the crooner Sinatra has been deferred because of a punctured ear drum.
>
> The ears are vital to a musician, vocal or instrumental, therefore if we judge by the salaries paid, Sinatra's ears are reasonably effective.
>
> Please have this looked into right away. If an Army doctor deferred him I want to know just why.

When the first contingents of draftees showed up at Army induction stations in 1940 and 1941, Army doctors rejected large numbers of them; the rejection rates in some states reached 30 percent. Since local boards had already done a preliminary medical screening, they and the physicians who worked with them came in for considerable criticism; but beyond that there was a flurry of public concern over the health of the younger generation. In fact, the health of American youth was reasonably good, and if there was a problem it lay with the Army's standards for induction. The issue of physical standards was one of several differences in viewpoint that developed between the Army and the local draft boards; in each case the public and its representatives in Washington sided with the boards, and the Army gave way.

The Army was proud of the physical standards it set at the beginning of the draft. A month before Pearl Harbor an Army doctor boasted: "A registrant who qualifies today and is inducted into the Army can feel distinctly honored." In 1940 men were rejected because they were overweight or underweight. "Edentulous individuals" were turned away because they did not have all the teeth the Army required; correctable defects of teeth and eyes were the basis for a third of the early rejections. The Army, accustomed to picking and choosing among the many potential recruits offered by Depression America, wanted men without a physical blemish; Selective Service was sending it men chosen primarily because they could be spared from civilian life. And even if the local draft boards had allotted manpower on the basis of physical condition, they could not have supplied enough flawless draftees for the massive armed forces the nation would eventually muster. The solution was obvious. As early as 1941 physical standards began to drop. By February 1942 the Army was taking men who had "sufficient teeth (natural or artificial) to subsist on the Army ration." Customarily the Army had provided little dental care; in 1939 it had only 250 dentists. By 1945 it had 25,000, and they had pulled 15,000,000 teeth and fitted 2,500,000 dentures.

As vision standards were relaxed the Medical Department had to develop an optometry service. By 1945 it had issued 2,250,000 pairs of glasses, and one soldier in five was wearing them. Ultimately the service took men with only one eye, and when it did so it found itself faced with an unusual problem: a shortage of glass eyes, most of which came from abroad. It was the Army's medical researchers who developed the acrylic artificial eye. It was much the same story with other defects: In 1940 a hernia usually meant rejection of a selectee; at one point later in the war, ten thousand men were in Army hospitals for hernia repair. By 1944 the Army could tell its soldiers, "Probably never in civilian life will you find greater care given your physical condition than in the service." Just supplying the dental needs of the G.I. has been called "the most momentous job in the history of dentistry." The overall effort at physical rehabilitation was immense, though it has remained little known to this day.

By 1942 the Army's standards were under attack on another front: The public was increasingly unhappy because the system permitted those with venereal disease to avoid service while those without it were compelled to serve. The Army took a very dim view of the "social diseases" and with strong support from the Surgeon General had virtually eradicated them among the Regulars; but here, too, it had to give ground. In October 1942 it began accepting selectees with uncomplicated gonorrhea, and by the end of the year it was taking some syphilitics as well. By war's end it had taken in and treated two hundred thousand men suffering from venereal disease; fortunately for the Army's Medical Department, recently developed sulfa compounds greatly simplified the task.

The Army's educational standards at the outset seem quite modest today: a fourth-grade education and the ability to use the English language. But draft boards read these requirements differently. Why should illiterates stay at home while those who had taken the trouble to educate themselves go off to war? Then, too, the draft boards and the communities they represented were insistent that the nation's ethnic minorities contribute to the quota even if their knowledge of English was limited or nonexistent (at least one draft board in Chicago communicated with its registrants in Chinese). By the summer of 1942 Selective Service's Washington headquarters reported that local boards were "raising hell at healthy young men being rejected because of illiteracy." They ultimately had their way, with the Army absorbing eight hundred thousand illiterates, aliens, and hyphenated Americans, cycling them through Special Training Units where they learned to read and write the language of the country whose uniform they wore. They packed into hastily improvised classrooms, where they struggled through primers especially written for them: *Meet Private Pete*, and *Private Pete Eats His Dinner*.

Almost from the beginning, the draft boards collided with the War Department over its policy of refusing any man who had a felony conviction in his past. As early as January 1941, the draft board in Lebanon, Tennessee, complained that it had a registrant ready and willing to be drafted but barred because he had been in the state prison for "lifting a chicken or two"—even though he had later received a pardon from the governor. Two months later the board in Franklin County, Virginia, reported it had twenty-five able-bodied registrants it had been obliged to classify IV-F because they had been convicted of making moonshine whiskey. The board pointed out that Franklin County had been called the wettest county in the country; since whiskey making was one of its principal occupations, the county would be hard put to fill its quotas. And to many the War Department policy seemed one of discrimination against the law abiding. The chairman of a local draft board reported: "The people living in our community are more or less incensed with the fact that the hardened criminal and the social misfit is allowed to stay at home and permitted to hold any job which he may obtain." Members of Congress echoed this theme. A Pennsylvania congressman estimated that there were "at least 500,000 hoboes—bums—wife beaters—drunks—and dissipaters of all kinds who should be put into uniform."

The outcome was inevitable. In July 1941 the Army indicated it would accept convicted felons in special "meritorious" cases; gradually, draft boards lost sight of the "meritorious" designation, classifying large numbers of ex-felons as I-A. By 1944 Special Panel Boards of the Selective Service System were visiting prisons and arranging paroles for inmates who agreed to enter the service. Ultimately, over a hundred thousand felons wore the Army uniform, and the vast majority of them wore it with honor.

But as the war proceeded many senior officers became alarmed at the lowering of barriers and other transformations in the service to which they had dedicated their lives. War Department officials were alarmed that the Army was getting more than its share of the less desirable manpower, and they resented the favored status the Navy enjoyed in this regard, as it did in so many others. The War Department saw itself as the underdog in interservice rivalry, since President Roosevelt had once served as Assistant Secretary of the Navy and retained a very warm regard for the sea service. Secretary of War Henry Stimson, who was involved in most of the interservice battles, frequently confided to his diary his impatience with the President's pet service and its spoiled-child behavior.

For a year after Pearl Harbor the Navy continued to recruit its needs (the Army recruited, too, but with less success; to the generation of 1940 it did not have the Navy's allure). The Navy recruiting program was an aggressive one, so much so that Army officers claimed it was not unusual for Navy recruiting officers to approach inductees at stations who were waiting to be processed. The Navy's slogan—"Choose While You Can"—had its effect. In one month shortly after Pearl Harbor thirty-five thousand men scheduled for induction chose the sea service. The Navy did not take all those who volunteered, nor did it want to; rather, it wanted to skim off the best. And even after general recruiting was stopped at the end of 1942, through a fluke the Navy continued to enjoy the right of signing up seventeen-year-old volunteers, whom it placed in the Reserves for activation later. This was in essence another skimming operation, enabling the Navy to stake prior claim on the most promising men in the coveted eighteen-to-twenty age group, which both services identified as having the best health, morale, and resilience. Even though the Army could now draw eighteen-year-olds from Selective Service, General Hershey told Congress he would be lucky if he could get two out of three in that prime age group.

Even when the Navy began to take manpower from the Selective Service pool it got preferential treatment, arguing that the special nature of service at sea required greater selectivity in personnel. The Navy refused to take anyone who was shorter than five feet two or taller than six feet four. Since the Army's limits were five feet and six feet six, it received the outsize inductees. Color-blind men were not acceptable to the Navy, nor were those convicted of certain crimes, bigamy and "seduction" being among them. For much of the war the Navy successfully resisted taking its share of black manpower, and when Selective Service inducted twenty-one thousand Japanese-Americans late in the war, the Navy said it would take none of them.

The Army was no doubt still smarting from these things when a historian wrote in one of its postwar "Green Book" histories that the Navy and Marines had "the character of hand-picked organizations," which would lead the reader to the conclusion that the Army got the leavings. Selective Service was held largely responsible for this state of affairs. If the Army was not particularly happy with the men sent to it, the men themselves were not particularly happy, either—and everyone blamed the draft.

Actually, the Selective Service System was probably the most effective way to allocate manpower—and still be acceptable to the American people—that could have been devised. Despite its bias and its blunders, on the whole the system worked well; it would have worked even better had the armed services themselves not interfered with its operation. What made Selective Service superior was the fact that it was a "system," designed to allocate manpower on a rational and equitable basis. In this respect it was superior to voluntary enlistment. The machinist who left his lathe and the draftsman who abandoned his table in a defense plant and rushed off to enlist in the Marines did so from undeniably laudable motives, but quite possibly they could have contributed much more to the war effort by continuing their civilian trades—and only Selective Service could determine such things and place the men accordingly.

The Navy was instrumental in continuing voluntary enlistment for a full year after Pearl Harbor, for it was a device that served the Navy well. But, in fact, both services bypassed the Selective Service System in a variety of ways when it seemed to their advantage. Both the Navy and the Army Air Forces "reserved" prime personnel by signing them up in their air cadet programs, automatically rendering them "draftproof." Most importantly, they signed them up in excess of their ultimate needs. Since flight training took a year, and since both services liked to hold a six-months' backlog, any young man recruited into the program after 1943 would scarcely get into the war before it ended. The Army also removed thousands of young men from the draft pool with its ASTP (Army Special Training Program), which recruited students and then allowed them to pursue college studies in medicine, engineering, and other subjects useful to the Army. Like the air cadet programs, ASTP made sense up to a certain point. But that point was soon passed, in what Selective Service officials called "the childlike greed of each to secure the most capable personnel." The squirreling away of vital manpower contributed to problems on the fighting fronts: Toward the end of the war the Army ran desperately short of combat infantrymen and was obliged to dismantle the ASTP program. And there were problems at home as the draft cut deeper. A Selective Service official recalled: "I was in Northfield, Vt., and Durham, N.H., in September 1943, when fathers in their middle thirties were being inducted from their stores, garages, and other businesses. The presence of several hundred able-bodied students in uniform in that community created a situation difficult to describe."

Selective Service had some major flaws. It no doubt contributed to the Army's problem with overage soldiers. In 1944 the average age of the American soldier was nearly twenty-six, while that of the American sailor was twenty-three and that of the average Marine was twenty-two; by then the local boards, in their zeal to protect breadwinners and heads of families, had stripped their rolls of single men in their twenties and thirties and had sent off sizable numbers of arthritic bachelors in their forties. But the gravest failing of the system lay in its preoccupation with fatherhood. Until late 1943 this group had been largely shielded, but thereafter there was no one else left to send. Rather than draft fathers, the local boards failed to meet their quotas; in the last three months of 1943 they supplied only two thirds of the selectees asked for. In doing so they contributed indirectly to the military manpower crises that developed later.

The reluctance of the boards to draft fathers reflected faithfully the repugnance the public felt at the idea. A poll conducted in early 1944 revealed that the American people preferred drafting single women before fathers, and by a three-to-one majority. Congress wrestled with the problem and accepted the drafting of eighteen-year-olds late in 1942 in hopes of protecting family men. But in the end there was no other recourse. The local boards bit the bullet: In October 1943 fathers had figured for only 6 percent of the month's quota; by April 1944 they were over 50 percent.

The immense mass of manpower Selective Service supplied represented the upper two thirds of the nation's manhood in the draftable age group, selected by the most sophisticated means then available; the other third of the pool remained IV-F despite repeated siftings by local boards. As a group the selectees were physically sound, certainly when compared to men mobilized by other belligerents. Whatever else foreign populations would think of the G.I., they would be impressed by his physical appearance and his bloom of health. German army leaders consistently rated American troops as superior physical specimens. Intellectually, the World War II soldier had impressive credentials; the average G.I. had finished a year of high school, a far cry from the sixth-grade education of the doughboy of 1917. But the term "average G.I." must be used with caution, for it represents a midpoint between widely separated parameters: The soldier with a year of high school behind him might well rub shoulders with a Ph.D. in linguistics, and also with a semiliterate who could barely pick his way through *Meet Private Pete*. The G.I. Army was a juxtaposition of opposites, a blending of extremes. Extremes there were, and the soldier's weekly *Yank* loved to point them out. The biggest foot in the Army belonged to a private who wore a specially made shoe in size 18½EEEEEE. The heaviest man in the service weighed 407 pounds. The oldest sergeant was seventy-four, having enlisted in 1895; the youngest sergeant was fifteen—though he was discharged as soon as the Army learned his true age.

But the essential point is this: Despite the concerns voiced by the Army's personnel experts, the G.I. Army was neither dregs nor leavings. It was, to be sure, an ethnic and cultural potpourri—but then, so was the country. It had its share—and no doubt some of the Navy's share—of color-blind men, "edentulous individuals," seducers, and former moonshiners. But if the other services were to a degree "hand-picked" from the nation at large, then the Army was the nation itself, an authentic slice of American society with all its many layers. Given the amount of manpower mobilized, it was probably necessary that the Army be that way; given the principles for which the nation fought, it was also somehow appropriate.

★ 2 ★

Greetings...

For any young man who carried a Selective Service card in his pocket in the early forties, the daily arrival of the mail was an event of more than casual interest, for the local boards used the mails to communicate with registrants. And once a man had been classified I-A, sooner or later the postman would come, like an emissary of the fates, bearing the notice to report for induction, universally known as the "greetings" (the salutation on this form letter was "Greeting"). In the meantime, the young man curious to know what lay in store for him could find out from such books as Major John Kenderdine's *Your Year in the Army*, or *How To Get Along in the Army*, by "Old Sarge." These books struck a positive, reassuring note. There was also counsel—often unsolicited—from World War I veterans, who assured the prospective soldier he would never know anything as bad as the Argonne.

Ultimately, the postman brought the "greetings" that indicated the date and time the selectee should report to his local draft board, from which he would be transported to the induction station. (Southern draft boards sometimes ordered black inductees to report to the local police station, where they got an armed escort.) Since the induction process was to be completed in a single day, and the stations were sometimes at considerable distance, draft boards had the men report as early as four or five o'clock in the morning. They gathered outside board headquarters in the pre-dawn darkness, smoking and making acquaintance, often discovering that men unknown to them were close neighbors. Their trip to the induction station was generally not a one-way affair; all of the men would be returning that evening, but those found acceptable would already be in the Army, with a two-week furlough to wind up their personal affairs. (This was generally the procedure during the middle years of the war, the Army having learned that if it sent accepted selectees back home without swearing them in they often enlisted in the Navy.)

The Army's manual on operating induction stations stressed that since they were the new soldier's first contact with the service, "He should be impressed by the fact that he is joining an effective and businesslike organization," and the manual contained flowcharts to show how the processing should be done. In keeping with these instructions the physical examination, which was the chief operation, was conducted on an assembly line basis, with about twenty-five men passing through the line every hour. The inductees came in one end of the line and went through most of it naked, wearing identifying numbers around their necks or marked on the back of their hands; they came out the other end as accepted or rejected. It was the most comprehensive physical examination most inductees had ever had. They were impressed by the procedure, but they were also intimidated by it. Some were uncomfortable in their nakedness; many had difficulty urinating on demand into the specimen bottles handed them. Examining physicians recognized that rapid and irregular heartbeat was often the result of simple nervousness in selectees. A draftee from Oklahoma who was herded through induction in a vast and cheerless armory recorded: "There, for the first time, we met the Army. It was sobering."

In many contingents of draftees there were at least one or two men who had spent the previous night saying farewell to civilian life with friends and considerable drinking. They came to the induction station showing the effects, or at least the aftereffects. There were no stern words or raised eyebrows from the Army personnel who received them. Nor would drunkenness be regarded as a serious offense later, when the selectee was in uniform. A psychiatrist who worked with the military found that "the indulgence of the Army was particularly marked in the case of alcoholics, who were given repeated chances to reform, especially if they were pleasant fellows or performed well when sober."

An Army doctor attached to an induction station described the work as "stimulating." One encountered every conceivable type of congenital and acquired deformity. In older men it was possible to see the effects of child labor and prolonged malnutrition. The Army discovered curious regional variations in body types. "The highest percentage of muscularly superior and well developed types come from the New England states," one study found, "with the foreign born second and the Pacific and mountain states very high. The largest assortment of thin weak and plump weak types comes from South Atlantic and East South Central Districts." The Army kept monthly figures on rejection rates by states. The West and the Far West sent the highest proportion of healthy men, with the Dakotas often figuring among the top five. The southern states usually had the higher rejection rates—for whites as well as blacks.

The inductee of the Second World War proved on the average to be an inch taller and eight pounds heavier than the doughboy of 1917. There was less evidence of undernourishment, though the new soldier gained from six to nine pounds in the first few months in uniform. Dentists were in agreement that the teeth of inductees were in a deplorable state. Dental officers who had served in the previous war claimed dental health had declined, but they could not agree on why.

The doctors were trained to detect malingering. Selective Service frequently got tips about such things: An anonymous correspondent in Gainesville, Georgia, reported that "a lot of the boys are eating a lot asperns to upset their heart." When an unusual number of Florida inductees showed up with elevated blood pressure, doctors suspected they had been eating Octagon soap, but an investigation gave no conclusive results. Malingering was a less serious problem than one might think. An Army psychiatrist claimed, "The number who are likely to malinger are so few, their services so poor, that it is best to do without them." Another reported: "Many more are disturbed by being rejected than are upset by being accepted."

Examining physicians related that generally inductees seemed anxious to pass the examination, as though it were an affirmation of their manhood. This tendency was so strong that it produced "negative malingering," in which inductees tried to conceal or deny a disqualifying infirmity or condition. Epileptics often tried to hide their affliction: Where epilepsy was suspected, physicians were advised to look for scars on tongue and lips and other evidence of past seizures. And men with other chronic ailments tried to hide them, imagining that somehow the wholesome, spartan military life would help them. A selectee who was planning to plead a weak back found himself in line behind a man with a clubfoot. The physician examined the foot and told the man he was not fit for service, but the man would not accept the verdict. "He taps the doctor's shoulder and says, 'Watch how I walk.' He walks without a limp, but not with ease. He makes the doctor watch him run. He is in a stew of supplication." When the next man's turn came, he did not mention his back.

A selectee who passed the exam was ruled physically fit for "general service"; later, when he was sent to an arm or branch of the service, it was without reference to his physical suitability. A soldier of five feet weighing 105 pounds (the Army's weight minimum) might thus be assigned to the infantry, even though it would be hard for him to carry a heavy pack under field conditions (the infantrymen who struggled ashore in the North African landings of 1942 carried an aggregate of 132 pounds). The British, on the other hand, graded their manpower into a dozen categories.

The Germans did likewise, and even had special criteria for *Tropendienstfähigkeit,* a suitability for service in the tropics. After a brief and unsatisfactory experience with a "limited service" category, the U.S. Army adopted a "profile" or PULHES system modeled on the Canadian one, but it did not go into effect until 1944, when most of the manpower was already committed.

The man who failed to pass the induction tests went back home, no doubt in the grip of mixed emotions. In the early days of the draft, selectees had been instructed to settle all their affairs when they received the "greetings"; sometimes men gave up their jobs and said good-bye to their families, only to find themselves back home a few hours later with the news they had been rejected. Even later, when induction procedures were changed, rejected selectees did not enjoy the experience. They could be called up for reexamination, of course, for there were no permanent deferments, not even for the blind. Some of the draft boards regarded them as casualties of a sort.

In addition to the physical examination there was a screening session with a psychiatrist. This was supposed to give some preliminary indication of intelligence and also help weed out potential "neuropsychiatric" undesirables. This second goal was the one the War Department stressed. The First World War had revealed in a dramatic way the emotional strain to which men in combat were subjected. The number of doughboys who broke under that strain was so large that in the summer of 1918 General John J. Pershing cabled the War Department from France, urging that future draftees be screened to winnow out those who would be most susceptible to "shell shock." Nearly a hundred thousand such cases entered Army hospitals through 1919, and in caring for them after the war the Veterans Administration spent close to a billion dollars. In 1940 the War Department was anxious that the screening be done from the outset, and that it be done with care. Local draft boards could not be counted upon here, given their inclination to send off the community's expendables. In fact, General Hershey had to remind them in 1941 that "an individual not feeble-minded enough or not insane enough to require institutional care in civil life may still be too feeble-minded or too disordered in mind to make a good soldier." Thus the Army psychiatrist joined the staff of the induction center.

The press made much of the psychiatric screening and spoke of "inkblot" tests, but the examination usually took the form of a brief interview. The psychiatrists were told to look for neuropsychosis, or NP, a term that covered a wide range of emotional disturbances from phobias to excessive sweating. The examiner began by observing the selectee's coordination, at the same time looking for evidence of nail biting and other clues. Then he asked a series of questions, probing further into any area in which he got a suspicious reaction. The psychiatrists discovered there were advantages in interviewing a naked man. One of them noted: "It is indeed surprising how defenses are shed with one's clothing."

The pattern of questions varied. If the examiner suspected mental deficiency he might ask: "Why does the sun rise in the morning and set at night?" This interview was also for screening out homosexuals, so often the psychiatrist would ask: "Do you like girls?" One psychiatrist recommended excluding any man, homosexual or not, who was "so effeminate in appearance and mannerism that he is inevitably destined to be the butt of all the jokes in the company." But homosexuals were often negative malingerers—and successful ones. Some concealed their sexual preference out of fear or shame, others because they wanted to serve.

The psychiatric examination at induction was a noteworthy innovation in screening procedures (the British army used only consulting psychiatrists, who could be called in to examine suspicious cases). Yet a U.S. Army historian acknowledged after the war that "the Army's standards on mental defects were inadequate and ineffectively administered"; one participating psychiatrist admitted the screen was "not very effective," and another said most NP rejections were "by guess and by God." General Hershey protested that the psychiatrists were rejecting men "no queerer than the rest of us." The experience of the war proved that the predictive value of the screen was very limited. Though 1,846,000 men were rejected for neuropsychiatric reasons (of fifteen million examined), the Army was subsequently obliged to discharge a third of a million more for the same cause. And there were men, initially rejected as NPs, who later got into combat and acquitted themselves quite well; we will encounter these "misdiagnoses" again when we consider the soldier under the stress of combat.

At the outset the psychiatrists were too optimistic about their ability to screen. Most were accustomed to working in depth with few subjects and found it difficult to reach conclusions after a single brief interview. As the tempo of induction picked up, the interview was more hurried. One examiner recalled: "There were hectic days during which my examinational procedure consisted of four rapid-fire questions: 'How do you feel? Have you ever been sick? Are you nervous? How do you think you will get along in the Army?' One day I saw 512 men."

There was another unanticipated difficulty, and General Hershey put his finger on it when he claimed that the NP rejection rate was high because "Yankee" psychiatrists did not know how to communicate with boys from the rural South. Examining psychiatrists confessed there was a communication problem: "Boys from the Southern hills . . . looked withdrawn, autistic, and were often diagnosed as schizophrenic, with no reference to their taciturn culture pattern."

Those who passed the physical and psychiatric examinations went on to be fingerprinted—this, too, was a test of sorts, since the fingerprints were checked against FBI files, and a number of criminals were thus detected. The inductees also had a preassignment interview, in which they got a chance to say the type of service they preferred. The U.S. Army Air Forces were the most popular choice, the new soldiers feeling that while flying was full of risk, it also offered the best chance of distinguishing oneself. The infantry was an infrequent choice: It was regarded as dangerous and unglamorous. The new soldiers then signed their induction papers, and were given serial numbers and told to memorize them. "That Army serial number is yours for keeps," confided "Old Sarge." "No one else will ever have it." Finally, the inductees were assembled for the administering of the oath. Army regulations required that it be administered "with proper ceremony." Very often an officer spoke to the men for a few moments before he asked them to raise their right hands. For almost everyone who did so it was a solemn moment. The ceremony over, the men headed back home. They were now soldiers on furlough, expected to report at reception centers within a few days; to drive home this point authorities at the induction station usually read to the new servicemen the fifty-eighth and sixty-first Articles of War, those covering the crimes of desertion and absence without leave.

The real farewell to civilian life took place when the men left for one of the score of Army reception centers scattered across the country. Into 1942 communities organized "send-off" ceremonies with bands and speeches at the railroad stations. An inductee from Illinois recalled that the local Elks Club treated him to breakfast and sent him on his way with a supply of cigarettes and a dollar bill; a Houston draft board presented to each of its departing selectees a sack of Bull Durham tobacco and a Bible. As the war went on the departures came with less fanfare. For one thing, there were so many of them; then, too, the increasing number of family men preferred to say their good-byes privately, in the warmth and intimacy of their homes. But most of all, departing draftees did not care for patriotic send-off ceremonies.

Some celebrated their last night in civilian life the same way they had celebrated the night before induction: by getting drunk. Others brought bottles along with them. The larger the party of inductees traveling together, the more likely it was that they would become boisterous. A postwar treatise on the problems of Selective Service recorded soberly that on occasion the men did "considerable damage to trains and buses." But for most men it was not a time for hilarity. One recalled that he bought a newspaper to read, but found that the sports page and the comics no longer had the savor of the "old, old civilian days." Another remembered: "It was cold and windy, the perfect day for a novelist to begin a mystery or a tragedy, and this was both. We were well on our way when it started to snow, and soon it was a raging blizzard. We passed through a small town. I could see a man fighting his way down the street as I looked out the window. You are free, I thought, but I am in a trap."

The reception center was often located inside a sprawling installation such as Fort Dix, New Jersey, or Fort Bragg, North Carolina. The new arrivals found themselves in a sea of uniforms, their own civilian clothes motley and inappropriate. As they lined up with their overnight bags, soldiers passing by would shout at them, "You'll be sorry," or "Jeep"—the popular term for a rookie in the beginning of the war. The reception center gave the inductee his first taste of Army life; he might be there four days or four weeks, depending on how long it took the Army to process him and decide where to send him (the average stay was nine days). He was shepherded by noncoms and soldiers attached to the reception center, and some of these assumed the role of fraternity brothers put in charge of a new group of pledges. There were dark hints of ordeals to come, including inoculation with square needles and a mysterious device called "the hook."

Usually, the first procedure was for the men to drop their trousers for what the Medical Department called a "short physical inspection" and the rest of the Army called the "shortarm," an examination of the genitals. A new soldier who underwent the shortarm for the first time at Camp Upton, New York, wrote his wife: "If you can't guess what it was, don't ask anyone." The practice went back to the Spanish-American War; its purpose was to discover whether or not soldiers had contracted venereal disease, and it was repeated periodically and whenever a soldier reported to a new post. As further proof of the Army's concern over sexual matters, processing called for a "sex morality lecture" by an Army physician. He sometimes concluded his remarks with the admonition, "Flies spread disease, so keep yours buttoned." Early in the war the new soldier received a pamphlet that told him: "Famous explorers have proved many times that a man can keep perfectly healthy, strong and active without sexual contact. . . . The truth is that using the sex glands too much exhausts them and weakens a man." Later, Hollywood came to the Army's assistance with graphic films on the subject, made by such talented producers as Darryl Zanuck, for use in the camps.

Actually, the Army's attitude toward sex, like its view of alcohol, was a relatively liberal one, certainly more liberal than that prescribed for civilian Americans by religious leaders and health authorities alike, one of whom proclaimed: "Our present social structure demands chastity before marriage." The Army, accustomed to the hard-drinking, hard-living ways of the Regulars, did not demand so much. The soldier would find a woman, just as he would find a bottle; if he were incautious in his indulgence, if he compromised his service, he would be made to pay.

At an early stage in the reception process the new soldiers received an issue of clothing, and the fitting of uniforms was sometimes accompanied by the supply sergeant's ritualistic humor. "The Sergeant asked if everyone had a lovely fit," one inductee recalled. "Those who did not were to take three steps forward. Then the Sergeant said if something could be buttoned it was not too tight. If it stayed with you when you stepped forward it was not too loose." In the first months of the draft there were not enough uniforms; quartermasters had to rummage through depots and the stocks of the National Guard, and many soldiers received clothing that was secondhand. Inductees sometimes found PX receipts dated 1918 in the pockets of their uniforms. Bill Mauldin recalled receiving an entire World War I uniform, from choke-collar "monkey jacket" to wraparound puttees: "They had to be coiled around your legs like anacondas; if you still had circulation in your feet you knew your leggings were too loose and would work their way down to your ankles like a schoolgirl's stockings." Another soldier received the high-peaked overseas cap of World War I. Because of it he found himself constantly addressed by noncoms as "you in the funny cap." He tried to lose it several times, but those who found it recognized it and brought it back to him.

Shoes were another matter. At most reception centers a great deal of care went into the fitting of them, sometimes under the supervision of an officer or with the use of an X-ray device. It was common for the soldier to try them out while carrying two buckets of sand to represent the weight of his pack. The Army of 1941 showed almost as much interest in a soldier's feet as in the condition of his genitals. Old-timers advised toughening the feet by baths in alum water. Lieutenant General Walter Krueger, who commanded the Third Army at the beginning of the war, was known for his surprise foot inspections. Bill Mauldin encountered Krueger once during prewar maneuvers. "It is an awesome experience," wrote Mauldin, "when a man with three stars on each shoulder steps out of the bushes and demands to see your bare feet." The reason for this preoccupation was simple—the prewar Army used its feet a great deal. When the 20th Infantry Regiment took part in the Louisiana maneuvers of 1941, it went from Fort Leonard Wood, Missouri, and back by foot, a round trip of a thousand miles.

Another Army tradition was the reading of the Articles of War, which went back to the days of the Continental Army. The articles were the Army's criminal code. The new soldiers had already heard the AWOL and desertion articles, now they listened to a long list of unfamiliar crimes: fraudulent enlistment, false muster, and provoking speeches and gestures. A young soldier wrote home: "We also had the Articles of War read and explained, which roughly means don't say anything about anyone or do anything to anyone, be real polite to everyone, and be at the proper place at the proper time or you can get everything from six months' labor to a sunrise shooting—mostly shooting." There were also orientation lectures on such subjects as military courtesy—especially how and when to salute—and some instruction on close order drill.

The fabled shots, then commonly called "injections," were only the first of a series, usually smallpox and typhoid. Few men fainted despite the folklore that surrounded the "hook." But since there might be a reaction, the shots were never given until the inductees had taken the tests that were a key part of the reception process. While various aptitude tests were given when soldiers indicated a particular skill, such as radio code, the most important test was the Army General Classification Test, or AGCT. In its classic form it consisted of 150 multiple-choice questions with a forty-minute time limit. There were three types of questions, including block counting, the matching of synonyms, and simple arithmetic problems: "Mike had 12 cigars. He bought 3 more and then smoked 6. How many did he have left?" The tests were machine graded, and the results were used in the placing or classifying of the new soldier, which was the main function of the reception center. The men were placed in five "classes" according to their scores. Class I was over 130; Class II, 110 or over; Class III, the "average" group, had scores between 90 and 109; Class IV went down to 70; and Class V was 69 or below.

The men usually tried their best on the AGCT. Many of them hoped a high score would help them find a better Army slot. It took a score of 115 to get into ASTP, and 110 was required for admission to Officer Candidate School. A high score also helped a man's chances of getting into the Army Air Forces. The AGCT was not a true intelligence test, as the Army never tired of saying; it was supposed to measure "usable intelligence," or "trainability." Test scores were affected by level and quality of schooling and the breadth of "social experience." Blacks, who were often deficient in both, tended to get lower scores. These results served to confirm an opinion widely held by the Army's leadership—that blacks made inferior soldiers. Secretary of War Henry Stimson felt they were adequate only if led by white officers, General Marshall lamented their "relatively low intelligence average," and General George S. Patton held that they could not think fast enough for armored warfare.

The black inductee's Army job was determined less by his test score than by the color of his skin; in the early years of the draft most blacks were shunted into the Engineers and the Quartermaster Corps and placed in all-black units used in construction, stevedore work, and the like. There was a general tendency to make them the Army's hewers of wood and drawers of water. The parachute school at Fort Benning, Georgia, agreed to take a number of blacks because it wanted them to relieve white soldiers of KP, policing of grounds, and other menial chores; not until late in 1943 was the first black parachute battalion activated. A black soldier who wanted to get into combat had a long wait; not before 1944 did any sizable black unit see action.

Japanese-Americans (or Nisei) who volunteered or were drafted into the Army later in the war were also segregated, essentially for security considerations. The Army's Judge Advocate General warned that if they were inducted like everyone else, "disloyal elements" among them would have "unlimited opportunities to commit sabotage, espionage, and other acts of treachery." Though the Nisei protested bitterly over their segregation, some twenty thousand were inducted, and a number of them saw action in Europe (the Nisei 442nd Infantry Regiment fought in Italy as part of the black 92nd Division). There were a few other "ethnic" units, notably infantry battalions for Americans of Austrian, Norwegian, and Greek extractions; the rationale for these is less clear.

These and a few other exceptions aside, the G.I. generally got his Army assignment on the basis of what he had done in civilian life; consequently, the fifteen-minute interview with the classification specialist was sometimes as important as the time spent on the AGCT. The specialist recorded the inductee's work experience, education, and training, as well as the sports he played, his hobbies, and even his talent for furnishing public entertainment. These attributes were then examined in light of the Army's needs and the assignment was made. At the beginning of the draft the enthusiasts of the "New Army" exaggerated its ability to employ various civilian skills; one of them wrote, for example, "The Army today is a huge corporation, highly industrialized and in need of all types of men except salesmen accustomed to direct selling." The Army itself tended to perpetuate the idea. Its film *Classification of Enlisted Men*, shown in 1944, showed the evaluator interviewing a tractor driver from a lumber camp, then assigning him to tanks; a telephone lineman went to the Signal Corps. A grocery clerk posed a momentary problem until he said his hobby was photography; then he, too, was suitably placed. The fourth interviewee was a "mountaineer." When the evaluator asked him what he like to do best, the mountaineer replied "shootin'"; he was thereupon sent to the infantry.

By that time the Army's misplacements and malassignments were legendary. There was the often-repeated story of the banker who became a baker because of a typing error. In one unit there was a cook who had been a garbage man; in another there was a medic who had been a butcher (the classification manual did recommend butchers and meat cutters for the Medical Department, as well as for the Quartermaster Corps). Well into the war a party of G.I.s encountered an unarmed soldier in the jungle of New Guinea; they asked him what he was doing there, and he said he was with Graves Registration and had formerly worked in the morgue at Bellevue. "As we listened to him," wrote one of the G.I.s, "we realized that at last we found the perfect example of a selectee placed by the Army's classification experts in the most suitable martial niche."

Once a man was put into a job, however inappropriate it might be, it was not easy to move him to a more suitable activity. When the 4th Armored Division received its quota of selectees in 1941, among the future tankers were five keypunch operators, seven airline pilots, two parachute mechanics, an optometrist, and an X-ray technician. Since the 4th Armored had not requested such specialists and did not need them, it tried to get them placed elsewhere. "After thirty pages of correspondence between 4th Armored, Second Army, and various War Department agencies, the five key punch operators were moved to a clerical unit; 4th Armored kept the rest."

Actually, the Army did a good job of using many of the skills the selectees brought it from a relatively sophisticated and technologically oriented society. In medical services, in the fields of transportation, communications, subsistence, and the like, the Army Service Forces made us the envy of other belligerents. These were areas where civilian and military skills overlapped. Unfortunately, there were vast areas where they did not. Artists, bookbinders, and newspaper reporters had no military equivalents, and rarely did such persons have hobbies of military value (these were for the most part uncommon, if not exotic: ballistics, cryptography, bird training, and the like). As a consequence, such persons were listed for "any arm or service." At the same time many, if not most, of the slots in the combat arms of the Army Ground Forces had no civilian equivalents. General Hershey liked to say, "I haven't seen a draft questionnaire yet in which the guy said he shot people for a living." The infantry was the most extreme case: Of a thousand infantrymen, only 164 would hold jobs for which there were civilian counterparts.

The *Index and Specifications for Occupational Specialists* (AR

615–20), used by the classification specialist, did not help him find men for the infantry; the "mountaineers," skiers, north woodsmen, and parachute jumpers it recommended for that arm were relatively rare. As a result the infantry and other combat arms tended to be filled with the "any arm or service" people, the occupational leftovers, including a fairly high proportion of white-collar workers. Where a man went—and usually stayed—depended also on the time he entered the service, for the Army's changing needs overrode all other considerations. A man with clerical skills had a good chance of assignment to the Quartermaster Corps if he entered in 1941 when the Army Service Forces were expanding rapidly; if he entered in 1944, when the Army had heavy combat losses to replace, the chances were he would be given a rifle instead of a typewriter.

Within the Army there was a considerable amount of skimming of manpower, especially in the early years of the war. Not only did Army Service Forces drain off the technical specialists they needed, but also the Army Air Forces took a large portion of the men who finished in the two highest categories on the AGCT. As a result, a survey conducted in 1943 indicated, combat soldiers in the Army Ground Forces had lower AGCT scores than men in the Army Service Forces or the Army Air Forces; combat soldiers were also shorter and weighed less. A historian of the Army's Personnel Division went as far as to say, "Army Ground Forces got the dregs." But beginning in 1943, priorities began to shift. Army Air Forces lost their skimming privileges and Army Ground Forces were favored. The ASTP men fed into combat units were a valuable transfusion. By special order of General Marshall the prime eighteen-to-twenty-year-olds were funneled into the infantry; finally, from March to June 1945, the Army was able to take the Navy's share of selectees in that same age group. As a result the United States Army was probably the only army in the war whose manpower in combat units was improving at the end of the conflict.

If the Army made a fundamental miscalculation in training too many specialists and technicians—pilots, ASTP men, and automotive mechanics—it also made an error in assuming that men so trained could not be used effectively in another role. Happily, this second error canceled out the effects of the first. When the German offensive broke in the Ardennes, hastily raised levies of men from the Army Service Forces were transformed into infantrymen, and they surprised their leaders with their fighting capacity.

But then no one knew just what characteristics went into making a good combat soldier, or how to detect those characteristics at the time of classification. When a British soldier was inducted, the interviewing officer attempted to rate the soldier's "combatant temperament" as high, low, or average. The PULHES evaluation system of the U.S. Army did not even go that far; it sought only a judgment on the soldier's emotional stability. An Army psychiatrist acknowledged in 1943 that the Medical Corps had yet to devise "a workable, practical test for stamina, the ability to adjust to unfavorable environments, the aggressiveness and initiative necessary in modern warfare." He suggested the Army look for combat soldiers who possessed a spirit of adventure, a zest for competition, and "a love of blood sports."

While the reception center personnel were deciding on the new soldier's assignment, he was making further acquaintance with the Army and its ways. For most inductees the first day was the most difficult, with its hurry-up and confusion. The first night in the barracks was also memorable. If most members of the group were young, the atmosphere was that of a Boy Scout outing. One inductee wrote his parents: "There were the usual attempts to get laughs: imitation burps, synthetic breaking wind, and the whistle-snore routine." But finally the barracks grew quiet and each man found himself alone in an alien world. Some men also remembered a moment of emotion when they packed up their civilian clothes. "It was a low feeling we had when we parted with those clothes," wrote a draftee from Wisconsin.

At the same time, acceptance and adaptation had begun. When the roll was called, no one answered "Yeah, man," as they had done at the induction station. Men who had brought pajamas sent them home and went to bed Army style, in their underwear. An observer who spent any time at a reception center could see very quickly why the Army preferred its soldiers young. The twenty-year-olds were not in uniform twenty-four hours before they were shouting "You'll be sorry" and "Look out for the hook" when they spotted a ragged column of men in civilian clothes headed for the processing building. Playwright Arthur Miller watched them crowding in front of the mirrors in the barracks washroom, practicing their salutes and adjusting their garrison caps at a rakish angle. Miller had come to study Army life as preparation for a screenplay he was to write, and as he followed the men through their stay in the reception center he was struck by the contrast between the very young and the older men. For the latter, adaptation was more difficult. "Their patterns are set at home and will never really be broken by Army life," Miller wrote.

For a minority the adaptation was easy because the Army offered things they had not had in civilian life. In the America of 1940 one home in three did not have running water, and almost that proportion did not have central heat; for all its bleakness the barracks had both. For some men the switch to uniform was a step up. Reception center officials at Fort Benning, Georgia, reported that inductees sometimes arrived wearing shirt and trousers and nothing else. A new soldier at Fort Jackson, South Carolina, complained in a letter, "My shoes hurts my feet because I haven't been used to wearing shoes." A draftee who was inducted with some young New England farmers recalled: "One hayshaker from Maine was delighted with his new outfit and babbled his delight to anyone who would listen to him. He was even delighted with his overcoat, the bottom of which was almost dragging the ground." Later the same observer noted: "The hayshakers (Maine) all get up at four-thirty, wash, dress, make their bunks, and sit out on the steps waiting for chow. They can't seem to find the day long enough." And an enthusiastic new soldier from Texas wrote home "I like the Army fine so far. They let you sleep till 5:30."

Surprisingly, a number of men wrote their draft boards during their first days of service, and only rarely were the letters filled with recrimination. In some of them the germ of G.I. humor could be detected. A North Carolina draftee wrote his board: "Tell all of the boys to come on down for the Army is all right they are good to you down here for they will serve you breakfus in bed if you want them to all you have to do is tell thim the night before and they fixt you right up it is so easy."

The reception center was only a way station; every day men were shipped out to the training camps where they would learn the real business of soldiering. The men talked and speculated constantly about their possible destinations. The Army world was a world of rumor; it was said that long journeys always started at night, and that if a man was to leave in the morning, he could hope to be stationed not too far from home. This was the hope of most new soldiers, and those hopes were usually dashed when the men received their orders. A draftee from New England learned that he was headed to a training camp in Georgia—a thousand miles away. He was in the depths of despair, but he said nothing: "I just took my civilian clothes out and threw them in the trash can. It was my supreme gesture of acceptance. Why struggle any more? I was in the Army now."

★ 3 ★

The World of
the Training Camps

THE NEW SOLDIER who left the reception center could be headed
almost anywhere in the country; by the spring of 1945 the Army
Ground Forces and Army Service Forces (formerly Services of
Supply) were operating 242 training centers scattered all over the
United States. Whatever the soldier's destination, it probably bore
one of two designations: fort or camp. If the new G.I. had any
lingering notions that forts had battlements and that camps were
collections of tents, he would soon abandon them for the Army's
definition. The fort was a continuously occupied installation that
possessed permanent structures; a camp was either a site that had
been used previously on a part-time basis—by the National Guard,
for example—or a completely new installation. In either case, the
camp's structures were of the temporary sort: "mobilization"-type
frame buildings, prefabricated hutments, or tents.

For the New Army there were new camps by the scores, and
even on the older posts there was much building. Sometimes in

the first year or two of the draft, troops moved in before the carpenters and plumbers moved out. An officer with the 31st Division, sent to Camp Blanding, Florida, late in 1940, recalled: "A regiment of 1,815 men was moved in with not a single kitchen, latrine, or bathhouse available." At Camp Gruber, Oklahoma, where buildings were going up at the rate of one every forty minutes in the spring of 1942, the camp lacked the most essential services. Trainees received medical attention at a nearby veterans' hospital, clergymen from the vicinity filled the function of base chaplain, and the local police played the role of MPs.

It wasn't supposed to happen that way in the mobilization scheme the Army had devised before the war. Well into the 1930s the War Department had planned on a mobilization without the sprawling camps of World War I. This time the troops would be assembled and trained in smaller units, using public buildings, leased structures, athletic fields, and the like; thus a War Department spokesman suggested the 29th Division (National Guardsmen from the Washington-Baltimore area) might be housed in Baltimore's Montgomery Ward building and do its training in nearby Carroll Park. These ideas may have made sense in the 1930s, when the Army had slender budgets and planned only a limited mobilization effort; but in 1940 everything changed and the War Department had to launch a crash program of camp construction. The tempo of building was particularly frantic from the fall of 1940 through the summer of 1942; forty-six new camps went up in that period, and there were major expansions of the older installations.

Site selection had to be done hastily, with a number of people, particularly senators and congressmen, anxious to help the Army in its search. General Marshall got suggestions on the location of a divisional camp from a young congressman named Lyndon Johnson, and an Army historian hinted at "demands for special consideration which were sometimes too strong to be ignored." A forty-thousand-acre site near Leon, Iowa, had to be abandoned when it was discovered that the water supply was inadequate; but as a rule the Army built on the sites it had selected, whatever their shortcomings, for there was no time to do anything else. Lack of water was no problem at Camp Blanding—portions of the tract were twenty-four feet below the level of nearby Kingsley Lake. At another location the Army developed the surveyors had to get into rowboats to take the property corners. In time the climatic and topographical peculiarities of various Army posts became the subject of a rich folklore. It was said that Fort Benning was the only place a soldier could encounter mud and dust at the same time, though this claim was also made for several other posts. Men stationed at Camp Barkeley, Texas, claimed the mosquitoes were so large and so discriminating that before they bit a man they sat on his chest and checked his dog tags for blood type.

Yet the Army had definite requirements for the camps it was building, and those requirements can be read in the letters General Marshall wrote to irate or importunate members of Congress. A divisional camp needed forty thousand acres of varied terrain for cantonments, drill fields, and ranges. It needed a good water supply, good road and rail facilities, and a stream so that engineers could practice their bridging techniques. Finally, the site should be near a large population center where the soldiers could find recreation. The Army tended to place its training camps in the Southeast because the area offered these advantages and some others as well. Land was relatively cheap, there was a suitable area for maneuvers stretching from the Carolinas to Arkansas, and most of all, the climate permitted year-round training. An inventory of Army training facilities early in 1945 indicates that only one of the really large training camps—those with an enlisted capacity of fifty thousand or more—was outside the South; that was Fort Lewis, Washington, an Army Service Forces Replacement Training Center with a capacity of sixty-two thousand.

Within the states of the old Confederacy lay the huge camps where the Army's ground forces learned their trades. There was Fort Benning near Columbus, Georgia, the biggest of them all with ninety-five thousand capacity in 1945. Benning specialized in training infantry, as did Fort Jackson (sixty-five thousand) near Columbia, South Carolina. Fort Bragg (seventy-six thousand) near Fayetteville, North Carolina, trained artillerymen; its vast area (129,000 acres, twenty-five miles across) offered ranges for the largest guns. Fort Knox (fifty-three thousand), south of Louisville, Kentucky, was the training center for the armored forces. Added to these forts was a host of camps that had sprung up in 1940 and 1941. There was Blanding (fifty-four thousand) in Florida, Claiborne (fifty-five thousand) in Louisiana, Hood (sixty-eight thousand) in Texas, and Shelby (eighty-six thousand) in Mississippi; and there were other training centers of more modest size, such as the Engineers' facility at Fort Belvoir, Virginia.

The training camp had its own police force and its own fire department; it had its own water, sewerage, and transportation systems. It was in many ways a city, and Army officials were so impressed by the similarity that they offered commissions to city managers who would help run the installations. But to the new soldier the camp that would be his home for the next few months was like no city he had known in civilian life. There was first of all the essential similarity of all the buildings, understandable since for the most part they were built from the Quartermasters' 700 Series plans, drawn up in the 1930s. The buildings were wood because that was the fastest and cheapest form of construction, and they had the bare, angular "institutional" look characteristic of the 700 Series. The structures were of one or two stories to reduce fire hazard, and most Army posts could boast "nothing above two stories except the flag pole." The layout of the camp was in relentless rectangles, though Mrs. Roosevelt had suggested that curved streets might make the camps more pleasant places. The original intention had been to leave the structures unpainted, but here the President's wife and the Painting and Decorating Contractors of America had prevailed. Still, the buildings were all painted the same color, camp streets were not prominently marked, and one intersection looked like another; new soldiers frequently got lost.

Men who had just arrived had little time to explore their new home; they found their way to their barracks—usually a two-story, sixty-three-occupant affair with banks of toilets, lavatories, and shower heads—and the mess hall. Then they made acquaintance mostly with classroom and field, as they plunged into their training activities.

The Army's wartime training program suffered from the same

basic handicap as its building program—a hasty and imperfectly controlled expansion. In June 1940 General Marshall told a convention of the Veterans of Foreign Wars that the Army had "definite plans for a step-by-step coordinated increase," and he warned against "an ill-considered overnight expansion which would smother well-considered methods and leave us in a dilemma of confused results, half-baked and fatally unbalanced." Then came Pearl Harbor and a dizzying acceleration in the pace of mobilization. By the summer of 1942 men were pouring into reception centers and training camps at the rate of about fourteen thousand per day; not surprisingly, there were times when no one seemed quite sure what to do with them all. Those were the days when draftees spent part of their time draining the swamps around their unfinished training camps, men threw stones in the grenade course because there were not enough practice grenades, and future artillerymen stood in line for their chance at the 105-mm fieldpiece because there was only one gun for every five crews. (It may have been then that the saying "hurry up and wait" became part of the G.I. language.)

Lieutenant General Leslie J. McNair, who headed the Army Ground Forces from 1942 to 1944, frankly acknowledged that "the machine was a little wobbly when it first got going. The men knew it. The officers knew it. Everybody knew it." By the middle of the war the machine no longer wobbled, and the quality of training was probably on a par with that of the other belligerents; still, there were men who had gone through the system and emerged incompletely or improperly trained, and some went into combat unfamiliar with their weapons. A sergeant in Italy told a *Yank* reporter that in the middle of a firefight near the Rapido River, with the Germans some ten yards away, a recently arrived replacement fighting near him had held up his M1 rifle and shouted, "How do you load this thing?"

From 1942 on, the Army was divided functionally into three parts: Army Ground Forces, Army Service Forces, and Army Air Forces. Each of these set up its own training programs. Here, as in other matters, the airmen formed a class apart, but for the ground and service forces the approach to training was similar. The first or basic phase was instruction of the individual with the purpose of transforming him from a civilian to a soldier. Since he was taught what *every* soldier needed to know, the Army sometimes called this phase "branch immaterial training." The new soldier learned the elements of drill, beginning with the "facings" (right face, left face, and so on), military courtesy, and generally how he was expected to conduct himself in his new environment; at the same time the soldier was started on the physical conditioning process. The second phase of training, which often emerged very gradually from the first, taught the soldier to develop his specialty and to do it in cooperation with others in what was essentially "team" or unit training. Army Ground Forces had a third stage, combined-arms training, in which the various arms—infantry, artillery, armor—went through exercises together.

The Army Service Forces stressed training in technical specialties. Engineers mastered such subjects as searchlight maintenance and powerboat operation. The Transportation Replacement Training Center taught loading techniques, using a "landship"—a replica of a cargo vessel with booms, hatches, and space in its hold for 1,500 tons of cargo; the Ordnance School had a watch repair course. The tendency was to train people in rather narrow specialties, and some postwar critics said they were too narrow. The Army trained both cooks and bakers at Fort Sheridan, Wyoming, but it did not teach them each other's specialty. Mechanics were trained to work on diesel or gasoline engines, but not on both. In an emergency, service personnel might well be mobilized for combat, so they received some instruction on this subject as well; from 1943 on, Army Service Forces strove to see that each of its trainees was at home with the basic infantry weapon, the M1.

The Army Ground Forces' training activities fell into two major periods. The first, from 1941 to 1943, centered on the training of whole units at a time, especially divisions, which were the Army's major building blocks: through August 1943 some ninety divisions were activated, along with a large number of smaller, non-divisional units. Thereafter the Army created no more divisions, but bent its efforts to maintaining those already in existence; consequently, in 1944 the emphasis shifted to the training of replacements for those divisions. According to the formula used in 1942, the training of a division took exactly a year: forty-four weeks of individual, unit and combined-arms training followed by eight weeks of exercises and maneuvers. Replacements were trained in cycles of from eight to seventeen weeks, depending on the arm or service for which they were destined.

There never was complete uniformity in training, even for troops learning the same specialty at the same time. Some facilities were better equipped than others; troops who trained in divisions probably had better instruction than those in smaller units, for division commanders could more readily obtain training "props" —tanks, for example. And at each camp the instructors had their own ideas about teaching techniques. On one post, mock tombstones were erected to drive home a training point: "Here lies Brown the Clown, who wouldn't keep his head down." At Camp Shelby a major taught concealment by driving over the exercise course in a jeep, firing a slingshot at those who were exposed. An observer at another post recalled: "In a quiet moment of instruction a half stick of dynamite went off five yards behind the group of trainees. It almost blew my brains out. 'This is a method of keeping them awake,' as the major said."

In World War I the troops had been prepared for combat in the trenches in France, a specific type of warfare in a single locality. But World War II was fought in jungles, in deserts, and in mountains, with the nature of warfare varying from one theater of operations to the next. Army leaders decided quite early to train all the men and units to fight according to a standard program, though there were considerable misgivings among the General Staff. Its secretary, General Paul S. Robinett, noted in his diary: "It is believed that we must back up and establish sound basic training in task forces created for a particular role in a particular theater." The change was never made.

When special training was needed, it was generally given after the troops had finished the standard cycle; then units might be sent for amphibious instruction or for exercises at the Army's California-Arizona Maneuver Area. This was possible because divisions spent an average of just over two years in stateside camps before they were shipped overseas (as late as D-Day half of the Army was still in the United States, though virtually all the fighting divisions were abroad by the next spring). Then, too, training continued overseas. In the Pacific there were jungle warfare courses; in 1944 in France the various corps conducted their own "battle indoctrination" courses, held just behind the lines, for replacements. There new men were shown the tricks of the trade and given a chance to see and hear enemy weapons. And there was more instruction when new matériel was introduced; in a sense, training never ended.

During 1943 the training system overcame most of the serious problems that had troubled it in preceding years. By 1944 the equipment shortages that had plagued early hands-on training were largely over, and there was plenty of ammunition for the ranges and for simulating the sounds of battle. The camps were completed, and they now had classrooms to replace the barracks and mess halls where instruction had sometimes been given. Classroom techniques had improved, too. The crusty sergeant who knew everything about the SCR-131 radio and nothing about the presentation of information had been replaced by a teacher with lesson plans, charts, and diagrams. In other cases, what someone called the "army-style, pay-attention-you-fuckers lecture" had been replaced by a film. Eventually there were over four hundred training films, many of them high-quality Hollywood products. "It is doubtful that the draftees appreciated the moving parts of the M1 rifle as much as the moving parts of Betty Grable," a historian wrote recently, "but the films did prove an asset in assuring uniform instruction at a time when qualified instructors were spread so thinly."

But the most important changes in the training programs came as a result of combat experience. At the end of 1942 the first lessons filtered back from the fighting fronts in New Guinea and North Africa. Combat veterans joined the teaching staffs, with a generally beneficial result for the programs, though there were occasional problems. A veteran returning from Europe insisted it was a waste of time to teach men to fire from sitting or kneeling positions—until he was taken into a field of waist-high grass resembling the kunai grass often found in the Southwest Pacific. As the war moved into the more populated areas of Europe, training schedules were revised to include street fighting; as the end of the fighting in Europe neared, training courses stressed subjects of special use in the Pacific: night operations, malaria control, swimming, and amphibious operations. There was always something of a time lag before the training program reflected conditions in the theater of operations, but from 1943 on the trainee generally got better marks when he showed up in the field. The colonel of the 162nd Infantry, then (June 1944) at Biak, expressed his being "more than satisfied" with replacements: "They picked up the little tricks of caring for themselves in the jungle, and it was soon impossible to tell whether they were old or new men." The most eloquent testimonial came from the men themselves, when they said, after their first taste of combat, "It was no worse than maneuvers."

From the fighting fronts came suggestions to stop making training films in which the "hero" did not have his face and hands darkened or helmet camouflaged, or had his equipment shining and did not use cover properly and realistically. There was a steady call for training activities that closely simulated combat, a call well illustrated by this report from the Pacific:

Training should be more realistic, in order that the individual may be habituated to the sounds and incidents of warfare before he enters it. He will not then encounter so many new sights and sounds all at once, and will conduct himself with more assurance and determination. The following should be incorporated in combat firing exercises: overhead fire by artillery, mortars and machine guns; concealed snipers on flanks of the unit should fire into the ground just ahead of advancing soldiers; surprise targets should appear at close range; mines should be exploded in the midst of assault waves to simulate enemy mortar fire, etc. Smoke should be used to accustom a soldier to it, and leaders should be declared casualties in order to force the second in command to take charge of the unit. I saw all of these things done at the Australian Weapons School.

Most of these "realistic" features were incorporated into the training programs by 1943, along with many others. Infantrymen fired live ammunition at "buttoned-up" tanks, and the tanks in turn rolled over infantrymen while they lay crouched in holes. Soldiers crawled through infiltration courses with machine-gun bullets passing thirty inches above them. They moved through "Nazi" villages, kicking in doors and blazing away at pop-up targets. In a number of these techniques the Army was inspired by British and Australian training practices. The British made a particularly determined effort to reproduce not only the sights and sounds of the battlefield, but also its gruesomeness. The instructor referred to the battlefield as "the killing ground," and there were even experiments with spreading animal blood over the assault course and taking the troops on a visit to a slaughterhouse. An American officer who watched British "battle drill" in 1942 was impressed with it, but concluded, "The initiating of similar training in American units will probably be subjected to unfavorable comment by the press."

There were limits to the realism that could be introduced into the training of American troops, and those limits were reached as soon as live-ammunition exercises and other hazardous activities produced noticeable casualties. As a consequence, though the Army Ground Forces used 240,000 tons of ammunition and explosives in training between 1942 and 1944, realism was used with great precaution. Even so, there were casualties—at Fort Gordon, Georgia, for example, in May 1943, when an artillery shell exploded prematurely and killed three men. There were similar accidents elsewhere that spring when infantry practiced advancing with overhead artillery fire. Likewise there were casualties in the parachute exercises. Out of a thousand who jumped, there might be a man here and there whose chute would not function. The Army understood this and accepted it; so did the paratroopers, who were volunteers. But the public could neither understand nor accept. "When training casualties occurred," wrote an Army historian, "the mails were flooded with protests." In another country, under a different type of regime, soldiers could get greater battle realism in their training, though they paid for it: During the war, casualties in German Waffen SS training sometimes reached 10 percent. As for the U.S. Army, its training would be "as realistic as safety (and public opinion) permitted."

While officials in the Pentagon confronted such problems as battle realism in training, the rank and file of the Army—hundreds of thousands of young men in Fort Benning and Camp Claiborne and on other posts—were confronting training not as it might be, but as it was. We have some idea of what they were doing from a list of common "subjects" the Army Ground Forces laid down for Replacement Training Centers in October 1942. The purely "academic" subjects, at least those dispensed in the classroom, were relatively few in number. Six hours were allotted for military courtesy, discipline, and the by-now-familiar Articles of War; ten hours were dedicated to sanitation, first aid, and the inevitable sex hygiene. Three hours were allotted to the protection of military information (Darryl Zanuck produced a film on the subject), and there was an hour lecture on Army organization. Some seven hours were set aside for "Indoctrination." This was a presentation of the nation's war aims and of the progress in the war to date—the sort of information that was always labeled propaganda when dispensed in the enemy army.

Several of the subjects covered the practical aspects of soldiering, such as equipment, clothing, and tent pitching (seven hours), map and aerial photograph reading (eight hours minimum), and field fortification and camouflage (eight hours). Less useful, though no one could be sure of it at the time, was defense against chemical attack (twelve hours). There were thirty-six hours of physical training, twenty or more hours of marches and bivouacs, and, finally, four hours of guard duty, twenty of drill, and eighteen of inspection. In 1943 Army Ground Forces prescribed more physical training as well as instruction on "dirty fighting," night fighting, battle indoctrination, and mines and booby traps. Some subjects were reduced in importance; hours for drill and inspection dropped, as did those set aside for aircraft identification once the Allies gained air superiority in the various theaters.

As the war progressed, probably more subjects were added to the combat soldier's curriculum than were dropped; in any event, his schedule became more crowded and training hours lengthened. In 1942 the six-day training week was set at forty-four hours; but by 1944 it had become forty-eight hours in some camps. That's what it was in theory at the Infantry Replacement Training Center at Camp Fannin, Texas. The basic training schedule for December 1944 survives, and it gives us a good look at what the trainee's day was like. First call (and not reveille) was sounded at 5:55 A.M.; reveille and its roll call came ten minutes later. By 6:20 the soldiers had washed, dressed, made their bunks, and fallen in for the five-minute march to the mess hall. After a twenty-minute stay there they marched back to their barracks; they then policed the area, prepared their equipment, and made the forty-minute march to the training site, where they pursued scheduled training activities from 8:00 A.M. until 5:30 P.M., the nine and a half hours broken only by the midday meal, which the Army called dinner. By the time the men marched back to barracks, then made the trip to supper and back, it was 7:00. The working day was not really over, however: There was still mail call and announcements, housekeeping chores, fatigue details, and the cleaning of equipment. The schedule allotted thirty minutes for showering and preparing for bed, and at 9:45 the lights went out. The training day could thus take almost sixteen hours. In addition, there were occasional night-training problems, weekend cleaning details known as "G.I. parties," and guard and KP duties (the latter with a wakeup time of 4:55 A.M.); training time lost while on guard or KP duty was to be made up during "free time" in the evening—from 9:20 to 9:45.

The basic training schedule was thus a full and rigorous one, perhaps too much so. That was the conclusion subsequently reached by the general who headed the Army Ground Forces Replacement and School Command, which oversaw training activities: "The programs were too full, the days too concentrated, the men too seldom able to relax, so they were not fresh and fit each day for the training they were to receive." The men no doubt would have agreed. Their letters say as much, sometimes even in the way they were composed: A man would be overtaken by "lights out" or his own exhaustion after he had written a paragraph or two, so he would put the letter aside after promising the correspondent he would finish it the next night; sometimes he could not keep the promise. No one treated basic training lightly in letters home; the words the trainee used to describe it were "hot and tough," "mighty tough," "plenty tough," the same word reappearing consistently. Sometimes there are hints of apprehension that the trainee will not be able to make it through, and he tries to prepare his correspondent for his possible failure. An older draftee from Virginia wrote his wife: "It is hard, darling, and I hope that I have guts enough to really take it like I should."

The great majority of the men could and did take it, of course, and often in their letters it is possible to see concern and doubt replaced with a kind of pride as they realize this. A draftee wrote his parents from Fort McClellan, Alabama, at the end of May 1943: "I don't know whether I can stand to do what we have to do or not. I have to try it though." On June 8 he wrote: "No, I haven't fell out yet. I am going to stand it if I can." By July he is another man: "It was 106 today and when we are out drilling we really do get hot but I will tell you the truth, I have got so that I can stand it just as good as the next one. I sweat a lot but I go on like I was cool." Within about two weeks the training day became easier to bear; the shoes were broken in by then, sunburn had turned to a painless tan, and the body had begun to adjust to the new activity. "Right now I feel better than I have in a year," wrote an Indiana inductee at Camp Croft, South Carolina. "Most of the soreness has gone from my aching muscles and I can see the results from the 'toughening up' process."

An Indiana soldier in Texas explained the price of this "toughening up" even as he protested his inability to do so: "I cannot picture everything clearly to you for I cannot send you a box of Texas dust to pour liberally over your whole body. I cannot send you a long, hot road and a fine set of blisters or a pair of heavy G.I. shoes to be broken in. I cannot send you an overcoat which you will not be allowed to wear at reveille when it is freezing, but which you will be required to wear during the sweltering afternoon."

The summer heat is frequently mentioned in trainees' letters, and it was something that could scarcely be ignored in the Deep South. General Marshall, testifying about the rigors of training before a Senate committee, said the greatest endurance test was in the armored force because of the close confinement in tanks, where temperatures reached 130 degrees. The high temperatures were particularly hard on men who were not from the South. A Georgian wrote from Camp Stewart, in his native state, in June 1943: "The Northern boys are really suffering in this heat. They cuss the South in general and Georgia in particular and say they hope all us rebels suffocate."

The most grueling physical tests in training were hikes and obstacle courses, both of which varied in difficulty from one post to another. In 1943 the War Department prescribed a mandatory twenty-five-mile road march with full equipment to be taken by all personnel under forty years of age, but many infantry units in training exceeded this. The 351st Infantry Regiment once covered sixty-two miles in full gear in the space of twenty-nine hours without a single man falling out; for that feat it received a special commendation from General Marshall. But the supreme test at Camp Gruber, where the 351st trained, was considered to be its obstacle course:

> The culmination of physical training was the requirement that the soldier with rifle and thirty pound pack, negotiate a 1500 foot obstacle course in three and a half minutes. Specific requirements were that he take off with a yell (yelling or singing frequently accompanied physical activity), mount an eight foot wall, slide down a ten foot pole, leap a flaming trench, weave through a series of pickets, crawl through a water main, climb a ten foot rope, clamber over a five foot fence, swing by a rope across a seven foot ditch, mount a twelve foot ladder and descend to the other side, charge over a four foot breastwork, walk a twenty foot catwalk some twelve inches wide and seven feet over the ground, swing hand over hand along a five foot horizontal ladder, slither under a fence, climb another, and cross the finish line at a sprint.

Classroom sessions offered a pleasant change and a chance to catch one's breath. When the lights went out for a film many men were tempted to doze. Orientation was rarely an exhilarating experience. An observer who sat in on one of the sessions reported:

"The lieutenant droned off the news bulletins from a mimeographed sheet. Most of the men were scratching themselves or taking off shoes to straighten rumpled socks or just not listening."

Among the activities least liked was close order drill. Some training officials believed that having compact bodies of men march about over the drill ground was a means of subordinating the individual to the unit. It awakened "the desire for uniformity" among the men, "inculcating habits which will function spontaneously in the crisis of battle." While this view could be found among training cadre at the various camps, the Army's training manual warned against overdoing it, suggesting that such drills be kept "formal, precise and brief." When combat veterans in the Mediterranean were asked to list the training subjects that had been least helpful to them, they named close order drill, along with bayonet and hand-to-hand fighting, marches and hikes, military courtesy lectures, inspections, and chemical warfare training.

What the soldiers liked best were those activities that fitted their preconceptions of what a soldier should be doing, and to be precise, they liked those things that had the violence and the flavor of combat. They disliked cleaning their rifles but complained they did not get to fire them enough, or at moving targets such as airplanes. They liked grenade exercises, and wanted to throw live grenades. The closer the exercise approximated combat, the more enthusiastically they undertook it, and they particularly liked the village fighting course. Arthur Miller noticed this as a group of trainees prepared to move through a mock "Nazi" village. "The wonderful, horrible, strange thing is that they want to try themselves at the real thing. . . . They were all terribly excited by the village fighting. It was the kind of training they like. It has purpose. It is always obvious that when the lieutenant says not to do it that way it means life or death for them to learn it, and in the Nazi village they hang on his words."

Miller found the same enthusiasm and exhilaration among tankers roaring through their training course: "They are all Buck Rogerses in a way, driving through remembered newsreels, using fabulously expensive apparatus, wearing fierce looking goggles and helmets they would never have dared wear in civilian life."

By the time the trainee had begun these "battle inoculation" courses, he no longer felt awkward or ill at ease in his new life. His Army clothes, softened by many washings, had adopted the contours of his frame, and he himself had adjusted to the routine of the camp. The barracks had become a familiar refuge after a hard day in the field. The trainee's Sundays were his own, for while the Army encouraged church attendance, it issued no orders on the subject. In his first weekend or two the new soldier would spend much of the time in the barracks, writing letters, talking, or just taking it easy. Each company had a day room, with books and magazines and sometimes a radio. After 1941 there was a recreation building for each regiment, though in the early days the building was not well equipped. A soldier wrote from Fort Knox in October 1941 that the recreation hall was composed of a building, two Ping-Pong tables, and a pool table. The trainee soon discovered the post theater and found that after a day of training he still had the energy to take in a movie.

Though recreation facilities had low priority in the first rush of camp building, eventually all the posts were able to add service clubs. The first floor of the club was a lounge–reading room that could be converted into a ballroom; the upstairs had a small library and various rooms for meetings, indoor games, and other activities. The clubs were staffed by "hostesses" who had been carefully screened. "Only women of good character and nice personality need apply," ran the ad for hostesses at Fort Leonard Wood, Missouri. The hostesses served as chaperones for girls who were bused in to the weekend dances. They reported that "an astonishing number" of selectees, National Guardsmen, and regular soldiers did not know ballroom dancing.

More frequented than the service club was the PX, or post exchange. A venerable Army institution, the PX of 1940 was a modest retail store; but as the Army grew, the post exchange system expanded and diversified to bring to the camps a wide variety of services and amenities. In 1940 the PX at Camp Blanding was a one-room affair with a sales force of five; within a year it had six hundred employees and was taking in $350,000 a month. While Blanding's main PX expanded, it also spawned thirty-five smaller exchanges, one for each regimental area. The system at Blanding soon included three warehouses, eight trucks, three bus terminals, seven taxis, eight service stations, a garage, a restaurant, four cafeterias, a tailor shop, and a shoe repair shop. By 1945 the Army's PX system had become the largest retailer in the country.

But no matter what amenities or distractions existed within the camp, the trainee did not forget the world that lay outside the gates. It was an old Army practice not to grant passes to new soldiers—the measure was partly hygienic, designed to keep the new man in quarantine until any malady he might have brought in from civilian life declared itself. But sooner or later the trainee did receive a pass and found himself back in the world "outside." Some subtle, indefinable change had occurred: He could not just step back into civilian life as he had stepped out of it a few weeks before. Some men sensed this almost immediately, the instant they stepped into a bar to order a beer and realized that theirs was the only uniform in the room; for many this change would not register fully until they went home on furlough. But sooner or later the realization came to them all: The Army had put its mark upon them.

But if the soldier was no longer at his ease in the old, civilian world, by way of compensation he was beginning to feel at home in a totally new society, that of the training company and the barracks. That society began to take shape the moment the soldiers arrived at camp. Arthur Miller saw signs of it even in the reception center, as he watched new inductees examining the toilet articles the Army had given them: "Seemingly on the basis of having the same type of razor or other article, they began to fall into cliques—all at once there was something that they had in common. The buddy system was perceptibly germinating around a plastic razor."

Young sociologists who were drafted noted with a professional eye the budding relationships around them: "Frequently the choice of a buddy was fortuitous, growing out of arbitrary barracks or hutment assignment." Often men from the same region were drawn together; college men might initially be attracted to one another, but close relationships did not always develop among them. The basic social unit was from two to four men, the latter number being about the maximum for easy conversation. These groups often had overlapping memberships; clustered together they made up the training company, a body of about two hundred men. The company was a "work-related habitat continuum," in the sociologists' jargon. It was a relatively isolated entity, so that for all practical purposes the company represented the limits of the "known" world.

In the barracks one's former station in life was of little importance: "The essential fact about induction, reception center and basic training is the knifing off of past experience. Nothing in one's past seems relevant unless, possibly, a capacity for adaptation and the ability to assume a new role." In their new life the men felt themselves under scrutiny, and in a sense they were; the soldier said good-bye to privacy when he said good-bye to his civilian clothes. In the training camp a man ate, bathed, slept, and went to the toilet in the close company of others. In these activities, as in everything else he did in the barracks, a man strove to be like everyone else: "Most men attempt to divert attention from themselves by avoiding any erratic behavior," noted a sociologist-draftee. Conformity sometimes required fundamental changes in everyday habits and routines. Most veterans can relate stories of men who did not bathe—until they were carried off to the showers by their exasperated barracks mates and given a "G.I. shower," including a scrubbing with a stiff brush. Such things did happen, but much more often the nonbather changed his habits immediately and unobtrusively. Men who had never made a bed said nothing and imitated others.

College men faced another challenge, that of fitting in despite a diploma that marked them apart. A college man named Robert Welker found himself in this predicament and he confessed:

At the start I had been inclined to think of the soldiers beside me as "acceptable" or "good fellows," or "not a bad sort." There was something unhappily fastidious about that outlook. I was being consciously democratic. But that kind of thing couldn't last long. Contact with the same group, dawn to midnight, seven days a week, was bound to resolve such an attitude one way or another.

Either I would weary of egalitarian pretense and cut myself off from the rest, or I could drop my condescension and identify myself with the group. The decision was not made all at once nor even consciously; but when I thought about it I knew it was towards identity, not self-exclusion. Perhaps I was motivated by the merest desire for conformity, wanting group approval. But there was also a deep interest in each man as an individual, a single, separate person, an enigma to be wondered at.

Unless a man had traveled extensively and done a great many different things in his life, the chances were that the Army presented him with a much broader sampling of humanity than he had ever encountered. While certain units had a lingering regional identity—for example, a National Guard outfit such as the 36th Division, the "Texas Army"—the Army's personnel policies tended to scramble manpower pretty thoroughly; the thirty-odd draftee divisions formed in 1942 and 1943 were ethnic, cultural, and regional mélanges from the outset. As a result it was said that anywhere in the Army you could find a soldier who spoke Italian just by shouting for one. Within a company one could find the makings of a dramatic troupe or a hillybilly band. Within a division almost anything was possible. When the rabbi of the 88th Division needed an assistant, he sought a soldier who was a Jew, could drive and service a jeep, type, sing, and play a portable organ. Within the division he found ten men with all those qualifications. This richness and variety impressed the soldiers themselves. A former New York bartender confided: "I've seen all kinds of characters, but this place has got me doubled in spades." An ex-G.I. reflected: "A large number of Americans I met in the Army amazed me by their differentness. I had not known their like before, nor have I met them since." The same observation appears in soldiers' letters; they tell their correspondents that they have a friend who is an elephant trainer, or that a buddy "knows the Lone Ranger personally."

Teasing men about their home states was a barracks tradition that sprang up very quickly, and there was a particularly considerable amount of raillery between northerners and southerners.

Many Yankees took loud exception to the southern dishes served in the mess halls, to the climate, and to the *Tobacco Road* look of the countryside. They dated their letters from "Hotspot, Georgia," and "Somewhere in the Goddamn Alabama woods." A certain folk memory of the Civil War persisted in the generation of the 1940s, and they debated that subject with more passion than information. Apparently the debate never ended. A combat engineer from Georgia recalled that when his outfit was clearing mines on Omaha Beach, "We fought the Civil War every night, with the Yankee boys giving us hell."

Very soon, certain "types" emerged in barracks society. There was the loudmouth and also the brownnoser, who risked ostracism by answering the officer's questions at orientation. There was the goldbrick, skilled in doing as few as possible of the tasks assigned him. And there was that unfortunate who could be found in every company: the sad sack. According to *A Dictionary of Soldier Talk*, "The Sad Sack did his best, but he was not very bright, always had bad luck, and was often victimized." But in the barracks everyone came to be typed. The process was outlined in a study made by the Walter Reed Army Institute of Research in the 1970s: "In the slack times of the day and in the barracks at night, the individuals come to know their own potential. It is in gossiping, carousing, smoking and playing that consensus emerges as to who can talk, who has sound judgment, and who is a fool, who is reliable and who is untrustworthy, who gets into trouble and who stays out."

The constant contact with others in the training company and the isolation from those outside had a limiting effect on the topics of conversation. "As in a village, small talk and gossip are among the soldiers' means of diversion, often with persons as the objects of conversation." Incidents in training, especially humorous ones, were recounted many times over, as were adventures in town and collisions with officers and other symbols of authority. Such things were bonds that bound the unit together and gave it a collective identity. Sometimes an episode became so celebrated that it entered into the unit's folklore. In certain circumstances a word or a phrase sufficed to bring it instantly to mind and everyone burst out laughing—everyone except outsiders.

The unit was also bound by the adoption of a new language, which everyone took up. Within a week or two the trainee was referring to his first sergeant as "the Top Kick"; a little later he would respond to any complaint or lament with the admonition "Tell it to the chaplain." He might even briefly refer to canned milk as "armored cow" and to a shovel as an "Army banjo," before dropping such terms as too contrived. Embracing the new language was part of accepting the group and also of accepting the Army: "When a soldier begins to use the Army vocabulary and slang without deliberate choice, and when a situation automatically evokes the correct attitudes, he has unwittingly acquired the rules and regulations whether he knows it or not." The new language might well include terms peculiar to the unit, an oft-repeated phrase or slogan, which once again would be incomprehensible to an outsider. In a company that contained a large number of academics who spent much time in menial labor, the term "Ph.D." meant "post hole digger."

Anyone who considered Army talk from the clinical viewpoint was soon led to what has been called "the sociology of the obscene." Social scientists who found themselves in uniform did not hide their shock at the "constant and crude use of obscenity" by the soldiers. They sought to analyze the phenomenon in professional journals, but were handicapped because they could not use the very terms they wanted to talk about. They spoke of "a vital concern for the only major erogenous portion of the human anatomy that does not distinguish male from female," and they found "a rich expressiveness in the eliminatory functions." The rapidity with which the soldier seasoned his speech with obscenities intrigued both sociologists and psychologists. Some saw in the use of taboo words "an aggression against all of those who accept the taboo—in this case the entire civilian environment." Others saw obscenity as a gesture of defiance against the matriarchy under which the soldier grew up, or as an expression of rebelliousness against the Army.

The younger and more impressionable probably took to obscene expressions the way they took to wearing their overseas caps at a jaunty angle—it fitted their image of the soldier. The more mature were less influenced by such considerations. Though they, too, picked up the terms and used them, they did not immediately incorporate them into their vocabularies. In their diaries they would mark off such words as "fuck-up" and "shit list" with quotation marks, at least in the initial entries. But sooner or later such words fitted naturally into the speech of most soldiers, often because they were the most accurate and direct means of expression. Thus the word "chickenshit"—"chicken," in its milder form —conveyed instantly and unmistakably the idea of something that was demeaning or disagreeable in petty ways. In the barracks "chickenshit" was appropriate; "demeaning" would have raised eyebrows. Few men seem to have worried that their language was taking on a scatological cast. If there was any concern, it was that they might slip up and use a salty Army term when they returned to home and family. Sometimes it happened in an episode that burned itself into the memory. A nineteen-year-old private, re-united with his family around the Sunday dinner table, in an unguarded moment asked, "How about the fuckin' butter?"

In speech, then, as in deportment, the barracks imposed its canons. Obeying them was part of "getting along" with others, getting oneself accepted. And getting accepted was part of survival. "There is a final, overriding reason for becoming incorporated into the social order of the barracks," the Walter Reed study concluded. "The soldier's sanity and very life depend upon it. Impoverished and constrictive as it may seem, the social order of the barracks provides the individual with the only bonds of caring, respect, affection, and affiliation that he has in the Army." To avoid exclusion, a soldier might go to considerable lengths to find a buddy. A sociologist noted: "Soldiers acquire some very queer friendships, which would have a dubious future in a civilian background." Significantly, the same writer added, "It is rare to see a soldier or a sailor alone, whereas most psychoneurotic servicemen have few or no friends."

There were casualties in every training company, men who dropped out for one reason or another. Quite often the problem was emotional. There was the older man who could not make the adjustment to Army life in body or in mind. He would go on sick call, or enter the hospital, and not come back (generally, if a soldier missed as much as six days' training he was set back in the training cycle). There was the "shaky kid" who froze in the middle of the infiltration course. Though the instructors halted the overhead machine-gun fire, they could not get him to move. An ambulance came for him, and he never returned to the company. And there was the homosexual who went to the chaplain or the company commander and explained that though he had thought he could control his impulses, after a week in the barracks he knew he could not, and he wanted out before something happened. The next day he was gone, headed back for civilian life with a "blue" discharge that labeled him undesirable and deprived him of any veteran's benefits. The same discharge went to drug addicts, compulsory thieves, and others whose habits were revealed in the endless scrutiny of the barracks.

Barracks life produced other casualties; men broke down under the strains it imposed. Sometimes the man who broke down was what they called a "mama's boy." Nowhere did the Army provide for the "unweaned weakling," the passive, helpless dependent who survived psychologically in proximity to his mother or her equivalent. An Army general who had extensive experience with NP cases traced the "weakling's" course to the psychiatric ward: "He's scared to death the minute he gets into uniform and he never gets over it. The men in the barracks soon begin to make fun of him and he has no comeback. Then they begin to bully him. The noncoms bawl him out in hope of arousing some combative spirit in the poor drip, but he doesn't have any. As soon as that becomes known he gets beaten up a couple of times, by kids half his size, and then he begins coming to the infirmary with his nerves all shot to pieces."

But for those who did make it through the training cycle and went off with their division or headed for the replacement depot, the major adjustment to Army life had been made. Whether he ended up in an infantry company in Italy or an artillery battery in New Guinea, or as "permanent party" in a stateside installation, the soldier would find pretty much the society he had known in the training camp. And the priorities and the claims on his loyalties would be essentially the same. He might be inspired by the fighting traditions of his division or his regiment, or he might be indifferent to them. He might like or dislike his officers. What counted more was the rapport with the men who worked or fought beside him. It was his buddies who mattered.

★ 4 ★

The View from
the Barracks

THE JOKES, the pranks, the traditions, and the taboos of the training camp were all parts of a larger whole, which for a time neither the Army nor the young sociologists on the spot could see. Only gradually did this larger entity become discernible: The barracks were giving birth to a hybrid, quasi-military society the exact like of which had never been seen before and most likely will never appear again. Had mobilization proceeded at a more leisurely pace, had smaller numbers of men from civilian life been fed into preexisting regiments and divisions, draftees would perhaps have been absorbed or assimilated fairly completely; new soldiers would have come to share something of the regular soldier's regard for rank, discipline, and other military totems. But that was not to be. Pouring millions of men into the Army in a short space of time was something like pouring a rich chemical solution into a receptacle that already contained a quite different solution; an interaction, a reaction, was inevitable. And the precipitate, to continue the chemical analogy, was a compound of traits and attitudes that could be called "the G.I. way."

The Army's leadership discovered very quickly that National Guardsmen and selectees did not have the regular soldier's notion of subordination or his respect for channels. Citizen-soldiers who found themselves stationed in camps far removed from their homes clamored for transfers—this was the first major "gripe" of the G.I. Army. Some soldiers did not hesitate to write directly to the Chief of Staff on this subject, nor did their mothers, wives, and sweethearts. A young woman in Brooklyn, unhappy that her boyfriend was stationed in Louisiana, assured General Marshall that "with a distance of 1500 miles separating us and seven months away from the woman he loves he could never be a good soldier." Surprisingly, Marshall sometimes answered these letters himself. He advised a heartsick private in Camp Polk: "If you will wholeheartedly devote all of your energies to making the best possible soldier of yourself, I doubt that you will find time to be homesick."

In the summer of 1941 the Army passed through a morale crisis of sorts (it would pass through a second crisis after the war was won). The word "crisis" may be too strong to describe the events of that summer, but at the time the General Staff used such words as "shocking" and "appalling" to describe some of the attitudes it discovered among the men in the ranks. To begin with, the Army had public relations problems that summer, problems exemplified by the "Yoohoo Affair." Lieutenant General Ben Lear, commanding the Second Army, was on a Memphis golf course when a convoy of soldiers slowed to call to some pretty girls nearby. Lear tried to remonstrate with the men, who did not recognize him and told him to mind his own business. Ultimately, the soldiers paid for their mistake: They got a dressing-down from Lear and a long march under the July sun. The punishment was not unduly severe, but the press took up the affair and soon both Lear and the War Department got a cascade of hostile mail, much of it from the parents of draftees.

That summer there were also extensive maneuvers in Tennessee. Reporters covering the exercises often interviewed soldiers, who did not hesitate to pass judgment on the maneuvers or on the Army. They complained that they were kept in the dark about what they were doing, and they talked at length about the deficiencies in training and shortages of material. They felt they should be learning about the Blitzkrieg, but they assured reporters, "We've never even seen a tank." General Marshall sent a confidential radiogram to the commanding generals of the four armies, warning of a buildup in the press unfavorable to the maneuvers. He wrote President Roosevelt that press accounts of low morale among the soldiers were themselves generating low morale.

In truth, morale among the soldiers was not high that summer. This was particularly the case among National Guardsmen; they had accepted mobilization unhesitatingly in the fall of 1940, when a mood of crisis prevailed. But now, months later, the danger of war seemed less imminent, and the Guardsmen were anxious to get back to the families and businesses that many of them had left behind (they were more strongly motivated in this regard than the first contingents of selectees, who were younger and had fewer obligations in civilian life). By June most men were looking forward to their release in the fall. Then the administration asked Congress to extend the period of service by eighteen months, which the War Department said was necessary if the nation's preparedness program was to continue. After stormy debate, Congress voted the extension in August.

Among citizen-soldiers and their families the extension generated considerable hostility, and that hostility found several outlets. Soldiers wrote their congressmen, though in principle this was prohibited by the Articles of War. Wives and parents of servicemen wrote, too, and General Marshall admitted he was getting "a tremendous number of communications" about the extension. In the various camps there were efforts to organize demonstrations— or at least talk of organizing them. Here and there on barracks walls appeared the cryptic inscription OHIO, signifying "Over the Hill in October." At the very height of the agitation, *Life* magazine brought out its issue of August 18, with a story on "the growing restlessness and boredom of the great civilian army." It highlighted soldier's gripes and offered an in-depth look at an unidentified division (actually the 27th Division, then at Fort McClellan, Alabama). The article reproduced some vehement comments by the soldiers, including one that began, "To hell with Roosevelt and Marshall and the Army and especially this Goddamn hole."

The War Department was still reeling from this blow when *The New York Times* asked its cooperation in investigating the accuracy of the *Life* exposé. A. H. Sulzberger, the *Times* publisher, pledged that if the investigation did reveal the soldier's morale to be bad, then in the public interest the *Times* would *not* publish the story, the nation already being virtually at war against Germany. Such at least was the pledge conveyed by Hilton H. Railey, whom the *Times* chose to carry out the investigation. The War Department agreed and gave Railey full access to its various installations. In the late summer of 1941 he traveled some 8,000 miles, visiting most of the large southern camps and continuing on to the West Coast. He talked to over a thousand officers and men, taking copious notes. Then he and Sulzberger wrote a two-hundred-page report, "Morale in the U.S. Army," which they sent to Washington at the end of September. The American public never learned of Railey's findings. In the War Department the report was promptly classified "secret"; even today its existence is not widely known among military historians.

Railey was himself a veteran of World War I and was fundamentally sympathetic to the Army. He was clearly shocked by some of the things he found and he conveyed this shock to the General Staff very effectively. The Railey report made sobering reading. Generals with the troops confirmed the low state of morale. One spoke of "deterioration," and another said, "An abiding faith is lacking." Railey witnessed numerous scenes of what he called "flagrant and disgraceful" fraternization between officers and enlisted men. In one division the men had booed their officers; in another, Railey claimed the officers were in "physical fear" of the men under them. In Alexandria, Louisiana, he saw soldiers from the nearby camps in a carnival of drunkenness. A lieutenant had passed out on the front steps of the Hotel Bentley. On the road leading to a nightclub on the outskirts of town, Railey passed hundreds of soldiers in various stages of inebriation; one man staggered along carrying a rural mailbox, post and all, which he had evidently pulled up along the roadside. At one in the morning Railey watched a drunken soldier pound on the bar, demanding two drinks at a time. A major who was also at the bar leaned over and said, "Soldier, don't you think you've had about enough?" The soldier glared at the major, taking in his insignia of rank, and replied, "You take a good fuck for yourself." The officer then said, "All right, soldier, carry on."

Railey portrayed many higher officers as sitting complacently on a volcano of discontent, refusing to hear the rumblings of trouble. Such was the case with Major General Milton Reckord, commander of the 29th Division, then at Fort Meade, Maryland. Reckord told Railey that the "spirit" of his men was excellent. He could tell from their performance "in the field, out there in the heat." Then he added, "I don't pretend to know what my men think about the world situation, or anything else, for that matter, and I don't see the point of asking them." The view of the rank and file of the 29th was provided by a confidential observer, who told Railey that the men rarely mentioned General Reckord "except when someone says 'shit on him.' He may think morale is OK because all of his subordinates have to tell him it is," the observer continued. "If his powers of observation are any good at all, though, he should know better."

The basic warning sounded by Railey was unmistakable: "Command, vintage of 1917 (pretty general), appears naively and disconcertingly unaware that its men, vintage of 1940, are *a different breed of cat*. . . . The present breed (mark well) is questioning everything from God Almighty to themselves." The soldier of 1941 was also surprisingly well informed. Railey found that 95 percent of the men he talked with knew of the *Life* article; nine men out of ten told him things were even worse than the magazine described—they would then make telling criticisms of their own. Most seriously, they failed to understand the necessity of their own service in the Army. "They compare it to a football team in training but without a schedule of games," said Railey.

The immediate response of Army leadership was interesting. General McNair was so appalled that he proposed demobilizing the National Guard and sending it home. Other generals agreed with Railey that Nazi and communist "agitators" in the ranks were partly to blame, and that the FBI should take the camps under close surveillance. General Marshall took a less drastic view. He approved a plan to give early discharge to soldiers twenty-eight years of age or older, those whom the Railey report had indicated were the most disaffected. The measure was well received. Agitation seemed to die down and the desertion rate—the essential barometer of Army morale—remained low. And after December 7 the morale crisis was a thing of the past.

But the crisis of 1941 registered with Army leadership, and especially with General Marshall. During that hectic summer he had found no better way to gauge the mood in the barracks than to have the Adjutant General's people open soldiers' letters, a very dubious procedure at best. In October he took steps to find out the G.I.'s view of things by the simple but revolutionary expedient of asking him. Secretary of War Henry Stimson was opposed to opinion surveys among the troops, as were a number of generals, but Marshall had his way. In December the first cautious survey was conducted among men of the 9th Division at Fort Bragg. As time went on, the Research Branch of the Information and Education Division perfected its polling techniques and broadened the range of its questions until it was asking privates what they would do if *they* were company commander. By the end of the war the Research Branch had administered over two hundred surveys. It issued a periodic report called "What the Soldier Thinks," and after the war Samuel Stouffer and other veterans of the branch drew the polling results together in a comprehensive work called *The American Soldier*. Its two volumes are the point of departure for all inquiries into the average G.I.'s attitudes and preoccupations.

Given the incredible diversity in the rank and file of the G.I. Army, given the fact that each of several million soldiers had his own distinct set of experiences in the service and his own reaction to those experiences, is it even possible to talk about the "average" G.I.? It is at least possible to isolate the most widely held attitudes, relying in part on sociological data, but also on what the G.I. revealed of himself in the things he said and did, and even in the songs he liked and the jokes that made him laugh. It is possible, but it is not easy. The G.I. was a complex person. Arthur Miller sensed as much as he toured Army camps: "The American soldier is a much more complicated character than he is ever given credit for. He cannot be written into the script as though he were a civilian wearing a brown suit with metal buttons, nor can he be regarded as a 'soldier,' a being whose reactions are totally divorced from civilian emotions."

The G.I. was in a very real sense suspended between two ways of life and held in that state of suspension as long as he wore a uniform. Physically he left civilian life, yet mentally he never joined the Army; he was in the service but not of it. He spent part of his time thinking about what was for him the present—that is, his Army existence—and fully as much time thinking about his past—and what he hoped would be his future—in the civilian world. So if we are to understand the G.I., his attitudes toward these two worlds are the places to start.

The fact that most G.I.s remained emphatically civilians at heart, tied to the world they had left, is best demonstrated by the way they stayed in contact with that world. Periodic contact was essential to the G.I.'s morale, and the quickest and most direct means was a telephone call. During the 1941 maneuvers the Army discovered that soldiers would often stop at a farmhouse, ask to use the telephone, and call their homes collect to say hello from the field, a practice the authorities condemned as "unwarlike." Every Army camp had its telephone exchange, where men waited in turn for a booth while a bank of switchboard girls placed long-distance calls. In the evenings traffic was heaviest; the Bell exchange at Petersburg, Virginia, normally had four direct circuits to New York, but in the evenings, when the men at Camp Lee phoned home, the number of circuits was increased to twenty. At Camp Upton, New York, with thirty phone booths and five operators, the wait was sometimes an hour and a half.

For many men the contact was maintained chiefly through letters, and after troops went overseas this was virtually the only means of communication possible. Mail was a major concern in most soldiers' lives. Their own letters almost invariably started out with references to letters they had received or were expecting. The volume of correspondence was staggering: In 1943 the average G.I. was getting fourteen pieces of mail a week. He was also writing frequently. A survey among troops in Italy revealed that over half had written letters within the preceding twenty-four hours. Mail delivery was often erratic in overseas areas and was a frequent subject of complaint in soldiers' letters. If there was no mail for a considerable time, morale was affected. A black veteran recalled: "The mail had been sidetracked. We had no idea what was happening in the world outside. We had no outside. Psychologically it did something to me. I wrote a letter home: 'You've forsaken me. You don't write and I'm gonna die.' Finally my mother was able to get the Red Cross through to me."

While the soldier's morale required contact with his loved ones, an obsessive preoccupation with what was going on at home could lead the soldier to forget what he was supposed to be doing. Army psychiatrists kept an eye out for soldiers who spent all their time with their correspondence, and thus were in a sense absent. Then, too, the mail from home did not always bring good news. The soldiers felt powerless to aid in a family crisis, especially if they were overseas, and their anxiety could take many forms. "We had a saying," recalled an Army psychiatrist, "that as many casualties were caused on Guadalcanal by the mail from home as through enemy bullets."

The G.I.s' letters home offer the researcher an incredible variety in source materials. The two main themes are Army life—as much of it as censorship will allow them to tell—and talk of home. In MacArthur's command, a counterintelligence officer who screened G.I. letters found a fundamental sincerity in their judgments: "Opinions written to the folks back home can usually be taken as genuine." Garson Kanin, who censored G.I. mail, claimed it was one of the most significant literary experiences of his life: "I read some of the greatest prose in the English language, written by kids who couldn't spell. It didn't matter. It was the feeling." The most intense feeling, the most vivid images, often concerned home. "Tell me how my room looks," one G.I. wrote to his mother. "Did you change the furniture around? How are my records? My books?" Another wrote his father: "When your letters come I go up to my bunk to read them. Everything changes. I see you at the desk writing."

Nostalgia was a common ingredient in soldiers' letters. A G.I. in Sicily wrote a former teacher: "Life was so simple and uninvolved. We had problems then, of course we did, and at the time they seemed insurmountable; but as I look back, I believe that the most pressing problem I had was whether or not I would make the first five on the basketball team." A sociologist isolated among G.I.s a specific "nostalgia effect," which he described as "a sentimental overvaluing of everything the serviceman, by reason of his induction, had left behind." Army psychiatrists detected it, too, and saw potential dangers in it: "For the American the future has always been important. Suddenly, in the Army, the past becomes important. In his fantasies the soldier refashions so that only a fanciful expurgated past remains. All past pain is deleted, and he reminisces about the glory of what once was. This includes other people; for example the girlfriend toward whom he might have been rather ambivalent becomes a paragon of virtue. Hence the impulsive, erratic marriage with its attendant disasters."

When the soldier got a furlough and went home, he sometimes felt disillusionment the moment he stepped off the train and saw his hometown as smaller and shabbier than he had remembered it. Sometimes this "furlough syndrome," as it was called, was more subtle in its effects. Robert Welker recalled: "In those last weeks before embarkation we eagerly sought a three-day pass or a ten-day furlough, reaching back for that other life; but we found that the life had existed within ourselves, and was no longer there. I had that last Christmas at home, picketed round with friends and all the sweet remembered images of a loving family; yet each hour seemed to exist only in the past, real only as it could be remembered. I found that I could not even wear one of the civilian suits which hung in the closet of my room; the gesture would have been painfully empty, and a futile retreat, in a time when reality was decked in olive drab."

The man home on furlough was not alone in sensing that something had changed. Often parents and wives felt the returning serviceman was different, though they could not say exactly how. A sizable minority of soldiers were married (30 percent in the spring of 1943), and for them and their wives military service posed special problems. Many wives followed their husbands, finding what accommodations they could in crowded camp towns; thus husband and wife were able to be together, though in far-from-ideal circumstances. But even this arrangement was only temporary, for often it was too expensive to keep up, or the soldier was shipped overseas.

Separation placed severe strains not only on marriages, but also on engagements and on couples who were just "going steady." One soldier claimed a man's attitude toward separation was largely a function of his age:

> The older fellows, those who were married and settled, seemed to have their emotions usually on the same level. The youngest were happy-go-lucky boys, joking about their love life, and laughing about someone else's heartbreak. In between, there was a large crop. It included those who were married and those who were single and had girl friends to write to. The emotions of this group varied. There were some whose wives were calling it quits, and others who received "Dear Johns" from their sweethearts. There was an ever changing display of emotions whenever the mail truck brought those much wanted letters from home.

The "Dear John," also called the "Green Banana" in some parts of the Pacific, seems to have been a fairly common piece of mail. When a man received one, and if it were a serious affair, he could count on the sympathy and support of his buddies. A soldier in the Pacific got a letter from his wife that said simply, "I've found someone else, I want a divorce." His friends rallied around and did their best, but he was inconsolable. Not long afterward he was killed in action; the men in his outfit took a savage pleasure in knowing that three days before his death he had changed the beneficiary of his government life insurance policy. His faithless wife would get nothing.

Like other unpleasant things in the G.I.'s existence, the "Dear John" took on a humorous denotation. G.I.s in India formed the "Brush-Off Club," with admission only by Dear John letter; branches were formed in several other countries. G.I.s in Texas organized the "Jilted G.I. Club" with the same entrance requirement and a theme song: "Somebody Else Is Taking My Place." Army psychiatrists believed that under the hilarity there was considerable brooding and preoccupation. One psychiatrist cited the case of an emotionally disturbed soldier, brought to his attention because the unit censor had found the soldier's letters to his wife filled with wild and groundless accusations of infidelity. The same psychiatrist added: "Even in the normal person there appears to be considerable apprehension about the fidelity of the soldier's wife or sweetheart. Most often in the 'normal' the entire conflict is repressed. But if the question is ever raised, as during a 'bull session,' the conversation becomes charged with considerable feeling."

Psychological warfare specialists in all armies were convinced that the theme of "the woman left behind" was a highly profitable one to exploit; broadcasts and leaflets suggesting the infidelity of the enemy soldier's wife or sweetheart were frequently used. The Germans sometimes showered the American lines with leaflets portraying an attractive woman sitting on her bed removing her hose, while in the background a man was taking off his tie. The picture bore the caption "While You're Away." G.I.s tended to pick the leaflets up, chiefly because the woman was nude.

The G.I. view of women in the generic sense—the one that reigned in the barracks bull sessions—tended toward the earthy and the anatomical. Once again sociologists and psychologists in uniform observed the men around them; they spoke of a reversion to "adolescent erotic attitudes." A pair of psychologists observed that "the sight of a girl, a raised skirt in the movies, or representations of anatomy will evoke tremendous responses. Anyone who has ever attended a post theatre will be cognizant of this hyperaesthetic sexual attitude." A sociologist who had served with the French and with North African Moslem troops made some striking comparisons. The Frenchman spoke less about the sexual aspect of a woman and talked more about her personality than the G.I. did. The G.I.'s attitude closely resembled that of the North African, though the latter had fewer inhibitions; moreover, the G.I. shared certain sexual views with the Arapaho Indians, whom the sociologist had previously studied. His conclusion: "If animals could talk, their conversation about sex would doubtless be similar to that of the Moslems, Arapahos, and G.I.s."

Some psychologists believed that the frequent and graphic discussions of sex were attempts by the soldiers to reassure themselves that they were sexually adequate, even though deprived by their Army duties of the customary contacts with the opposite sex. They also believed that it was the desire to reassure and reaffirm himself that sent the G.I. on his forays into the bars and fleshpots that flourished near most large posts.

This was the kind of activity the Army understood and expected of its men. The Regulars were known for their fondness for women and their dislike of marriage. Few Regulars took wives in the Old Army, partly because a man's commanding officer had to give his consent, but mostly because it was hard to maintain a household on a private's salary (twenty-one dollars a month in 1940). The New Army imitated the old in its periodic "blowing off steam," with nights filled with liquor, women, and brawls in varying amounts. A G.I. sociologist provided the rationale. Once away from rules and regulations, "the soldier characteristically felt supremely 'free' and sought to release his impulses and feelings." Near almost every camp was a collection of bars, tattoo parlors, and beer halls, often called "the Strip," "G.I. town," or "Boomtown." There were places with colorful names like "The Pig Pen," "The Red Hound Bar," and "Frankie's Place." The historian of the 3rd Armored Division wrote nostalgically of nightspots near Camp Polk, where the division trained: the Red Dog Saloon, the Tip Top Inn, and the Roof Garden. In the latter place fights always produced "a flurry of slats jerked out of the railing which enclosed the dance floor." Soldiers stationed at Fort

Benning had at hand the most celebrated "good-time town" in the country. A soldier who knew it well penned this description: "The principal industry of the small town of Phenix City, Alabama [just across the state line from Fort Benning], is sex, and its customer is the Army. . . . The town is at least eighty percent devoted to the titillation and subsequent pillage of that group it affectionately calls 'Uncle Sam's Soldier Boys.'"

The G.I.'s affinity for casual sex and rowdy good times, cultivated in bars and bawdy houses all over the country, would manifest itself abroad and give Europeans a vivid and unflattering impression of American culture. Yet curiously, though the G.I. often scouted for easy women, he was also on a quest for "a nice girl"—"someone to go with." Soldiers confided this to Army hostesses, and they told Railey over and over again that they wanted "some place to go, some place to meet decent girls in real companionship." They trooped in droves to the on-post dances at the service club, waiting patiently to dance with a "nice girl," though men might outnumber girls ten to one. They sought acquaintance at the USO, and at church socials under the watchful gaze of chaperones. G.I.s in England were seen trying to strike up conversations with policewomen who were directing traffic. And in most cases they were just looking for "someone to go with." Hobbled by the Army regimen, set apart by the uniform they wore, they still followed the companionship-courtship ritual that had been part of their civilian lives.

It sometimes rankled them that they could no longer compete at best advantage. Resentment against those not in uniform often lay just under the surface, but it was not only their disadvantage in the competition for girls that rankled; there was a general ill feeling toward those who had stayed home to enjoy high wages and the pleasures of civilian life. Men overseas felt this resentment most keenly; in their letters they made frequent sarcastic references to "slackers," those with occupational deferments, and particularly strikers. The resentment went sufficiently deep for the G.I. to coin a derogatory name for the well-ensconced civilian: feather merchant.

For every derogatory term the soldier used to describe civilians, he used ten to describe the Army. For the Army was the other pole of the G.I.'s existence, and it seems at times to have repelled him quite as much as the civilian world attracted him. This phenomenon of attraction-repulsion could best be seen in little things. The soldier would pass up a chance to see a film at the post theater, then pay twice as much to see it at a theater in town—simply because it was in town. He would spurn a well-equipped recreation hall for a dingy downtown poolroom, because that way he could "get away from the Goddamn Army." This sort of behavior was all the more baffling to Army authorities, since post theaters and recreation buildings were designed to help the citizen-soldier adjust to military life. Ultimately, the Army's leaders, or at least the most perceptive of them, acknowledged that the G.I. would probably remain "maladjusted" despite all their efforts. To put it another way, the typical G.I. did not care for the Army and never would. If he commented on the service, that comment generally took the form of a gripe, for negativism reigned supreme in the barracks. Even those who liked Army life either kept quiet or joined the chorus of complaint. To do otherwise was to invite the most stinging rebuke one G.I. could inflict on another: "I think you've found a home in the Army."

The negative view of the Army developed early. Even before the draft began, the service had something of an image problem. In the popular mind it was a haven for misfits, filled with turbulent young men who had been given a choice between a hitch in the Army and a stretch in the penitentiary (in the 1930s some judges did offer this option to first-time offenders). Some of the early draftees noticed here and there that the uniform they wore carried a certain stigma; they might be refused a table in a fashionable restaurant, for example. Happily such discrimination faded quickly after Pearl Harbor. Into 1942 Hollywood adversely affected many a young man's view of the service with a series of films about tyranical sergeants, played by such character actors as Wallace Beery and Nat Pendleton (General Marshall went so far as to ask the film industry to drop the genre). Then, too, the Army suffered in comparison with the Navy and Marines; it could not offer the opportunities the Navy did for foreign travel, nor could it rival the impressive uniform of the Marines. The Army didn't even have a stirring song or anthem of its own (it still doesn't).

In the months before Pearl Harbor considerable ill will was generated when draftees and National Guardsmen clashed with the Regulars, who regarded the new arrivals as intruders and inferiors. Bill Mauldin remembered one post where the Regulars would not let Guardsmen use their PX. There was an especially serious difference between the Regulars and the "number men," as they called draftees, who saw the Army and the military life through very different eyes. A sergeant named Henry Giles, who had enlisted in 1939 after an impoverished youth, summed up the way many Regulars felt: "Nobody knows what the Army meant to me—security and pride and something good. . . . Putting on that uniform not only meant that for the first time in my life I had clothes I wasn't ashamed of, but also for the first time in my life I was *somebody*." Then, Giles recalled, the draftees arrived to disrupt his orderly world: "They came in bitching about this and that, regulations, the food, a cot instead of an innerspring mattress, barracks instead of private rooms." The draftee in turn had his view of the Regulars. Robert Welker said the Regulars "seemed to take a truculent pride in their own submission to the officer class and the system, and in their minor competences and little claims to caste among their fellow plebeians." And *Yank*, in its issue of September 2, 1942, defined "Old Army" as "a large group of first-three-graders who spent the pre-war years thinking up sentences beginning with 'By God, it wasn't like this in the ———.' "

This antagonism had important consequences in the first year or so, when Regulars moved into the noncommissioned slots in the expanding Army. Often poorly educated and vaguely intimidated by the draftees under them, the Regulars could be hard taskmasters. A draftee named John Toole wrote home from Fort Lewis, Washington, that "a brutal looking sergeant" had ordered all college men to take one step forward. When Toole and several others confidently did so, the sergeant told them, "I want you college men to dig a latrine twenty-four inches deep and thirty feet long right over there." Since the entire camp had modern plumbing, the punitive nature of the order was clear. A high proportion of the Regulars were southerners, and at the time of Pearl Harbor half the noncoms in the Army were from the South. Northern draftees wrote home that their noncoms did not like "Yankees" and made their lives difficult. The draftees had little recourse, though in at least one company the men got back at their persecutor by repeatedly singing the Civil War song "Marching through Georgia" while out on road marches. In training camps, where the men were new to the Army and looked for someone in authority who was sympathetic or at least fair to them, the strains created by the noncoms' animosity were sometimes severe. They became almost unbearable when the tyrannized draftees were well-educated blacks; psychiatrists found they were apt to become paranoid. Occasionally the pressures became downright explosive—Railey cited such a case at Camp Croft, South Carolina, in which several hundred Regulars had to be hastily transferred. As time passed and the composition of the Army changed, the problem went away, but it left behind a harvest of bitterness.

There was another matter on which the Old Army and the G.I. clashed throughout the war, and this was the uniform. In the pre-war Army there had been something of a cult of the uniform. The best troops were thought to be smart-looking troops, with impeccable dress a badge of both good discipline and high morale. Each regiment might have its leather a specified tint, and it was not uncommon for a company commander to stipulate the brand of shoe polish his men were to use. Soldiers spent an appreciable part of their meager pay to purchase commercially made leggings and brass items because they were of higher quality than the government issue.

That same dress code that was a hallmark of excellence in the Old Army was to the G.I. a particularly irksome manifestation of Army "chicken." A young soldier from the Middle West wrote home from Camp Croft in June 1943: "The other evening we lined up for retreat and the corporal verbally burned us in hell by his language because one of the fellows had not buttoned his buttons on his shirt pocket. Yet, here stood the corporal in front of us with his own shirt button open. It's a job to keep your mouth shut on occasions like this."

One of the most vexatious items of clothing in the first half of the war was the canvas leggings; putting them on was a tedious and time-consuming business, and the soldiers went without them whenever possible. An artilleryman in Italy told journalist Ernie Pyle that his battery was busy firing one morning when a new officer telephoned to ask if the men had their leggings on. "It made me so damned mad that I just pulled the gun out of action while we all sat down and put on the leggings," he said. In the Southwest Pacific, General Walter Krueger banned the practice of going shirtless, though he acknowledged in his memoirs that the order was unpopular and frequently disobeyed.

Even when he wore the full uniform, the G.I. did not wear it with the smartness and the swagger of the old Regulars. Hilton Railey complained that the new soldiers had a lack of pride in their uniforms, and an MP lieutenant told him, "We can't begin to cope with their dress." General Dwight D. Eisenhower wrote General Marshall in 1943 that the "natural proclivities of the American soldier" in matters of dress made a body of his troops look like "an armed mob." General Joseph Stilwell said that the G.I. was "superbly equipped, but happiest when in fatigues with a dirty baseball cap." General Patton's preoccupation with matters of dress was well known; he wrote an angry letter to the Army newspaper *Stars and Stripes*, complaining that the soldiers in Bill Mauldin's cartoons were slovenly, dirty, and unshaven. Mauldin's characters did not change their habits of dress—nor, for that matter, did the combat soldiers they represented.

Resistance to Army notions of conformity took another guise, one so subtle the soldiers themselves were unaware of it. The "armed mob" effect that Eisenhower complained of resulted not only from the way the soldier dressed, but also from his stance and his habits of movement. British officers remarked that the Americans had their own loose and free way of marching. Orval Faubus, who was an infantry officer, recalled that when his outfit assembled in occupied Germany, he noticed German civilians pointing at the troops and snickering at the raggedness of their formations and movements. It was not that the soldiers marched out of step, or that they could not move about in bodies with ease and dispatch.

It was that each man stepped out or swung his arms in his own way, giving European observers an impression of incipient discordance in any body of marching G.I.s. No amount of close order drill could completely erase that impression, for the G.I. never made that ultimate, intimate surrender of the individual to the mass. It was possible to see the lack of parade ground precision in another way. A Czech villager remarked to an American officer as they both watched American troops swing by, "They walk like free men."

It was not the iron law of conformity the uniform represented that G.I.s disliked most, but rather the institutionalized inequality they found. Railey saw evidence of this in 1941: "At one of the bivouacs, when the men had no food, not even water, a colonel and some other officers were seen drinking beer and eating sandwiches. . . . That infuriated their men." Quite often the resentment was directed not at the officer's superior status in itself, but at the material privileges he enjoyed. A G.I. wrote to *Yank* in December 1945: "What we EM [enlisted men] can't figure out is what God-given reason or military order says officers shall eat steak and drink whiskey while their subordinates eat hash." Separate wards in hospitals and reserved seats in theaters further goaded the G.I. Also resented was any menial service for the personal benefit of an officer—or noncom, for that matter. In February 1944 *Yank* published a letter from a soldier who had been confined for refusing to mop the sergeant's floor. He was unrepentant: "I'll sweat for my country, but here is one private who is never going to mop any sergeant's floor, even if it costs me six months' confinement." *Yank* gave such complaints a sympathetic ear. In its "Dogface Dictionary" it defined "rank" as "offensively gross or coarse; indecent; strongly scented."

In point of fact, the American soldier had less to complain about than his British or German counterpart. An American colonel reported after a visit to the British army: "There is an immeasurable gulf between the British officer and his enlisted men. My impression is that the comfort and welfare of the British soldier is not given the attention by his superior officer that the American soldier not only expects, but receives." And a captured German soldier named Erich Kuby witnessed a scene that is worth relating for what it tells about the G.I. Army. An American soldier had "liberated" a wristwatch belonging to a German prisoner. An American officer who was present ordered the soldier to return the watch; thereupon the soldier's sergeant intervened, and a loud and vehement argument ensued. Kuby reflected, "In our army such an argument, if not impossible, would have been accompanied by evil consequences for the sergeant."

The authors of *The American Soldier* discovered that resentment of privilege was basic to the G.I.'s makeup, and moreover that resentment increased as the war progressed. Samuel Stouffer and his colleagues concluded that privilege in the Army was objectionable because it was more precisely defined and more blatant than privilege in civilian life. A poor man might someday hope to receive an invitation to the country club; a private would never be invited to the officers' club. The Army's caste system came close to racial segregation in civilian life; for black soldiers adaptation to the military life was easier in this respect. There are no doubt other explanations for the American soldier's attitude toward officers and their privileges. There was no heritage, no cultural "memory" of legally distinguished classes as there was in Europe, and thus there was no tradition of deference to the officer-nobleman. The American officer's "title" was essentially his college degree, and among Americans the bachelor of arts diploma does not automatically inspire respect in those who do not possess one.

Just as the uniform was the badge of conformity, to many soldiers the salute was the symbol of subservience, and here the draftee's record is no more impressive than that of his observance of the dress code. The officer who delivered the military courtesy lecture might describe the salute as a "privilege," enjoyed only by those in the military service, but most G.I.s did not see it that way. They complained that they felt self-conscious about calling other men to attention when an officer approached, and they confessed that they avoided officers in order to avoid saluting them. What concerned the Army more was the soldier's failure to salute when he clearly should. At Fort Meade this neglect brought a five-dollar fine; at Camp Livingston, Louisiana (and a number of other posts), failure to salute resulted in a Saturday road march of twenty miles. A soldier who had been so punished at Livingston wrote a blistering letter to *Yank*: "The principles we are fighting for are being destroyed before our very eyes." There was a general tendency among the men to be more casual about "military courtesy" in the evenings and on weekends, when a man was not on "Army time," and especially when he was off post. To combat this tendency the authorities at Fort Meade, Maryland, sent "military courtesy teams" into Baltimore. An officer walked the downtown streets, followed by two MPs who picked up every soldier who did not salute the officer.

The Military Police were a problem in themselves. They became a separate organism of the Army only in 1941. Their recent creation and their lack of tradition may explain why they generally did not have high morale or a favorable self-image. But the fact is that the rest of the Army did not have a very favorable picture of them, either, and this was confirmed in the attitude surveys of the Research Branch. Even G.I.s who had no contact with MPs felt they were arbitrary and unfair. The citizen-soldier did not show the same hostility toward municipal police, and Arthur Miller tried to explain the discrepancy: "The difference between an MP and a civil policeman is that you are never asked to elect the MP or the people who control him. This difference is fatal." But the more likely reason for the unpopularity of the MPs is that they made it impossible for the G.I. to "get away from the God-damn Army." They followed him off post, enforcing "military courtesy" and making him roll his sleeves down and button his shirt. By 1945 there were over ten thousand MPs in the United States alone, patrolling the streets of towns like Alexandria, Louisiana, and Phenix City, Alabama; over three thousand rode the nation's railways, keeping an eye on the dress and deportment of soldiers on furlough. And the soldiers they watched perhaps savored the revelation in *Yank* that a former hit man for Murder Incorporated had been made an MP sergeant; at the very least they consoled themselves with the thought that the initials MP had another meaning in the barracks: Miserable Prick.

A number of rumors about the Military Police circulated in

the Army. According to one, an MP who let a prisoner escape had to serve out the escapee's term; according to another, if an MP shot a fleeing prisoner he was fined a dollar—and then presented with a carton of cigarettes. Both these stories were only service folklore, but then such stories circulated about every arm and service in the Army. There was, for example, the oft-told tale that Army cooks seasoned the food with saltpeter to reduce the soldiers' libido; men assigned to KP were told by their buddies to keep an eye out for the telltale chemical. Then there were stories, rooted in envy, about soft living in other arms or services. Men in the combat arms insisted that Quartermasters lived sybaritic lives, consuming rations that should have gone to the front. The U.S. Army Air Forces were filled with "glamour boys" who enjoyed inordinately high rank. *Yank* "reported" the case of a Western Union delivery boy who went into the Pentagon to deliver a telegram and emerged three days later as an Air Force major. Moreover, airmen were withdrawn from action after completing a certain number of missions, while there was no such arrangement in the Army Ground Forces; then, too, the "fly boys" got most of the medals. (These two gripes were well founded; with a more liberal policy on decorations, the Army Air Forces gave out three fourths of the medals conferred under authority of the War Department.) In the Pacific there was considerable rivalry between soldiers and Marines, for the latter always seemed to get most of the credit for victory there: "The Marines, the Marines, those publicity fiends," ran a piece of Army doggerel.

There were other rivalries between specific Army units. In the Louisiana maneuvers of 1943, the 88th Division was pitted against the 31st—the "Dixie Division"—which it regarded as its own personal enemy. Occasionally, fistfights broke out along the line of contact, and war games umpires had to call in officers of the two divisions to break up the fighting. More ominous were the confrontations between blacks and whites. Sometimes black soldiers clashed with police in southern towns; in one such episode in Alexandria, Louisiana, early in 1942, thirty blacks were wounded by police gunfire. Often the collision was between black soldiers and white MPs. But all too often there were white-against-black scuffles and brawls among the men themselves, both in camp and in town.

The animosities and the rivalries, even the barroom taunts and occasional brawls between units, had an important role in the soldier's life. They provided him with identity and affiliation beyond his immediate group and a sense of belonging to something more tangible and more appealing than that immense khaki sea called the Army. The division patch, worn on the shoulder, was such a badge of identity and belonging. In the early days of the war, when almost everything was in short supply, the soldiers clamored for patches and sometimes ordered them from commercial suppliers, paying for them out of their own pockets. Paratroopers had to have the high, laced boots of their specialty; when issued standard Army boots in their training camps they offered to pay for the lace-ups themselves. By the same token, men in the armored divisions prized their distinctive "tanker" jackets; those in the infantry cherished the oblong blue Combat Infantryman Badge, introduced in 1943 to give special recognition to the infantrymen. But the important thing was that, while each man found for himself an island of familiarity and belonging in that vast khaki sea, he continued to share with his fellows that common set of attitudes that made up the G.I. way.

We now know something of the way the G.I. regarded the two worlds to which he belonged, but how did he see himself? The answer probably lies in the term he chose to describe himself: G.I. The origin of this abbreviation is much debated, but it was undoubtedly used in the Old Army for "government issue." One story is that the Regulars used it as a derogatory label for early draftees, since they were content to wear what the Army gave them—i.e., government issue—rather than buy commercially made items of uniform that would have given them a smarter appearance. If obscurity surrounded the derivation of "G.I.," its various meanings were also a source of much confusion for the uninitiated. Thus, a man who had "the G.I.s" was afflicted with the Army's version of diarrhea. Used in another way, as in "too G.I.," the term meant a person or organization that rigidly adhered to regulations. When *Yank* began publication on June 14, 1942, the staff felt obliged to tell readers that the magazine was "not G.I. except in the sense that we are G.I." (That same issue contained a cartoon by Corporal Dave Breger entitled "G.I. Joe," which is probably the origin of that term.)

The use of "G.I." to simply designate a soldier probably began about 1941. In July of that year a *New York Times* reporter said no new name such as "doughboy" from the previous war had yet emerged; but about the same time another observer noted: "So common is the expression 'G.I.' that soldiers now apply it to themselves." Academics in the ranks, especially sociologists, were intrigued by the term; thanks largely to them we know some of its early nuances. They determined that "G.I." implied little or nothing by way of human qualities or values, but rather symbolized a mass-production commodity, a faceless creation as devoid of character as a bottle cap. Whoever took the label was thus putting himself down, and one early definition of "G.I." was "a good-humored expression of self-deprecation by the citizen-soldier."

Yet the same citizen-soldier could not accept the submersion in the mass or slavish submission that the term implied. There were indications that the soldier called himself G.I. for the same reasons that a man in civilian life might refer to himself as a peon—to describe a condition to which fate had consigned him and against which he inwardly rebelled. The G.I. appeared to be a man much imposed upon, even victimized: He was in the Army while others evaded the draft and remained at home; or he was in a combat unit while other soldiers lived comfortably behind the zone of operations. This being the case, it is easy to understand the popularity of Sergeant George Baker's cartoon character The Sad Sack —to a degree, the G.I. identified with him. Yet the G.I. did not wallow in self-pity; if he got the tough breaks and the dirty jobs, he took an almost perverse pride in coping with both and in enduring. He would generally do his job with a grim competence, perhaps lightly tinged with cynicism. What is more, like Bill Mauldin's characters Willie and Joe, he could find humor in his travails and somehow retain his dignity while hip deep in mud.

The element most difficult to isolate in the G.I.'s makeup is his positive motivation. From time to time throughout the war, Army authorities worried about a lack of commitment on the soldier's part; they tried to stimulate it with orientation sessions and a "Why We Fight" film series and a more liberal policy on decorations. Arthur Miller complained that he could find no expression of "social responsibility" in the barracks, and Hilton Railey questioned the patriotism of the soldiers he saw. Railey wondered if they got a lump in their throats when the national anthem was played. "I wonder also," he added, "if they love their country as we did in 1917?" In a sense the answer was no. The naive idealism, the noisy confidence of 1917 did not reappear, nor did the impetuosity that led the doughboys to dash forward into their own artillery barrage or to assault machine-gun nests frontally. The G.I. had a different "style" in combat, as we will see. He also had little taste for discussions on the justness of the American cause.

Patriotic themes and talk of war aims are the exceptions in G.I. letters. Intellectuals in the ranks would sometimes contrast fascism with the American way of life, but rarely did the rhetoric become very heated. Perhaps the only group that was persistently sensitive to moral issues in the war was that of the Jewish G.I.s; whatever their educational level, they understood that Hitlerian Germany was their implacable enemy. Nor do there seem to have been many impassioned bull sessions on moral and patriotic themes. In the barracks such subjects were apparently as out of place as complimentary remarks about the Army. And when Hollywood produced war films in which the heroes postured or declaimed, the G.I. audience would laugh and jeer. But that did not mean the real-life soldiers had no patriotism or sense of commitment. A G.I. in England tried to explain this to a friend in the film industry: "Tell the movie bigs to cut out the corn about the grand old flag and the great sacrifice the boys are making. It's nauseating from where we sit, not because it isn't true, but why bring it up?"

Somehow this aversion to flag waving and loud heroics fits in with the G.I.'s other character traits, perhaps because heroics clashed with his vow of cynicism or with his unheroic self-image. But it would be unfair to leave the subject of the G.I.'s makeup without acknowledging certain inconsistencies in it. The G.I. *Weltanschauung*, if there was such a thing, was not a mosaic of attitudes that neatly dovetailed. Notably, there were times when the unheroic and unenthusiastic soldier saw himself in quite a different light; it could happen on maneuvers, for example, when a gun crew was working furiously during firing exercises, and the realization spread among them that they were really good—it made them all proud and they worked all the harder. If he were awarded a Silver Star or a Bronze Star, the G.I. would say only that it was an accident, or he didn't know why the medal had come to him—but he would be proud of it. In sum, the G.I. could sometimes see himself as a warrior and like what he saw.

Finally, there were times when the soldier who hated the Army came close to loving the Army, times when, like the old Regular, he would find in it "something fine and good." Occasionally, G.I.s would confess this to their correspondents or their diaries. It was the sort of feeling that could suddenly well up in a man as he stepped off in unison with a thousand others just as a band crashed into "The Stars and Stripes Forever"—the kind of heart-plucking moment soldiers have known since the days of the Roman legions. But the feeling could also come in moments of reflection. It could come at night to a sentry as he stood watch over hundreds of men sleeping in some darkened encampment, or it could come to a man as he lay in some forward position on a mountain ridge in Italy and watched a relief column toiling its way up to him from the valley far below. At such times he saw the Army not as an immense khaki sea, but as a fraternity, close and dear.

⋆5⋆

The Compleat Soldier

"THE BEST-DRESSED, BEST-FED, BEST-EQUIPPED army in the world."
That phrase and variants of it were frequently heard in wartime
America. Government spokesmen and journalists were fond of it,
and the public liked the ring of it. It was an affirmation made with
pride, and the pride was justified, for the American soldier went
into battle sustained by a lavishness and sophistication of means
no other belligerent could match. The American people probably
would not have had it any other way. Being "best" in material
concerns—whether it be swords or plowshares—was an American
tradition.

But within the General Staff there was considerable disagree-
ment about how lavishly American troops should be equipped
and maintained. Manpower and other resources were after all
limited, so that a heavy commitment to the logistical or support
function could absorb men and resources that might better be
used on the battle line. To use a modern military expression, the

"teeth-to-tail" ratio would be a bad one. General McNair was an outspoken advocate of a "lean" army with lots of teeth up front and only the essential services behind. While General Marshall could sympathize with this view, he was very sensitive to the political implications and the public relations "fallout" of military policies. If the Army were to enjoy the full support of the government and the American public, it would have to accommodate itself to the citizen-soldier and make his stay in the ranks if not enjoyable, at least as bearable as possible. The new breed of soldier would require more delicate handling than the Regular; his various needs would have to be supplied, his wants anticipated, whether they be on-post tailor shops or portable showers—and such things did not make for a lean army.

Many of the steps Marshall took to make service less onerous did not require adding "fat." In the summer of 1942 the Army scrapped the irksome regulation that required a soldier to obtain his commanding officer's permission before marrying; the following year it banned liquor in officers' clubs, ending a privilege much resented among enlisted men. With the blessing of the Pentagon, local commanders took steps to soften or "humanize" the rigors of military life. Camp Funston, Kansas, had a soldiers' gripe box; other posts had something resembling a telephone "hot line." Soldiers no longer needed the First Sergeant's permission to see their company commander, and on some posts company commanders kept evening office hours when their men could see them. In August 1942 *Yank* reported that the commander of one southern training camp had painted on the sides of his command car the words "The Old Man." *Yank* approved wholeheartedly: "A breakdown in the old heel-clicking is being accomplished without injury to the discipline and power of command in an Army which is as modern as tomorrow's news." But if continued, the trend toward informality and familiarity would eventually reach the point where it began to erode authority—and the Army's hierarchy applied the brakes well short of that point.

The Pentagon set more store in other measures designed to improve the soldier's morale. The Morale Division (later Information and Education Division) of the General Staff was formed with morale improvement as one of its main functions; by the end of 1942 there was a morale officer in each regiment. Psychologists warned that once the soldier went overseas, increased isolation from all he had known could increase his morale problems: "Any symbol or representation of the culture that he has left assumes exaggerated value. A visitor from home, sports scores, moving pictures, American food or drinks are extraordinarily important for maintaining morale in expeditionary forces." Following this advice, the Pentagon encouraged overseas tours by American musicians and entertainers. It saw to it that men in uniform viewed the latest Hollywood films as soon as they were released, and sometimes before civilians saw them (the Army mobilized airplanes, landing barges, and even dogsled teams to speed films to remote posts in Alaska and the Aleutians). And the American authorities filled valuable cargo space to North Africa with countless crates of Coca-Cola, to the dismay of their British allies.

Field Marshal Sir Bernard Montgomery may have been thinking of the G.I.s when he wrote in his *Memoirs* that it was important not to spoil the soldier with too many conveniences and comforts. The British soldier, he wrote, "will do anything you ask of him so long as you arrange he gets his mail from home, the newspapers and, curiously enough, plenty of tea." The view in the Pentagon was that the American soldier needed something more, to be supplied by such agencies as Special Service Overseas Units. A captain in charge of one of these units told a *Yank* reporter in August 1942, "Our job is to get through to American front line troops and make 'em happy." For this purpose his eight-truck, four-trailer unit carried boxing gloves, basketballs and other sports equipment, shortwave receivers, a two-thousand-book library, and theatrical kits complete with costumes, wigs, and makeup. There was also a musical kit, which contained songbooks, harmonicas, and a "field" piano (especially designed with the assistance of the Steinway Company, the piano came in an olive drab case and could be carried by four men).

The Overseas Unit also had a mobile PX, for the Army's plan, ultimately realized, was for the PX system to follow the soldier wherever he went. But there was always a lag in setting up PX operations, and they were not feasible in forward areas, so beginning in 1942 theater commanders were authorized to issue toilet articles and sundries to the troops free of charge from Quartermaster supplies. This was done almost universally in the various theaters of operations. In his book *The March to Tunis*, writer Alan Moorehead recorded that among the Americans "things like cigarettes, chewing gum and toothpaste were handed out in a way that made the British soldier gape." G.I.s seem to have been offered cigarettes at every turn. Some local draft boards presented each departing selectee with a carton, and there was usually a Red Cross volunteer at pierside to give a carton to each soldier as he boarded his troopship. Cartons were also passed out to the heavily laden assault troops who landed on the coast of Normandy on D-Day—observers who visited the beach later said the shoreline was littered with the cartons as far as the eye could see. The Quartermaster ration was a pack a day (or the equivalent in pipe or chewing tobacco), and then there was the four-cigarette pack in the K ration. It would be interesting to know if the generation of Americans that fought World War II smoked more than their fathers; they certainly had the cigarettes available, and the tedium and the perils of wartime service supplied plenty of incentive. Ernie Pyle claimed that he had met ten G.I.s in Normandy who told him they had smoked their first cigarettes on the morning of June 6, 1944.

The largess the Army showed to its soldiers was only part of a general belief among the people and within the government that one couldn't do enough for the boys in uniform. Alan Moorehead recalled the country's mood in the fall of 1942: "Every stop in the propaganda organ had been pulled out wide in praise of the American soldier. There was religious fervor in the phrase 'our boys,' and while you could criticize everything else on earth, even the most hardboiled columnist or politician would never dare to question the skill and courage of the American soldier." One newspaper columnist, Henry MacLemore, did propose in the aftermath of Pearl Harbor that the American soldier be trained as a lean, relentless killer, formed in a regime of Spartan denial, but such arguments were shouted down. Shortly after Pearl Harbor,

Congress raised the private's pay from twenty-one dollars a month to a princely fifty dollars. A corporal who was captured in Italy recalled being quizzed about his pay by a German general flanked by two captains: "I told him my salary. He chuckled and told the captains, 'He's paid more than you.' " The government helped the soldier support his dependents, and delivered his letters free of charge; his former employer pledged to reinstate him in his job when he returned.

Making the United States Army the best-fed, best-dressed, best-equipped army in the world was largely the work of the Army Service Forces, an organization whose size and complexity was unmatched in any other army. As an example, when the initial contingent of fifty thousand American troops went ashore on D-Day, the operation was backed up by ten times that number of ASF troops, including Quartermasters (sixty thousand), Medical Corps (eighty thousand), Ordnance (forty-five thousand), Signal Corps (sixteen thousand), and Transportation Corps (sixty-eight thousand). As a general rule, for every American soldier engaged in combat in World War II there were three others behind him in support capacity—a greater proportion than for any of the other belligerents. (This disproportion could also be found within the major combat units, the divisions. In a German division on the Italian front about 40 percent of the personnel were involved in some way with logistical functions; in the American division it was 50 percent.) The heavy commitment of men to support functions was one of the reasons the United States Army fielded only ninety divisions, while the Japanese created a hundred, the Germans three hundred, and the Russians some four hundred.

If the U.S. Army trailed behind it an unusually large logistical "tail," it was probably condemned to do so, and not simply from any need to pamper the G.I. First of all, American armies in Europe fought at the end of a supply line three thousand miles long, and those in the Southwest Pacific were six thousand miles from their source of supply in the United States. The Army asked relatively little of its hard-pressed allies—the British were supplying only about 20 percent of the food for American troops stationed in the United Kingdom in 1944. As for matériel, the

Americans were usually the suppliers to their allies. Thus, Army Service Forces clothed the First French Army from the skin out and supplied all its equipment; American quartermasters had to supply woolen uniforms for the Brazilian division when its cotton clothing proved too thin for Italian winters. Then, too, motorization complicated the supply problem, and American infantry divisions used motorized vehicles exclusively, while a German infantry division used over four thousand horses. A Quartermaster study of 1942 showed that ground forces needed about six times the quantity of supplies required in the previous war; of twenty-seven pounds needed per man per day in 1942, fifteen pounds were petroleum products. Finally, the Americans were ready to make massive commitments in matériel in order to reduce casualties. This led them to lavish expenditures in artillery shells in order to produce the maximum "softening up" of enemy positions before the infantry made its assault; by the same token, when telephone wire was broken by enemy bombardment, it was quicker and safer to run new wire than to have repair parties hunt breaks in the old line and fix them.

The lavishness with which American troops were supplied impressed anyone who came in contact with them. This was notably the case with the British. All bread baked in the United Kingdom was made from a wartime flour known as National Wheat Flour. It contained barley and oats and was not to the liking of American troops. U.S. Army cooks therefore doctored it with sugar, shortening, and other additives in order to get a "silkier" texture. The British could not help but notice another sign of American prodigality: The British army stocked toilet paper on the assumption that the soldier would use three sheets per day; the American ration was twenty-two and a half sheets. The Germans, too, were impressed. Officers who interrogated German prisoners of war in Sicily told Ernie Pyle that when the Germans were first captured they were cocky and confident that their country would win the war; after they were transported to the rear and saw the masses of supplies stocked there, that confidence vanished. Prisoners who worked at the U.S. Army's Eastern Base Section, located at Tebessa,

Tunisia, found themselves in a supply dump that covered three square miles.

The only troops who were not impressed by the operations of the Army Service Forces were apparently the G.I.s. Many of them had that antagonism and suspicion toward those "in the rear" that frontline soldiers in all armies tend to feel. The supply service was a handy target for the G.I.'s frustrations, and the Army Service Forces seem to have understood and accepted this. The official history of ASF activity in Europe acknowledges that this was a common trait among American soldiers: "They will endure the privations, the fatigue and the serious injuries of war—not silently, but with that minimum of grumbling characteristic of good troops. But they protest vociferously against even minor hardships when not actively engaged in combat." The G.I. proved to be "demanding and individualistic in his relations with the supply services."

True to this pattern of behavior, G.I.s did not lavish praise on Army Service Forces when they introduced such things as non-mildew shoelaces, khaki-colored pipe cleaners, or the "health bomb" (an early, freon-charged aerosol insecticide); but they were loud in their criticisms at the slightest failings. G.I.s on several fronts set up a clamor because they were receiving only off-brand cigarettes—Chelseas, Avalons, and Wings—while presumably the supply people were keeping all the Camels and Luckies for themselves. When cigarettes ran short on the first day of the Salerno landings, and the men were down to a dozen smokes a day, the Quartermasters heard so much about the shortage that they took extra precautions with later amphibious operations. When American troops landed in southern France in August 1944, they were accompanied by sixty-three tons of tobacco and other sundries.

Some of the ASF's gaffes were monumental. At Aversa, outside Naples, a badly chosen dump site and heavy rains led to the spoilage of thirty thousand tons of rations, enough to feed ten million men for one day. Quartermaster operations were based on consumption figures: For example, within a twenty-four-hour period two hundred soldiers would need three toothbrushes, sixteen tubes of shaving cream, twenty-eight bars of soap, thirty razor blades, and four hundred sticks of gum. But sometimes the calculations were off, as when the Fifth Army's Quartermasters purchased six million pounds of Sicilian lemons in a single month—enough to supply each American soldier in Italy with a bushel. Then there was the time the Base Section at Tebessa sent out a trainload of what were supposed to be balanced rations for fifty thousand men. When the train arrived it was found to contain sixteen carloads of peanut butter, a car full of crackers, a case of grapefruit, and a single sack of flour. But if such things were memorable, it was because they were exceptions. The Army's supply and support services were the envy of the other belligerents, and justly so. Their overall efficiency and their rare failures contributed a great deal to the combat efficiency of the American soldier.

Though most G.I.s did not like to believe it, they were fed better than the soldiers of any other army (soldiers who had been on the British "compo" ration, with its mutton stew and kidney pie, were easier to convince of this fact). The Quartermasters Department could back up that claim, since it made a point of acquiring rations of both allied and enemy armies and making comparisons. The Army's own rations were devised, tested—and tasted—in the Subsistence Research Laboratory of the Chicago Quartermaster Depot. *Yank* sent a reporter there, and he related his findings in the issue of November 18, 1942. The laboratory was then deep into research on dehydrated foods, which the Germans had pioneered, making air deliveries to their troops in the Scandinavian campaign of 1940. Every time the Chicago laboratory devised a new ration element it was submitted to the "Guinea Pig Club," a panel of lab workers who gave the concoctions various ratings, including "it stinks."

The Army's standard garrison ration, the one found in stateside training camps, provided about 4,300 calories daily (it also provides the explanation for weight gain among new soldiers). It offered considerable variation, and since the Quartermasters bought foodstuffs in local or regional markets, fare at southern camps contained more grits and sweet potatoes than most northern soldiers were used to or cared for.

In the field the Army prepared A or B rations in mobile kitchens. These closely approximated the garrison ration, the A differing from the B only in that it contained perishables. Though the soldiers griped about a number of dishes served there, especially powdered eggs, British soldiers who tried the American field ration sang its praises. "By European standards the American rations were lavish to the point of extravagance," wrote one British officer. "Vast quantities of tinned meats, fruits and vegetables." The tinned meat referred to was carried on Army inventories as luncheon meat, canned; among the soldiers it was known universally as Spam and almost as universally denounced. When the Hormel Company, producers of Spam, protested that they did not supply their product to the Army, *Yank* published a photo showing cases of Spam in what was apparently an Army storage depot. The photo carried the caption, "We still say it's Spam and we still say to hell with it." Records show that the Army continued to place its confidence in "luncheon meat, canned"; through 1945 it bought 272,000,000 pounds of it.

While it was theoretically possible to carry hot food from Army kitchens all the way to the most forward positions by means of insulated marmite cans, this was only rarely done. The comings and goings that such service required and the noises made in manipulating mess gear could attract the enemy's attention and provoke a mortar barrage. In such situations the soldiers used one of three combat-type rations. The U ration, also called the 5-in-1 and later the 10-in-1 ration, provided, as the name implied, a day's food for five or for ten men. Most of the food came in cans, with five different "meals," each providing about 3,700 calories. These rations were much used by armored troops and artillerymen, who had the vehicles to transport the large cases they came in. More practical in many situations was the individual C ration, composed chiefly of cans, providing something over 3,400 calories per day. The canned dishes were not very palatable unless heated and the meat and vegetable hash was not to the taste of most G.I.s even then (it was ultimately withdrawn). The soldiers usually ate straight from the cans, thus avoiding use of the mess kit; the mess kit's knife and fork were not ordinarily used, either, so that the only utensil the soldier usually needed was his spoon, model 1926. He might even avoid dirtying that if he used a biscuit to dip food from the cans. Wherever the G.I. Army went in Europe or Asia, it left in its wake millions of tiny, golden C ration cans. Enemy reconnaissance planes could sometimes use them to spot the Army's routes and bivouacs (the cans later got a coat of green paint).

The C ration had one major disadvantage in that it was bulky. The K ration, which came in three small boxes, was better suited for men obliged to carry their food, and was hailed as "a triumph of the packager's art." The K ration provided 3,100 to 3,400 calories a day; it contained a can for each meal (meat, meat and egg, processed cheese), biscuits, crackers, dextrose tablets, soluble coffee packet, fruit bar, chocolate bar, bouillon, lemon juice crystals, and sugar tablets. Fixing a K ration breakfast was an easy matter, as a G.I. named Walter Bernstein remembered it: "I got a breakfast ration from one of the men, slit it open, ate the fruit bar, made the coffee and opened the chopped ham and eggs and placed it near the fire. I put the biscuits in my pocket in case I was someday reduced to absolute starvation." The officer who designed the K ration included a stick of chewing gum because as an old cavalryman he felt the soldier would need "something to cut the dust"; he confessed that he had included a pack of four cigarettes as an afterthought to keep the meat can from rolling around in the package. Finally, there was the emergency D ration, a four-ounce bar of fortified chocolate with a nutritional value of about 600 calories (a smaller version came in the K ration). The D bar was reasonably popular, but if a man wasn't careful he could break a tooth on it.

The Quartermasters Department tinkered constantly with its menus, soliciting troop reaction to one food after another. It fretted because the G.I. would not consume all the elements in his K ration, which had to be eaten in its entirety to assure proper nutrition. The department substituted caramels for the unpopular dextrose tablets with some success. It was not successful with its lemon drink crystals, which were almost universally scorned. Any bivouac in Europe or the Pacific that had been inhabited by K ration eaters would be littered with little glassine envelopes, still containing their lemon crystals. On the other hand, the instant coffee was extremely successful; the product was scarcely known before the war, so the Quartermasters served to popularize what has become a national staple. There were some disasters, such as cabbage flakes, of which the Army improvidently bought twenty million pounds. The special butter known as "Army spread," in which the subsistence laboratory took such pride, was not well received by the troops, nor was an apricot spread; both substances acquired obscene names. All in all, the Quartermasters seem to have had more misses than hits in their efforts to please the soldier's palate. But Quartermasters and cooks did have one success that ex-G.I.s will usually acknowledge with a point of pleasure and a nod of gratitude—that was the tour de force of serving turkey dinners for the Thanksgiving and Christmas holidays in 1943 and again in 1944 to the troops on the fighting fronts.

The soldier in the field was rarely without adequate supplies of food of some kind, the situation on Bataan in early 1942 being the most notable case of deprivation; but sometimes local conditions reduced the G.I. to eating a monotonous and therefore unsatisfying diet—when a contingent of American paratroops was informed that a planned drop on German-held Sicily was definitely on, someone in the ranks was heard to say, "Thank God, no more C rations." Sometimes inertia or lack of foresight at command levels created problems. When General Robert Eichelberger took command of American forces on New Guinea, he found that while food supplies were plentiful, the condition of the men in the front lines was "pitiful." Eichelberger wrote a friend: "At three o'clock in the afternoon these men had had nothing to eat since the previous day and had had no hot food in ten days. Somebody had read a book about lighting fires in the presence of the enemy. They were getting two tins of C-rations per man per day or . . . about 1800 calories a day. No rice was going forward to supplement their diet. The men had no cigarettes, although there seemed to be no shortage back in the base section."

Whenever the G.I. had the opportunity, he showed considerable initiative in introducing variety into his diet. He would get himself invited to eat with French troops, only to find they were on American rations, or he would have dinner with the British and regret the experience. In places like France or Italy he would strike a bargain with a local woman who would improvise a meal with army rations as a base. And the G.I. was capable of creative cooking of his own, as this recipe for "D ration fudge" indicates:

Ingredients: 1 block D ration chocolate,
1 package sugar, 1 can condensed milk,
1 large shell fragment.

Directions: Pound chocolate with shell fragment until chocolate is powdered. Throw away shell fragment. Mix chocolate with sugar and milk and cook over Coleman stove. Test by dropping samples of mixture in canteen cup of cold water. When sample congeals in water, pour fudge into shallow pan, cool and slice.

If the G.I. was the best-fed soldier of World War II, at the beginning of that war he was by no means the best dressed. The niggardly appropriations the Army received in the interwar years compelled its soldiers to use the same uniform for both dress purposes and field use—a light tan cotton outfit for summer and a darker wool uniform for winter. The woolen clothing was difficult to keep clean in field conditions (American troops in Iceland sometimes sent their uniforms to Scotland by air to have them drycleaned). The cotton khaki clothing was described by a observer in the Pacific as "useless as a combat garment due to color, fit, and lack of pockets." The same observer reported that a newly devised coverall-type jungle suit was also unsatisfactory. Half of the men in a regiment might have diarrhea or dysentery, and it was "a physical impossibility to remove all web equipment and the garment from the shoulders in sufficient time under the circumstances." Men sometimes cut a flap in the seat of the outfit, but this was also unsatisfactory since "it was an opening for insects and invariably rode up while sitting."

The G.I. ended up doing most of his fighting in ODs, the olive drab cotton twill shirt and trousers originally conceived as fatigue clothing; over that he often wore the 1943 field jacket, which was probably the best single article of clothing in the G.I. wardrobe. For colder weather the soldier could wear wool trousers under his cotton ones and a short woolen jacket, the ETO or Eisenhower jacket, under the field jacket (the soldiers regarded the Eisenhower jacket as an article of dress and rarely wore it in combat). The Army's solution for cold weather was called the "layering system": The lower the temperature, the more clothing the soldier put on. A G.I. who was on sentry duty along the Belgian border during the bitter cold of December 1944 carried the principle to its limits: "I wore a set of cotton underclothes, a wool undershirt, a set of wool shirt and trousers, a wool knit sweater, a set of fatigue shirt and trousers, a field jacket, an overcoat, a wool cap under my helmet, gloves, at least two pairs of wool socks, boots, and galoshes. It was almost an impossibility to wear another article of clothing, and it didn't give me much freedom of movement, but I wouldn't have parted with a single thread."

The American soldier's clothing, like his rations, was the subject of constant innovation by the Quartermasters Department. Army underwear went from white to khaki in 1943 after troops reported that their wash attracted enemy fire when they hung it out to dry. New clothing ideas were derived from manufacturers of hunting apparel, arctic explorers, and from the gripes and suggestions of G.I.s. New models got extensive testing in both laboratory and field. *Yank* reported in May 1943 that the Quartermaster Depot at Philadelphia detailed two hundred G.I.s to do nothing but jump up and down in rubber sacks. Their perspiration was then collected in bottles and used in tests of clothing.

The soldier's footwear evolved during the course of the war. The Army field shoe of 1941 was an early victim to jungle humidity; moreover, its leather sole deteriorated rapidly in contact with abrasive soils. In Tunisia, 80 percent of the troops operating over areas of volcanic rock wore out their shoes within twenty-four hours. The canvas leggings that complemented the field shoe were tedious to put on, and once wet they were slow to dry out. Soldiers in Italy had a tendency to leave their shoes and leggings on for long periods of time, and in doing so a number of them developed trench foot, a condition in which the flesh takes on a dead look and breaks out in sores. A daily "sock exchange" program was launched, and in 1943 the leggings began to disappear as the Army introduced the combat boot, a shoe with rubber composition sole and heel and a leather cuff to encircle the lower part of the trousers. For jungle warfare the Quartermasters developed a jungle boot derived from the athlete's sneakers. In cold and wet weather the best footwear was the shoepac, a high moccasin with a leather top and rubber foot. These were scarce and highly sought after when they were first introduced on the Italian front. An officer in the 88th Division related that a soldier wearing almost new shoepacs had a leg mangled by a shell burst. At the aid station the leg was removed, and the soldier was evacuated on a stretcher, after the doctors removed the shoepac from his remaining foot. It then occurred to one of those present that they should remove the other shoepac from the severed leg so that someone else might have use of the precious footwear: "There were men in that aid station who had seen many grim operations, but Griffo said when the shoepac was finally removed, he and Stoner had the aid station to themselves."

Of all the items the G.I. wore, the Quartermasters seem to have considered the M1 helmet as their greatest triumph—in 1944 they devoted a whole monograph to recounting its development. Well before the war they had studied the possibility of a new helmet to replace the Model 1917 "tin hat," which had been copied from the British army. The 1917 model was so heavy that it sometimes gave wearers a stiff neck; moreover, its design offered little protection from shell fragments thrown up from the ground. Then another problem appeared. Early in 1941 General Marshall inspected troops in the Southwest and found that they had no headgear that would protect them from the sun or rain other than their M1917 steel helmets. The Army's traditional "Montana Peak" hat (the kind still worn by drill instructors and Smokey the Bear) was unsuitable. As it turned out, these two separate needs were satisfied by the introduction of the M1 helmet and liner.

The new helmet and liner combined weighed three pounds and were designed to protect the wearer from a .45-caliber bullet fired at a range of five feet. The steel helmet itself was simply a shell that fitted over the liner. The new helmet gave enhanced protection to the wearer—reports from the field were unanimous in this regard. Its form had only one disadvantage; to many people it resembled the German helmet, and for this reason the British requested that the first American troops sent to Northern Ireland in 1942 wear the 1917 model. The helmet liner was the really new element. As the Quartermasters history put it: "The concept of a hat-shaped liner for a helmet had never before been considered in the long history of warfare." Finding a suitable material was a difficult challenge. The Quartermasters ordered four million liners made from impregnated fiber, only to find that they split too easily and turned "mushy" in the jungle. They tried redwood bark, macerated canvas, and a number of other exotic substances before they came up with the answer: laminated phenolic resin-impregnated fabric.

The liner contained the suspension, or headband, so it could be worn with or without the helmet; in the latter case it gave good protection from the elements and a decent military appearance. The M1 helmet had other uses, including those of stool and pillow. The steel outer shell could be used as water bucket, washbasin, or mixing bowl; by using the visor rim like a shovel blade, it could even be used for digging. An Army nurse claimed to have devised twenty-one separate uses for the M1 helmet. The chief function was always the protection of the wearer, and for that purpose it was generally worn with the chin strap unfastened. In Patton's command, where rigid enforcement of the dress code prevailed, the fine for not wearing one's helmet was twenty-five dollars. Yet Patton issued orders that chin straps were *not* to be fastened; it was said that he had lost an aide in Tunisia when concussion from a shell caused the man's helmet to snap his head back and break his neck.

What has been said of the G.I.'s food and clothing also applies to the weapons and equipment that were the tools of his trade: They evolved and improved significantly during the war. The author of a recent study of an infantry division found that "virtually all items of personal equipment, packs, barracks bags, ammunition carriers, shelter halves, sleeping gear, entrenching tools, web gear, etc. changed significantly during 1942 and 1943." In the case of the Antiaircraft Command, there was only one major item of equipment from 1941 that was still being used in 1944. Some of the improvements were borrowed from other armies. Just as the British battle dress inspired the Eisenhower jacket, the jerrican —as its name implies—was taken from the Germans via the British. The G.I.'s folding shovel, which could also be adjusted for use as a pick or hoe, was copied from the German entrenching tool.

The basic tool of the American infantryman was the M1 rifle. The only semiautomatic rifle that was standard issue among all the armies of World War II, it gave the American foot soldier impressive firepower; thanks to the M1 an American platoon in World War II had the firepower of an entire company of doughboys in World War I. The M1 had some minor disadvantages. One was that the slide could pinch the unwary soldier as he loaded an eight-round clip, giving him a case of "M1 thumb"; then, too, the mechanism was delicate and could become inoperable in extreme cold or when fouled. The hazards of surf and sand encountered in amphibious operations posed such serious problems that the Army developed a special plastic bag for the soldiers to put their M1s into. Once closed, the bag was watertight; if the soldier blew into it to inflate it before closing, the bag had enough buoyancy to keep the rifle afloat. Finally, in case of emergency the G.I. could fire his rifle without taking it out of the bag.

If the M1 was the infantryman's most essential item, the bayonet that accompanied it was among the least useful. In the combat zone old-timers could often tell replacements because they carried their bayonets affixed to their rifles. The tendency was for the veteran soldier not to carry the bayonet at all if he could avoid it. When the U.S. Seventh Army was moving up through southern France, one platoon leader ordered his men to fix bayonets in preparation for an assault and discovered that not a single soldier had a bayonet. Even more useless to most G.I.s was the gas mask. The devices were sometimes used as breathing aids in very dusty conditions, and Army cooks were sometimes seen wearing them as they peeled onions, but the masks were often shed by their owners. Occasionally, there would be false gas alarms, creating something of a panic. Once in France a diligent sentry detected the odor of new-mown hay, which every G.I. had been taught was characteristic of the deadly gas phosgene. The sentry duly gave the alarm. When the uproar subsided, investigation revealed that the odor was coming from a field of new-mown hay.

American artillery was also well equipped, chiefly with the 105-mm howitzer. There was a tradition of excellence in the artillery that ran all the way back to the Mexican War. General Patton, whose first love was armor, paid the American artillerymen the supreme compliment when he said at the end of the war, "I do not have to tell you who won the war. You know our artillery did." Patton's own armor suffered from a single major handicap: American armor lacked a heavy tank to match the German Tiger and Panther models. The mainstay of the American armor, the Sherman or M4 medium, was outgunned by such behemoths, but American tankers could usually rely on numbers, mobility, and altered tactics to limit the German advantage. The hallmark of the Sherman was its rugged dependability (its motor was designed to run for three thousand miles without major overhaul), and the same could be said of all the vehicles used by the Army. The jeep was probably the most universally popular vehicle in the war; it was the one the Germans most liked to capture for day-to-day use. American trucks also had an excellent reputation; the British liked them better than their own, perhaps because they considered American engines to be superior. Army historian Hugh Cole, who interviewed German generals after the war, found that they expressed more admiration for the 2½-ton truck than anything else in the American arsenal.

The truck was the most sophisticated means of transport an army could have, and usually it was the best. But the Army soon learned that the truck made it roadbound in areas where roads were inadequate—in Italy, for example—or simply nonexistent, as in many areas of the Pacific. Here the ASF had to improvise. In the jungles the supply system sometimes rested on pack bearers, either G.I.s or natives when they could be recruited. In mountainous areas of Italy the solution tended to be the mule. At one time the Fifth Army used over four thousand of them. The fighting in Italy produced other improvisations. Mortar crews sometimes transported mortar rounds in baby carriages; units that were particularly isolated sometimes received their essential supplies by air, wrapped in reclaimed blankets and packed inside belly tanks, which were then jettisoned by low-flying planes. Orval Faubus recalled that when a battalion of the 120th Infantry Regiment, 30th Division, was marooned on a hilltop in France, vital medical supplies were also sent by air—in this case packed inside 155-mm artillery shells fired at them.

The G.I. seems to have been something of a tinkerer and improviser by nature. Many of the ideas for improving weapons and equipment came from him, and often he made the changes before the Army Service Forces did. While waiting for their khaki underwear, soldiers sometimes dyed their white underclothing in coffee. Some soldiers felt the rolled rim on the canteen cup retained heat too long and made them burn their lips, so they filed it off. They improved the warmth of their sleeping bags by making them "four-ply," encasing them in an outer bag sewn from blankets. There was a good deal of improvisation and experimentation among tank crews. They enhanced the Sherman's resistance to antitank weapons by welding brackets onto the hull and placing sandbags on them, and they reinforced the steel floor of the light tank when it proved too vulnerable to German mines. When the 3rd Armored Division ran into a formidable obstacle in the Normandy hedgerow, it also improvised a solution. According to the 3rd's historian: "After a few days of experimentation, a double plow chopper, designed by the armored engineers, was evolved. In one week 100 of these gadgets were fitted to tanks."

To sum up, the G.I. went to war fed and clothed, armed and equipped, in a fashion that compared very favorably with the other belligerents. The testimony of foreign observers is eloquent in this regard. According to Alan Moorehead: "Most of the American stuff was first class, and even as good or better than the German. Their mess tins, water-bottles, rubber soled boots, woolen underclothes, shirts and windbreakers were all superior to the British equivalents and their uniforms in general made of finer stuff. The Garand [M1] rifle and the officer's carbine were already regarded by many veterans as the best small arms on the front."

And the German assessment was hardly different. Hugh Cole found the Germans chiefly criticized the Americans' tanks and their lack of very heavy artillery. German experts got their first chance to examine and test American arms and equipment in the North African campaign; in general they found them to be first class. Rommel described the Americans as "fantastically well equipped."

Here was perhaps the most graphic impression the Americans made on those who fought against them or beside them: In the sophistication and the lavishness of means and material put at their disposal, the G.I.s were truly "the rich Americans." But this very plethora of means carried with it a potential danger. If the U.S. Army were denied its extraordinary material advantages—and in the hazards of war that was bound to happen—how would it function? And how would the G.I. fight under such circumstances? The Army's leaders no doubt speculated on this, and so for that matter did leaders in the Allied and the enemy armies.

★ 6 ★

Aboard and Abroad

THE DAY PEARL HARBOR was bombed a small American convoy was en route from Hawaii to the Philippines. The convoy was composed of the cruiser *Pensacola* and eight cargo vessels loaded with supplies and reinforcements for the Philippine garrison; on board were about 4,700 soldiers and airmen. When hostilities began the Navy wanted the ships to simply reverse course, but the War Department had other ideas. On December 12, the convoy was renamed Task Force South Pacific; it altered its course toward the Fiji Islands, then toward Australia. The new task force reached Brisbane on December 22; its commander set up headquarters in a local hotel, and the G.I.s took up quarters in a local racetrack, where they were fed by the Australian Army. The men of Task Force South Pacific were not the first American soldiers to go abroad; small contingents had been sent to Trinidad, to Iceland and to Greenland well before Pearl Harbor. But the men who came ashore at Brisbane were the first of the wartime expeditions to Allied countries, the first wave in a vast tide that would take several million Americans abroad.

After Pearl Harbor the overseas movement of American troops accelerated. In January 1942, 4,000 sailed for Northern Ireland, followed by another 8,500 the next month. In the course of 1942 the Army's Transportation Corps embarked 953,000 persons in all, the vast majority of them G.I.s. A few of the embarkations were unusual in that they were for hostile shores, and so arranged —"combat-loaded" was the term—that the troops would be able to come off fighting. This was the case with forces sent to the Aleutians and with a portion of the North African invasion force, those elements under General Patton that sailed for Morocco from Hampton Roads, Virginia. In 1943 Task Force Husky was similarly loaded at Hampton Roads for the invasion of Sicily. But the combat-loaded convoy was the exception. Most G.I.s who went overseas could anticipate a stay in an Allied country—most often the United Kingdom or Australia—for an appreciable length of time before they reached one of the fighting fronts.

In 1943 troop movements overseas virtually doubled over the previous year, but 1944 was the year of the diaspora for the G.I. Army, with nearly three million embarkations from the United States. The heaviest flow was to Europe. On the eve of the Normandy invasion there were 1,671,000 American troops in the United Kingdom alone. The movement to the Pacific was smaller and peaked later. From January 1942 to August 1945 a million troops took ship for the Southwest Pacific; 36 percent of that number left in the eight months of 1945, and the peak embarkation— 129,354—came in August 1945, the month the fighting stopped. While the great bulk of troops went to the two major theaters of operations, in fact G.I.s were scattered quite literally from Adak to Zanzibar, passing by way of Ascension Island, Curaçao, Kenya, and other unlikely places.

Sooner or later almost all Army units became involved in that complicated process known as POM, or Preparation for Overseas Movement. The first clear sign the men had that they would shortly be going overseas was the preembarkation furlough, usually of about ten days. Though the granting of these furloughs appreciably increased the time it took to get the unit ready for movement, the Army had learned that for most soldiers a brief trip home was essential—so essential that unless furloughs were granted, some men would simply take off. As it was, the weeks before movement overseas saw an increase in absences without leave. The AWOL rate showed what the Adjutant General called an "alarming increase" toward the end of 1942. It reached disturbing levels again in the spring of 1944, and the headquarters of the Fourth Service Command offered this explanation:

> The current movements of large numbers of troops overseas have stimulated AWOL in two ways: some enlisted men absent themselves for the purpose of taking care of personal business and for personal enjoyment prior to embarkation, leaving with the intent to return to their organizations prior to departure for port, or to rejoin their unit at the port. There are others who have a fear of going overseas and leave their units as a last resort to remain within the continental limits of the United States.

The idea of leaving the United States troubled a good many men. There was first of all the strangeness of it, for few G.I.s had ever traveled abroad; then, too, there was a special finality about going overseas in uniform—the civilian tourist always came back, the soldier sometimes didn't. An Army psychiatrist noted: "Psychoneurotics had a rough time of it as their units prepared for overseas shipment. Some broke down at that time. Others were able to get up the gangplank with the 'help' of the medical officer, the chaplain, or military police. It was only after exposure to combat—or after assignment to an isolated outpost—that they actually broke down."

Among the emotionally stable the state of mind varied greatly. One veteran recalled that as he headed across the Pacific at age eighteen he was "young, innocent, ignorant, and rarin' to go." Others were vaguely apprehensive as the time for embarkation approached (the same phenomenon had been noted in the previous war). Part of the POM process was a further screening of the men to make sure that those going overseas were up to the rigors of campaigning, and the screening tended to become more intensive as the war progressed. Army physicians sought to differentiate between temporary "gangplank fever" and more-serious psychological problems, and at the same time they did physical screening. Most units would lose men in this process; most likely they had already lost others to illness, training accidents, transfers, and separations. POM was thus a period of "personnel turbulence," as the Army called it, as here and there men were removed and others set in their place.

Replacements frequently were drawn from other organizations of the same arm or service; thus, infantrymen might be drawn from another infantry division, for example. Sometimes the men received this way were inferior to those whose places they took. Many division commanders considered an order to provide men to another outfit as an opportunity to purge their own ranks of problem soldiers, misfits, and "losers." So common was the practice that once, when the 88th Division received replacements from another division, its commander had guards posted around the train carrying the newly arrived replacements. He and his officers went aboard the train and inspected the records of the new men. These made such grim reading that the commander of the 88th refused the entire draft of replacements and sent the train back where it came from. It should be said that commanders of departing units also did their best to shed their undesirables. When Military Police picked up a sizable number of men who had missed the sailing of one particular regiment, they discovered it was because regimental officers had given the men passes to "see the town" the same day the regiment embarked. The men were sent overseas on the next ship, as were virtually all AWOLs, for that matter. The Army reasoned that if it meted out stateside prison sentences, it might even spur the tendency toward AWOL among men apprehensive about going overseas.

As the time for departure grew near, the men entrained for a brief stay at one of the camps that served as staging areas for the major POEs (or ports of embarkation—there were eight POEs in all). Camp Patrick Henry served Hampton Roads POE, Camp Planche was the major staging area for New Orleans, and Camp Stoneman served San Francisco. Boston's and New York's POEs had several camps that fed them embarking troops. The stay in the staging areas was fairly brief; at Camp Patrick Henry it aver-aged from one to two weeks. For some troops the training exercises ended because their equipment was already crated for shipment, but there were special skills to be acquired in preparation for the voyage, especially abandon-ship drills. Frequently, the troops also went through a gas chamber to make certain their gas masks functioned well, and they got another battery of shots in prepara-tion for service overseas. For the last day or two before actual embarkation the troops were placed under "blackout"—no one was allowed off the post, visitors were forbidden, and no telegrams or telephone calls were permitted. A G.I. who was shipped to Europe recalled: "Early the next morning we were lined up and given boat numbers. Then about ten o'clock a platoon of military police drove up and surrounded the company area, standing armed and ready about every fifteen yards. We were 'under re-striction' for movement to a port of embarkation; we were on our way."

The trip to the port was usually by train, and in some cases the troop train rolled out onto the pier. Transportation Corps men with red and gold armbands directed the movement of men from train to ship, and a common feature of embarkation was the port band, which played First World War tunes such as "Over There" and songs representing the states that the National Guard divi-sions were from (the same band, or a similar one, would play "There's No Place Like Home" when the men came back in 1945 and 1946). And inevitably there were Red Cross volunteers serving doughnuts and coffee. The boarding was done "by the numbers." In fact, the soldiers usually had numbers chalked on their helmets. As each man came forward his last name was called, he answered with his first name and initial, and he was checked off. He then struggled up the gangplank, usually wearing full equipment—helmet, pack, rifle, cartridge belt, bayonet, canteen, and gas mask, and generally carrying or dragging two barracks bags or a duffel bag. Once on board, he was directed straight to his berth, which was usually far deeper into the bowels of the ship than he had imagined it would be. Sometime during or shortly after embark-ing, each soldier received a letter from President Roosevelt. In part, it read: "You are a soldier of the United States Army. You have embarked for distant places where the war is being fought." The War Department had hit upon the idea as a boost to morale, and the President had agreed (while the letter was ostensibly on White House stationery, it had been printed, signature and all, for mass distribution).

The first few hours on board ship were novel and exciting, but the novelty wore off quickly. Any soldier who had imagined that accommodations on a troopship would resemble those on an ocean liner was in for a cruel disappointment. Even the liners that had been pressed into service, the *Queen Mary*, *Queen Elizabeth*, and *West Point* (formerly *America*), had been completely refitted for transporting the maximum number of troops. Berthing accommodations were pretty much the same everywhere: canvas and metal-frame bunks, six feet long and two feet wide, suspended by chains or standees and stacked one above the other—as many as six high—with a two-foot space between bunks. Getting into the bunks and turning over in them required a certain adroitness. Sitting upright on them was impossible because of their closeness. The tiers of bunks so filled the living compartment that there was almost no place to sit; in such conditions the ship's ventilating system was insufficient, and the compartments became hot and dank. In daylight hours troops could usually go up on deck, but at nightfall the ship's public address system announced "All troops lay below," and the decks were cleared.

The troopship had other peculiarities. On some vessels there was "double bunking," with men sleeping in two shifts. Troops got only two meals a day, which was all the overworked galleys could manage. On the troopship, KP duty was much coveted for once, because it got a man more food and more chance to get above decks. It was impossible for the ships' evaporators to supply sufficient fresh water for normal needs, so the showers and the washbasins ran seawater; the Quartermasters supplied a specially developed soap that lathered in salt water. Even for drinking purposes fresh water was in short supply. On some ships there were permanent lines at water fountains, and soldiers sometimes stored water in their canteens. The PX, which had become a fixture in the soldier's life, was replaced by a sparsely supplied ship's store; to reduce the store's traffic, the men were obliged to pool their orders and confide them to an emissary who stood in line and made purchases for the group. Finally, smoking was greatly restricted. The toilets drew not only smokers, but also gamblers and insomniacs, as well as the customary traffic.

Tempers sometimes frayed in the packed holds and fights broke out. The soldier's unhappiness with his lot was further deepened by rumors that officers had better food and the run of the decks at night; a man thought about such things as he lay wedged in his bunk in the middle of the night, surrounded by a vast chorus of snoring. It is easy to understand the vehemence of a private named Sam Shapiro, who wrote *Yank* in June 1942, "We'll win this damn war but I can't face that trip back."

The liners *Queen Elizabeth* and *Queen Mary* scarcely offered any improvement over other vessels in accommodations, since they sometimes used *triple* bunking (sleeping in three shifts), and they served English fare, which never commended itself to the G.I. Their chief advantage was their speed. They ran without escort and could make the Atlantic crossing in six days. Refitted so they could each carry fifteen thousand men—a division—they did yeoman service on both oceans. Together they transported well over a million G.I.s. "The Queens" had an excellent safety record, though there were some close calls. Off the coast of Scotland the *Queen Mary* was once hit by a freak wave of gigantic size; the ship heeled over alarmingly and hung there before righting herself again.

The worst way to cross the ocean was by Liberty Ship. In 1943 these were pressed into service as troop transports on the Atlantic run because of a shortage of larger ships. A Liberty could take a maximum of 550 equipment-laden soldiers, but under conditions that the Army Transportation Corps admitted "lowered morale." The Liberty Ship did not give a particularly good "ride," and its slowness was such that a voyage in convoy from Hampton Roads to the Mediterranean took three weeks. The messing facilities were barely adequate, and the main deck was usually so heavily loaded with matériel that there was scarcely any space for troops to relax on deck. The Liberty was used extensively in the Pacific for ferry-ing troops from one spot to another, with even more primitive accommodations. One division commander gave it as his opinion that passage on a Liberty ship was a good preparation for the hard-ships of campaigning.

Every soldier gave thought to the possibility that his ship would be sunk; with the frequent abandon-ship drills, he could scarcely do otherwise. As the ship moved farther across the ocean, those thoughts became more frequent. A corporal from the New York area who had worked in a shipyard wrote during his crossing of the Atlantic in November 1944: "It seems hard to conceive that there is but ¾ of an inch of steel now between me and the ocean; that the steel was made by man, and that other men in turn seek even now to break that thin sheet and allow the sea to swallow all." Sometimes submarines were reported in an area and safety measures would be reinforced. The men would sleep fully clothed and in their lifesaving vests.

Fortunately, troopships were rarely attacked. In the Atlantic the convoy system provided good protection; in the Pacific the Navy said after Pearl Harbor that it could not escort more than one fast troop convoy per month to the Southwest Pacific. From late 1942 on, troopships in the Pacific usually traveled without escort and without danger, save in the forward areas. The German navy and air force offered a greater threat than those of the Japanese, but even in European waters the losses were very low. According to a compilation made in June 1945, 4,453,061 American soldiers had been sent from the United States to Europe with a loss of only 1,094 lives, or 0.024 percent of the troops transported. Even add-ing later transshipments (Great Britain to North Africa, North Africa to Sicily, etc.), the loss rate was only 0.081 percent.

There were four particularly costly sinkings of troopships in European waters: the *Rohna*, sunk off Algeria on November 26, 1943, with a loss of 1,015 lives; the *Leopoldville*, which went down with 764 men off Cherbourg on Christmas Eve, 1944; the *Dor-chester*, sunk south of Greenland on February 3, 1943, with 404 men lost; and the *Paul Hamilton*, lost off Algiers on April 20, 1944. The *Paul Hamilton* was a Liberty Ship headed for Italy with a special demolitions team aboard. It was attacked, as were other ships in its convoy, by six German torpedo planes. There was a thunderous explosion; the *Paul Hamilton* vanished under an enormous geyser of smoke and water that—incredibly—brought down the Dornier 217 that had torpedoed the *Hamilton*. The 504 G.I.s on the *Hamilton* were all lost, as was the entire crew.

If the crossing was generally without danger, it was often monotonous. Men lost track of what day it was. With little by way of recreation facilities, many men spent their time writing letters. By the time the ship reached port they had stacks of outgoing correspondence. Because the voyage was a new chapter in their lives the men wrote about it in great detail—but often those details never reached their designated reader. These letters were the first that fell under the Army's censorship regime; though the men had lectures on the system and were told the necessity of it, they always resented it. The censors were the men's own officers, an arrangement that did not go down well with many G.I.s; then, too, the officers censored their own letters, a privilege the men resented even more. Not a few G.I. letters from overseas contain ironic references written especially for the censor.

The adventure and the hazards of an ocean crossing were followed by an experience that was equally novel to most G.I.s—living in a foreign country. The reception was generally cordial, at least in the beginning. To the inhabitants of Australia and the United Kingdom, particularly, the first Americans showed up at a time in the war when any help was bound to be appreciated. In Australia in the first dark months of 1942, people would sometimes break into spontaneous applause at the sight of American troops. The British were more reserved, but they, too, conveyed their satisfaction at the arrival of the G.I.s. In the early days of the American presence in England, an American soldier who entered a pub would usually find someone who wanted to buy him a drink (if he wore a marksmanship medal he could count on it; the British thought they were decorations for heroism). But after a first flurry of excitement the novelty of having the Americans wore off, and hosts and guests settled down to living side by side—not without problems. After a few months of American presence in Northern

Ireland, one G.I. reported a pattern that would be repeated elsewhere in the English-speaking world: "The children are nuts about us, to slip into the vernacular. We get along very well with the girls, a fact which isn't calculated to endear us to the boys, and the older people take us pretty well as we come. The visiting fireman aura has worn off now."

The affinity between G.I.s and children would be repeated in every country the Army passed through. The American soldier had candy and chewing gum, but he also had a quick friendliness and an easy, unaffected manner that drew children as much as it sometimes disconcerted their parents. The G.I. found it easy to establish rapport with people his own age, especially girls, because Hollywood films and American music had preceded him as goodwill ambassadors. One British psychologist argued that one reason the G.I. seemed to fascinate British girls was that he spoke with the same accent as the Hollywood stars. The Americans usually had an immediate impact on popular music. Wherever the G.I.s stayed for any length of time swing bands would spring up. A G.I. wrote *Yank* from Australia in November 1942: "The bands are playing 'I Don't Wanna Set the World on Fire,' the top hit of the moment. They are months behind American bands in the latest numbers and years behind in the technique of swing." With the Americans also came innovations in dancing, especially the jitterbug. In Northern Ireland, a G.I. organized the Ulster Hepcats, which soon had four hundred card-bearing members.

The G.I. presence inevitably had an economic impact, which might be modest if the host country were England, or staggering if it were a primitive area such as the Fiji Islands. The "rich American" image emerged very quickly. In the Army, money took on a different meaning, especially overseas. Almost all the soldier's needs were provided by the Army, so virtually everything he received on payday was spending money; then, too, the G.I. was often paid in foreign currency, and as one ex-G.I. put it, "It was like Monopoly money; it didn't mean a thing." The Army and the local authorities knew there could be problems with the G.I.s' buying power, and the Army tried to get soldiers to put more of their money into savings, especially war bonds, but the G.I. remained a prodigal spender. This prodigality would have effects on the labor market. In the Fiji Islands, a considerable portion of the indigenous population went into the business of washing clothes for the Americans. In New Guinea, the Americans paid such high wages that the Australian authorities could get no natives to work for them for the customary rate of pay: thirty-five cents and two plugs of tobacco per week.

The American soldier offered an inexhaustible market for curios and souvenirs. He was fascinated by the square nickels used on Curaçao. He sent them home as mementos and had them made into bracelets in such numbers that the coins became scarce. Throughout the Pacific he sought grass skirts; in some places where they had been abandoned, the natives went back into their production for American customers. On one island grass skirts that had sold for fifty cents brought five dollars. Carved canes could also be sold for five dollars, the monthly wage of a worker on a rubber plantation. In Australia the favorite souvenirs were black opals and boomerangs, and almost everywhere there was a strong demand for souvenirs from the fighting areas, especially enemy weapons and equipment. Among the most desirable items in the Pacific were the personal battle flags, which Japanese soldiers carried or wore wrapped around them, bearing such inscriptions as "fight bravely" and "we are invincible." Supply was limited, the demand great, and the prices sufficiently high to bring counterfeiters into the market. The bogus flags were made from parachute silk; the counterfeiters, ignorant of the Japanese language, simply copied any inscriptions they could find, including those on abandoned packing crates. Consequently, the bogus battle flags bore inscriptions such as "inflammable" and "this end up."

Barter was common, and *Yank* offered G.I.s tips in the art of haggling, including the recommendation to "walk up to the trader in a nonchalant manner." Cigarettes were the most common item for barter; in Labrador, for example, men traded them for husky puppies. In Australia the G.I.s in one unit acquired a baby kangaroo. "After supper we planned his whole life," wrote one of the soldiers. "After the war we were going to take him back to America and have him give exhibitions in boxing, take $10,000 worth of insurance, make dog tags for him, outfit him in half American and half Australian uniform." These plans fell through when the kangaroo died; the men buried him in a large field with full military honors.

Each time an American soldier went to a foreign country he was given lectures on how to behave and usually a booklet about the country he would be visiting. These booklets were ambitious efforts that often treated the country's history and geography before passing on to practical tips on getting along; the booklet on Australia went to fifty pages. The more different the culture, the greater the effort the Army's Information and Education Division made to impress the soldier with the importance of his role as ambassador and to warn him of the pitfalls he might encounter. The booklet on North Africa contained these injunctions:

> Never smoke or spit in front of a mosque.

> Don't kill snakes or birds. Some Arabs believe the souls of departed chieftains reside in them.

> When you see grown men walking hand in hand, ignore it. They are not "queer."

The booklet probably went into more detail than was necessary, for few G.I.s were entertained by Arab hosts, and consequently most of them did not read the numerous pointers on etiquette at the table. In the case of North Africa the Army seems to have had an exaggerated fear of incidents with the local population over treatment of women. There were special admonitions against staring at Moslem women or touching their veils, and a warning that "serious injury if not death at the hands of Moslem men may result if these rules are not followed." The Army's fears on this score were groundless, for the G.I. did not often seek intimate contact with populations of very different culture. In the case of the North African population, the intellectuals in the ranks might express a curiosity about their culture and lament the way the French ruled over them, but the average G.I. took a less kindly view. A sergeant wrote, after a tour of the fabled Casbah: "I have never seen such filth, squalor, primitive and crude methods and people." Another explained in a letter home that the North Africans "would come around to steal food, and they'd dig up graves to steal clothes from the dead. It's because they never had any bringing up."

The G.I. who arrived in the United Kingdom got reminders about subtle differences in language that could cause problems. *Yank* warned G.I.s: "Don't use 'bloody' in front of a doll." It also urged caution in using the word "bum": "For instance don't say 'I feel like a bum.' In England that means you feel like your own backside." And the British were coached about the peculiarities of the G.I.'s speech: "Try not to appear shocked at some of their expressions. Many of these may sound remarkably like swearing words to you, but in fact they are words in everyday use in America." Actually, the G.I.'s penchant for profanity had less shock effect than one might think. In other English-speaking countries his favorite terms did not have the same impact, or were simply unknown. American military engineers in Australia succeeded in naming an airstrip they built Lacka Nookie, having assured the Australian authorities that this was an old Indian name much revered in the United States.

There were potential problems that went far deeper than the nuances in language. The G.I.'s high pay (four times that of the British Tommy) meant that the American had first call on food, drink, and female companionship. Whenever Americans were present they were the prostitutes' preferred clientele. At the same time, the American was better able to offer a "nice girl" a good time. Both the Army and the governments of the host countries worried about the consequences of G.I.–local girl relationships. The American authorities were concerned that prostitutes would take advantage of gullible soldiers and marry their way into the United States; consequently, in 1942 the Army reimposed marriage restrictions for men overseas. Local authorities feared that the G.I.s, who gave every appearance of being sexually enterprising and hyperactive, would take advantage of local girls—a fear summed up in the admonition "Look before you jeep or you'll be Yanked into maternity." (G.I.s took some eighty thousand "war brides" in the United Kingdom and twelve thousand in Australia.)

There is probably a point at which foreigners, however well behaved, become objectionable simply because there are so many of them. At one point, Americans may have constituted 5 percent of the Australian population, and there were parts of England that were literally packed with Americans by the spring of 1944. If food was scarce it was natural to associate the scarcity with the visitors from America; in the case of Australia, which supplied the Army with great quantities of foodstuffs, the civilian population did make sacrifices. And at some point the admixture of American culture must have been irritating—for example, to the Briton who found jazz on his radio, baseball scores in his newspaper, and a chunk of ice added to his scotch. And there were the little shocks produced among people of different customs living cheek by jowl. American soldiers were taken aback by the barmaids they found in Ireland, and by women who smoked on the street in London—and just as taken aback to find that those women were not particularly interested in their propositions. The British were shocked in turn at the American's habit of drinking in excess and in public, and the aggressiveness with which he drove. Drunkenness and traffic offenses, along with short-term AWOL, were the chief disciplinary problems in the United Kingdom. Drinking and reckless driving were to be problems virtually everywhere the G.I. went. In Iran, where thirty thousand G.I.s kept a truck supply line open to the Soviet Union, death and injury of villagers living along the supply line were daily occurrences, as were cash settlements for such mishaps. (Traffic accidents were the leading cause of nonbattle casualties among G.I.s, with 12,000 killed and 230,000 injured.)

Americans abroad tended to be loud and boisterous in public places (they still do). In restaurants, they seemed to talk as though they wanted people at other tables to hear them and they were loud in complaint if the waiter could not furnish separate checks. There was one national shortcoming that was remarked everywhere Americans went—they tended to be braggarts. As early as July 1942 *Yank* warned: "Don't brag. Don't tell an Englishman we came over and won the last war for them. We didn't. England lost a million men; we lost only 60,000." But the same magazine had to acknowledge two months later that when one of its writers asked an Australian to comment on the Americans the Aussie had said, "Well, I wouldn't mind if you bloody blokes would stop telling me of the toughness of the Louisiana maneuvers." At the same time, agents of the Army's intelligence service, planted in bars and taverns in Australia—and in other countries, too—reported that the American's tendency to brag about his weapons and equipment could provide the enemy with valuable information. (G.I.s were prosecuted from time to time for such breaches of security, receiving prison sentences of up to five years.)

The Germans also came to know the G.I.'s assertive confidence in his Army. One technique of German officers who interrogated American prisoners was to ask, "Do you Americans really think you can beat us Germans?" When the prisoner replied "Damn right, we can," the officer would ask, "What makes you think so?" Then, unless the prisoner was careful, he was likely to commit the same sort of indiscretion he was sometimes guilty of in his favorite bar.

The American soldier's self-laudatory habits can be explained in part by the fact that he went abroad well into the war, after America's entrance and after the tide had turned in the conflict—and for most Americans, in uniform or not, it was our entrance that had turned the tide. Then, too, even before Pearl Harbor the government and the media had sold the country on the Army's excellence and its superiority over all others—especially in the realm of matériel. Once during the war the Information and Education Division had G.I.s pick out one question they would like to ask President Roosevelt. Almost no one thought to ask him if we were going to win the war—they already knew the answer. The G.I.'s confidence in his country's armed might was sometimes inappropriately expressed, but in time of adversity it stood him in good stead. One of the more arresting photographs of World War II shows a group of American prisoners being marched through the streets of Rome sometime in 1943 on their way to internment in Germany. The German guards are grim as death; the G.I.s are smiling and waving at the camera, their fingers held up in the V-for-victory sign.

The stay of American troops in the United Kingdom and Australia in sizable numbers and for a considerable period of time gave soldiers of the Allied armies a chance to take the measure of each other. The resulting views and perceptions—most of which did not change later, when the armies fought side by side—for the most part confirm conclusions we have already reached about the G.I. Army. For example, the British government did opinion sampling in the British soldier's letters, and found that the Americans were portrayed there as being splendidly supplied and holding a very good opinion of themselves. And an Australian concluded, "The Yanks taught us two things: how to use weapon power in battle, not manpower, and how to soldier and live like human beings at the same time."

A British officer named Anthony Cotterell spent considerable time in American camps in England, and he sketched out what seemed to be the differences between the two armies:

> Their marching by our standards was very loose, though maybe none the worse for that. . . . Americans seem to spend just as much time on spit and polish as we do, but their standard of results in this direction is lower. Perhaps this is an expression of their constant determination to resent being ordered about. Englishmen, of all ranks, take orders with far less question. The ignominies of K.P. (fatigues to us) are much less keenly felt. . . . Americans look on the Army more as a nine-to-six job. Their loyalty is more akin to the pride of a businessman employed by a first-rate firm, whereas the British soldier's loyalty is based on the feeling that we mustn't let the old place down, plus personal attachment to officers, which I think Americans are too independent to develop to the same extent unless their officer is an acknowledged hero . . .

While British and American soldiers generally got on well together, there were differences in temperament that were sensed by the men themselves. Many American soldiers felt their British counterparts could have performed better than they did. When asked to rate the fighting men of other countries in an Army opinion survey, the G.I.s rated the Russian soldier best, followed by the German. The Tommy gave the impression of being too slow and leisurely about the business of war. Faced with a problem, the British soldier's first impulse seemed to be to "brew up" (G.I.s commented frequently on the tea break). Orval Faubus recalled: "Because they did stop for tea, or for other causes on occasion, at what appeared to be inopportune times, the thought developed among us that they did not go as far and as fast as they might have." On the other hand, in the view of the Tommy, and also of the Aussie, the G.I. was almost too active, too loudly enterprising and impatient to "get the show on the road," to use the uniquely American expression. Captain Cotterell remarked on "the American flair for being purposeful and significant about anything, however trifling"; a British veteran of the fighting in North Africa complained that the Americans had "an urge to get going which is inclined to get on the nerves of an old desert rat."

Here we may be close to fixing on that essential impression the G.I. Army made on its allies, an impression in some ways more important than the lavish means and endless supply that distinguished the Americans. If the G.I. brought anything really distinctive (if not always welcome) to the Allied war effort, it was probably best summed up by an Australian writer named Maureen Meadows: "The entire keynote of this amazing Army seemed to be enthusiasm. They possessed an 'Oh, Boy' attitude towards everything, and it wasn't only beer and blondes or candy and Coca-Cola. Nothing represented trouble to them, nothing augured of the impossible."

★ 7 ★

The Challenge
of Combat

ONE OF the more unusual museums of Western Europe is housed in a red-brick school building in Reims, France. In 1945 the building served as General Eisenhower's headquarters, and it was there that representatives of the German armed forces came to sign their capitulation in the early morning hours of May 7, 1945. The room in which the signing took place has been left intact. The table and chairs used in the signing ceremony are in place; a slate board hung on the wall still carries the number of air missions flown on May 6. The most prominent feature in the room—one the German delegation must have regarded with some emotion—is a gigantic map of Western Europe indicating the progress of the Allied forces. The battle line for May 6, 1945, is meticulously marked out by a scarlet thread that zigzags from one pin to the next across the face of Germany.

There are other lines on the map. Some run perpendicular to the front, and these serve to separate the zones or areas of operations of the various Allied armies. There is also a line that roughly parallels the front, serving to mark off the rear of the areas of operations and distinguishing them from the areas then known as the Communications Zone or Com Z, where the ASF maintained the Army's supply lines. As the armies progressed, the "band" they occupied thus moved across Europe, while behind that band the area of the Communications Zone steadily enlarged. Normally the band, or zone of operations, was many miles deep, so deep that virtually all of the enemy's blows fell within it, including bombardment by his heaviest artillery; normally only enemy aircraft and the V-1 and V-2 rockets the Germans developed at the end of the war could penetrate into the Communications Zone. There were exceptions to this rule. When the army fought in a very restricted space, as on a beachhead, the support personnel were only yards rather than miles from the front lines and they suffered casualties; at Anzio some of the Quartermaster units on the beachhead lost 10 percent of their effectives.

Even within the area of operations there were gradations. When a man crossed from the Communications Zone there was no abrupt change—unless he entered the area of General Patton's Third Army, in which case he encountered signs with stern warnings against appearing in improper uniform. But as he continued toward the front he entered, successively, the corps area, the division sector, the battalion sector, and finally he reached the line of contact with the enemy, a line usually held by a string of rifle companies. Thus one passed gradually from safety into danger, as one came within range of the enemy's various weapons and offensive means and finally within the closest proximity to the foe.

Just as it is difficult to fix on a precise "combat zone," so is it difficult to determine which soldiers were in combat and which were not. G.I.s themselves did not agree on this, as the Information and Education Division discovered when it quizzed them on the subject. There was general agreement that those troops who fought in close proximity to the enemy—within sight of him— were indeed combat soldiers: This would include frontline infantrymen, tankers, tank destroyer crews, combat engineers, and the medical aid men who worked the battlefield. There was less agreement on the status of men who usually participated in the battle from a greater distance—thus, about half of the G.I.s queried would accord full combat credit to men in field artillery batteries and chemical mortar outfits. As for headquarters and service troops in the divisional sector, not one G.I. in four would recognize them as having full combat status. But combat took place in such a great variety of ways that any blanket categorizations miss the mark: Japanese infiltration techniques meant that G.I. cooks and clerks could find themselves face to face with enemy soldiers, and the same could be said of the men in the trains of the armored divisions who encountered enemy forces missed or by-passed by the heads of the advancing armored columns.

What is clear is that the combat soldiers, however broadly defined, were only a minority of the Army. While no reliable general statistics are available, Samuel Stouffer and his colleagues estimated in *The American Soldier* that when American forces in Europe peaked at three million, only about 750,000 were in units engaged in fighting. The combat soldier very quickly emerged as the elite element in a new Army caste system, which replaced the old Regular Army–National Guard–Draftee hierarchy. In the Army milieu, the combat soldier enjoyed status and respect not accorded to the men stationed in the Communications Zone; when men came out of the line on pass to a city such as Paris or Naples, they made the distinction obvious to those stationed in Com Z. Robert Welker, who was with the Army Service Forces in Naples, recalled that in the summer of 1944 "there were still combat troops visiting Naples, and poseurs, too, studiously unkempt and loud of mouth. . . . 'Typewriter commandos,' they called us, or 'ball-bearing Wacs.' " And Herbert French, who was stationed in Paris, recalled an encounter with a combat veteran on the *terrasse* of a Paris restaurant: "He was a great big tough fellow, the kind of soldier that makes another fellow glad he is not a German soldier. From his table next to ours, he leaned in my general direction, examined my lieutenant's bars critically, and told me without blinking, 'I hate all lieutenants.' "

Actually, one of the few advantages of service in a combat unit was the easier relationship that prevailed between officers and men. One of the more curious results of the Army's opinion surveys was the clear indication that men in the front lines were far more favorable in their view of officers than those in rear areas. Some sociologists thought this might be a by-product of combat, since the men were able to work out most of their aggression against the enemy. But the front lines were distinguished by their general lack of "chicken" and "military courtesy." The salute often went by the boards, as did the use of "sir"; under combat conditions they seemed as stilted and out of place as separate quarters and food for officers. Company-grade officers and their men were thrown together more than they had been before, and the formalities usually eroded away. A journalist visiting the front joined five G.I.s around a fire, and as he did so he noticed that among their helmets, which they had placed together on the ground, one bore the insignia of a second lieutenant. None of the men at the fire was wearing a lieutenant's bars, so the journalist decided to see if he could guess from their conversation which man was the officer. He listened to them talk for twenty minutes —without getting an inkling.

While there was a blurring of the distinctions between officers and men, combat outfits tended to have a caste system all their own. At the top of it were the old-timers, the steadily shrinking number of officers and men who had been with the unit since basic training, which they referred to as the "Camp Howze days," or the "Fort Benning days." Ernie Pyle noticed that the dwindling number of them—sometimes no more than a dozen in an infantry company of two hundred—formed a family of their own, apart from the newer men. Orval Faubus carefully recorded the disappearance of each of the "old originals" in his battalion. To a degree one's status depended on time in the unit; unquestionably on the bottom rung of the social ladder were the latest replacements, who arrived friendless and forlorn and stayed that way until the other men decided to accept them.

While a general permissiveness pervaded the battle zone, it varied considerably; some senior officers reacted very strongly to an atmosphere they felt to be "unsoldierly" and downright harmful. A lieutenant colonel in the 9th Division artillery lamented the tendency "for officers to become familiar with the men with whom they are closely associated. Officers who do so will regret it. Undue familiarity between officers and men should not be allowed." He also noted an inclination of the men "to get and look as dirty as possible. They won't shave—they won't wash—they won't use straddle trenches. Discipline dictates that they do otherwise—sanitation requires it. . . . For us it took several weeks of combat to convince our men that one could lead a normal sanitary life in the field."

When a new commander took over there was often a tightening up. When General Eichelberger took command of American forces in New Guinea, he found a general slackness and indiscipline up front: "There was no front line discipline of any kind. Our men were walking around and the crew of the heavy Browning at the right of our line were entirely exposed. . . . There were many soldiers at the rear, at aid stations and on the roots of trees. Undoubtedly some of these men had been sent back for a rest, and others had left the front without permission."

The men explained to Eichelberger that the casual atmosphere and lack of security were possible because of a tacit truce with the enemy: "They won't shoot at us if we don't shoot at them." Eichelberger thereupon fired a burst in the direction of the Japanese, but there were no answering shots. The general wrote to a friend that same day: "There will be a straggler line tomorrow and the tendency to sympathize with every little whimper will vanish. . . . Our soldiers have been sympathized with by our officers until they forget that the Japanese are having a harder time than they are."

Even when officers and commanders were most sympathetic, many of the objectionable things about the Army became more objectionable in the combat zone, particularly the material conditions of life. Life was simply harder—even leaving aside that hardest of realities, combat. There might be an order to shave every morning, but no hot water to do it with. The Army had devised portable showers, but the trucks could not be brought up to the front and the men could not leave their positions. There was an Army laundry service, but it functioned well only in rear area installations such as hospitals. Men who kept diaries (though the practice was forbidden) would note that they put on a suit of woolen underwear at Thanksgiving, and then record that they had been pulled out of the lines for showers and a change of underclothing—in January.

Men did not sleep well; even in quiet sectors of the Italian front the Army discovered soldiers were getting only about four hours of sleep a night. On the very front lines the men could not even have the minimal comfort of a sleeping bag—in the event of enemy attack they could not spare the thirty seconds it would take to get out of the bag and ready for combat. The food tended to be C or K rations, cloying and monotonous over a long period of time. Even when the Army got Christmas turkey, some of the frontline units got it later than everyone else. Then, too, there was often a sense of isolation as complete as that of the training camp barracks. Mail deliveries were irregular, and the *Stars and Stripes* and *Yank* were not always available. The taboo against talking about national war aims and other patriotic topics was even more pronounced than elsewhere. Conversations tended to turn on the doings of the group, everyday problems, and reminiscences. A sergeant named Myles Babcock reported that in his unit in the Pacific "important thinking is rare."

The front lines offered a hothouse atmosphere for rumors. Nowhere else in the Army did they thrive so well. In the Pacific there was the persistent story that the United States government paid an American soap manufacturer seventy cents for every palm tree destroyed in operations, and the rumor that the first wave of Marines on Guadalcanal consisted of ex-convicts who had been promised their freedom if they survived the war. According to another story, Mrs. Roosevelt had arranged for all servicemen who had contracted venereal disease to be quarantined on an island off the coast of the United States, rather than come straight home when the war was over. The story circulated so widely that Mrs. Roosevelt had to issue a denial. And some of the rumors reflected the specific fears and preoccupations of men in combat. The government, it was said, was secretly shipping back to the United States hundreds of "basket cases"—quadruple amputees. And to the combat soldier there was the most tantalizing and persistent rumor of all, the one the men would not let die despite endless official denials: G.I.s who had been overseas for two years—another version said eighteen months—were to be sent home.

But the central, inseparable feature of life in the combat zone was, of course, combat. It was something few of the men looked forward to, even back in those early, naive days of the training camp. In 1942 the Army polled some fifteen thousand men at fifty-four different installations, and it concluded that from a quarter to a half of the men lacked strong motivation to fight and preferred to avoid combat service. If men said they preferred service in the United States to that abroad, and in a noncombat unit rather than a fighting outfit, they were classified as "not wanting to fight." The findings were so disturbing to the War Department that it launched several programs designed to "raise morale." That was at the beginning of the war, when people still remembered the scrappy "let-me-at-'em" mood of 1917. Later, the Pentagon learned the temper of the G.I. Army and the truth of an observation made by Ernie Pyle after he visited a company of the 34th Infantry Division: "A lot of people have morale confused with the desire to fight. I don't know of one soldier out of ten thousand who wants to fight. They certainly didn't in that company. The old-timers were sick to death of battle and the new replacements were scared to death of it. And yet the company went into battle, and it was a proud company."

By the time the war ended, the Army knew a great deal concerning how its men felt about combat and how they performed in it. Indeed, the I and E Division conducted the most extensive study of men in battle ever made to that time. An entire volume of *The American Soldier* was dedicated to the G.I. in combat; an I and E Division officer named S. L. A. Marshall analyzed infantry combat in a volume entitled *Men against Fire*, one of the classics of the art of war. What is more, the Army accepted the findings of all these inquiries and shaped its policies accordingly, developing a more realistic notion of what it could expect of men in combat and a more understanding attitude—some said too understanding—toward those who did not meet expectations.

The Army frankly told potential combat soldiers that they would know fear. "You'll be scared," it said in *Army Life*, the official handbook issued to trainees. "Sure you'll be scared. Before you go into battle, you'll be frightened at the uncertainty, at the thought of being killed. . . . If you say you're not scared, you'll be a cocky fool." Telling a man he will be frightened is laudable, but it didn't make the first time in combat less traumatic. One cause of fear and poor performance among soldiers new to combat lay in the fact that the fighting was quite different from their preconception of it. Many of their notions, probably most, came from training and maneuvers; but strangely enough their image of war also owed a great deal to Hollywood. Over and over again in their letters and in their conversations they made the same remark. If two buddies were advancing across a field, with bullets kicking up mud around their feet, or if they were walking up the main street of a seemingly deserted Italian town, their rifles at the ready, one would invariably say to the other, "This is just like the movies." In the movies, and in training, the men almost invariably worked with others, with the objective or the enemy clearly defined. Then they went into combat and found the situation could be completely different.

This was a particularly serious problem for the infantry. A brigadier general named H. J. Matchett explained the difficulty in the *Infantry Journal* in June 1946: "In combat we found that green troops would invariably freeze when first coming under fire. They would stop, seek cover, and then try to find the enemy. They could not see any clear, distinct targets. Therefore they did not fire. Their casualties increased. The conditions under which they had been trained to open fire simply did not exist." And something even more disquieting happened. In scattering and taking cover, the soldiers lost contact with one another. No enemy was visible, but much more disconcerting, no friend was visible, either. In such circumstances a man had the terrifying feeling that he was all alone; he would cease all motion, all activity. Said S. L. A. Marshall, "I hold it to be one of the simplest truths of war that the thing which enables an infantry soldier to keep moving with his weapon is the near presence or the presumed presence of a comrade."

In one respect the counsel *Army Life* gave to new soldiers was overoptimistic. There is an implication that the soldier will eventually put his fear behind him: "After you've become used to the picture and the sensations of the battlefield, you will change. . . . That first fight—that fight with yourself—will have gone." But the essential change that came as the soldier became battle-wise was an ability to discriminate among the sights and sounds of the battlefield and to fear only the dangerous ones. The historian of the 3rd Armored Division observed in this connection: "There was nothing basically wrong with the division . . . but, in common with every other American force new to combat, the 3rd had to get over the feeling that every shell was an 88 and it had to realize that no matter how much noise an automatic weapon makes, it is still so much scrap metal unless properly directed."

The combat veteran could distinguish between the "incoming" German fire and the "outgoing" American fire, and so dive for cover only when he heard the former; he would not panic at the appearance of the relatively innocuous German dive-bomber, but his blood would still freeze in his veins every time he identified the clatter of an approaching Tiger tank. For the veteran, the aggregate of fears should theoretically have declined as his powers of discrimination increased. It doesn't seem to have worked that way. When infantrymen in the Mediterranean were polled on the question, three quarters of them said they found the war more frightening as it continued. The fear the men knew was not just the minor apprehension mixed with excitement that produces the proverbial cold sweat and trembling fingers. Combat veterans told interviewers that they had known intense anxiety with a whole gamut of physiological manifestations, including violent pounding of the heart and shaking or trembling all over. Of those queried in one study, 10 percent acknowledged that they had lost control of their bowels.

While fear of such things as the dive-bomber might abate, the fear of enemy artillery did not; indeed, it may have increased for many soldiers. Lying helpless and exposed in a heavy shelling was for many the worst experience of all. Men who felt they might crack up would say they didn't think they could take another shelling. Walter Bernstein recalled that it was "something inhuman and terribly frightening. . . . It is like the finger of God." During one intense bombardment, Bernstein suddenly remembered a handbag that his wife had admired but which they had not bought because it was too expensive. "And I thought now, the shells falling like the end of the world: We should have bought the bag, we should have bought the bag." And the nightmare of being shelled was one of the most common "battle dreams" seen in Army hospitals. An Army psychologist who witnessed a number of such episodes wrote: "In some . . . the patient executes strenuous digging and scraping movements in his bed, reproducing the common experience of a soldier lying in a shallow depression under heavy fire, and attempting to convert it into a deeper hole for better protection by digging with his hands, and even the head. Frequently they bury themselves under their covers during such dreams, or even get under the bed, and wake up wondering where they are."

At the beginning of the war the Army's training methods were designed to produce a kind of "automatic" response; through frequent repetition the soldier would become so accustomed to manipulating his weapon—so "grooved," as one general put it— that when called upon he would do the task virtually without thinking, even if his mind were partially paralyzed by fear. But it was soon clear that the modern battlefield and sophisticated weaponry required soldiers who could control their fear, think with some clarity, and use initiative in situations where they were not under direct supervision—and do all these things along with considerable physical exertion. As a result the Army found the ideal battlefield soldier needed youth, intelligence, and a proper physique; in the second half of the war military manpower was allocated accordingly. Though the Army's basic conclusions were sound enough, it proved exasperatingly difficult to predict which men would perform well in combat. One can cite as an example a frail Texan who joined the Army in 1942. He had already been turned down by the Marines. His educational accomplishments were minimal—four years of schooling. He was only five pounds over the Army's minimum weight, and the men in his training company called him Baby; he once fainted during a training formation. But his name was Audie Murphy and he became the most decorated combat soldier in American history.

Within any infantry company there were men who would be lions in combat and others who would be sheep. A Marine division commander in the Pacific told an Army observer: "About ten percent of a unit do all the fighting and will never cause you trouble—they are the backbone. About eighty percent are half-trained, scared to death, and waiting to see what someone else is going to do. The other ten percent never were and never will be any good." S. L. A. Marshall reached similar conclusions. He estimated that in any battle only about 25 percent of an infantry outfit would fire their rifles; but the basis for his estimate is unclear, and many combat veterans say it is far too low. Marshall also wrote: "Company by company we found in our work that there were men who had been consistently bad actors in the training period, marked by the faults of laziness, unruliness, and disorderliness, who just as consistently became lions on the battlefield, with all the virtues of sustained aggressiveness, warm obedience, and thoughtfully planned action. When the battle was over and time came to coast, they almost invariably relapsed again. They could fight like hell but they couldn't soldier."

This was a mystery for a psychiatrist to explain, but here the psychiatrists of the war period were inclined to throw up their hands. They had rejected men as psychologically unfit for military service based on their most studied professional judgment, and then had seen those men reclassified, put into uniform, and awarded decorations for their performance in the battlefield. Some psychiatrists called such cases "sources of the greatest perplexity"; others confessed that the predictive value of their psychiatric scanning was nil.

Yet the battlefield produced specimens to pique the curiosity of any serious student of the human mind. There were, for example, men who from the very first actually enjoyed combat. There were others—not very many, apparently—who came onto the battlefield absolutely without fear. Some said such men were "the best of the best"; James Jones claimed to have known two, both of whom were "certifiably insane." They could be as great a menace to their comrades in arms as they were to the enemy. They would observe no firing discipline, blazing away at any enemy they saw, sometimes exposing their unit to a riposte by vastly superior enemy forces. If admonished, they would accuse their fellow soldiers and even their superiors of cowardice. According to psychiatrist Eli Ginzberg, "Many of the outstanding combat soldiers were hostile, emotionally insecure, extremely unstable personalities who might well be termed clinically 'psychopaths,' whatever that may imply, who fully enjoyed the opportunity of taking out hostilities directly in a socially acceptable setting of warfare and who in the absence of such an outlet not infrequently end up in penitentiaries."

What Dr. Ginzberg wrote may very well be true. It is no less true that in the main the war was fought and won by American men whose minds were not so ordered—or so disordered—that combat was any easy thing for them. Four decades later, many will acknowledge that combat was the most redoubtable challenge of their lives. What was it that enabled them to cope? What qualities, what resources, saw them through their ordeal? Samuel Stouffer and his colleagues asked them such questions, and they got a range of answers, some of which are surprising. When asked what most helped "when the going got tough," the men most frequently designated "prayer," though this meant many different things to them. And there is other evidence that the spiritual factor was an important one in the soldier's life. This was true in the training camps, where chapels were usually filled although attendance was voluntary. Men told the researchers for *The American Soldier* that they had become more religious in the Army, and this is often borne out in their letters. "In civilian life I was never very religious," wrote one G.I. "Now I somehow want to be very much." And undoubtedly prayer figured in the preparation for combat—in many accounts there are references to the men of a unit's briefly praying together before they went into action. There may have been much truth in the often-repeated saying of the war years: "There are no atheists in the foxholes."

The second most important factor in keeping a man going when things were toughest was the thought that he couldn't let the other men down. We have already seen that the bonding process began in the training camps; the more arduous the training, the stronger the bond. In combat the bond became strongest of all. Many veterans will say they never had such profound friendships before or since their Army days. Louis Rossetti, an artilleryman with the 75th Division, observed that "when you've been around the same men for months, work, eat and sleep together, you get to know them pretty well. . . . You get to know their personal feelings and all about their families and wives and sweethearts." He recalled that whenever the men had night guard duty and challenged someone they heard approaching in the dark, the person would often say, "It's me"—and be instantly recognized. "It got so we knew every member of our unit—there were only about sixty of us—in the dark. We recognized their voices or even their coughs and actions in the dusk."

So powerful was the cohesive force of the fighting unit that men who were for some reason removed from it had feelings of guilt that were sometimes as strong as their sense of relief. When Ernie Pyle visited a tent hospital in Sicily he found that at least a third of the less severely wounded wanted to return to duty immediately. Another journalist visiting a frontline unit was introduced to a soldier obviously still recovering from wounds who was described as "AWOL from the hospital." (There was another consideration the wounded soldier kept in mind: If he stayed away from his unit too long he would be replaced—and then become a replacement himself in some other outfit.) Though virtually everyone dreamed of being miraculously withdrawn from combat, when an opportunity presented itself the men did not automatically seize it. The authors of *The American Soldier* even argued that the soldier's most important fight was here, in "the conflict between loyalty to one's outfit and buddies and the desire to escape from combat." One who wrestled with the problem was a young

7th Division soldier named John Hogan who had a chance to move from a rifle company to a much safer message center. He explained to his parents: "There is something about the spirit of the men in this platoon that I have grown to love and I want to help guard it." Hogan, who was deeply religious, concluded that "danger is a sacrament too"; he stayed with his friends. When his patrol encountered the enemy in the Gaja Ridge area of Okinawa he shouted for the other men to take cover and returned the enemy's fire until he fell. He was awarded a posthumous Silver Star.

S. L. A. Marshall believed that one could draw around a soldier in combat a circle that would include only those persons and objects the soldier could see or that he thought would have an immediate impact on his chances of survival, and that what the soldier perceived within that circle would determine how he fought. It may well be true that in the heat of battle the soldier was aware only of his immediate surroundings. But when he had a chance to look back and to reflect, he revealed a more complex pattern of motivation. In 1944 the I and E Division asked veteran infantrymen in the Mediterranean this question: "Generally, from your combat experience, what was most important to you in making you want to keep going and do as well as you could?" The incentive the men cited most—39 percent of the times—was "getting the task done," that is, putting the war behind them and getting back home. For another 10 percent the thought of "home and loved ones" was an incentive; so those various considerations summed up in the magic word "home" dominated all others. Solidarity with the group, the "buddies," is less important (14 percent) than it was in helping a man pull through a specific, "tough" combat situation. A sense of duty and self-respect was cited by 9 percent of the G.I.s questioned. Finally, what could be called "idealistic" reasons figured in only one answer out of twenty. If the men who were polled faithfully represented their several million fellow soldiers, they were fighting mainly so they could go home again.

Scarcely one soldier in a hundred cited leadership among the incentives that kept him to his task, and this is an interesting and significant omission. The authors of *The American Soldier* concluded that the character and qualities of a commanding general probably had little impact on the American soldier; while Eisenhower was in a sense "popular" with the men under him, his popularity and prestige were not major factors in determining how they fought under him. No one could be indifferent to a colorful commander such as George S. Patton; those who served under him tended to be outspoken admirers or equally outspoken critics. G.I.s who did not like Patton claimed he was wasteful of their lives in the pursuit of his objectives: "Our blood, his guts," they said. According to an apocryphal story that went the rounds in his command, Patton had said he would be the first Allied general in Berlin even if it took three trucks to haul the dog tags of Third Army soldiers killed in the process. General Mark Clark was similarly criticized by some of those who served under him, particularly those in outfits that had fought and sustained heavy losses at Salerno and Anzio.

In the Pacific, the rating General MacArthur received from his troops was periodically established by extracting and collating opinions found in G.I. letters (about 5 percent of the letters written by servicemen were censored a second time at the base section in Australia, and it was there that opinion sampling was done). Elliott Thorpe, MacArthur's chief of counterintelligence, supervised this work; he found that the general's standing among his troops rose or fell according to his military fortunes, though even in the darkest hours the men recognized that he did his utmost to support the frontline soldier. Interestingly, MacArthur read the monthly reports scrupulously, including favorable and adverse comments G.I.s made about him. "It always seemed to me," Thorpe recalled, "the military censorship section outdid itself in the adverse comments given on the matter of the general himself. I recall such unflattering quotes as 'brass-hatted old bastard,' 'flannel-mouthed fool,' 'egotistical ass,' et cetera."

If leadership at the higher command levels had little impact on combat motivation, that was not the case at lower levels, where officers and men were in constant contact. Here, in fact, good leadership was absolutely critical to the G.I.'s performance in combat; as one G.I. put it, "Everybody wants someone to look up to when he's scared." And G.I.s did not hesitate to point out the qualities they looked for in those who led them: They wanted officers—and noncoms—who led by example, who had confidence in themselves, and who knew their jobs; but they also wanted leaders who knew and cared about the men, shared jokes and hardships with them, and were careful to keep them informed and to explain the purpose of their missions.

Where leaders did not have these qualities, the results could be disastrous. Army psychologists noted that one infantry company might have ten times more neuropsychiatric casualties than another company of the same battalion engaged in the same operations—the character of the company commander being the key variable. A senior noncom who was insecure in his position and a martinet requiring rigid conformity, and "riding" certain men, could utterly demoralize his unit. The G.I. could be led, it was often said, but he could not be driven. S. L. A. Marshall reported in this connection a particularly tragic episode that occurred in the Marshall Islands. The American infantry had been pinned down on the invasion beach by heavy Japanese fire; a "prodding" order came down from division headquarters, and a lieutenant cautiously worked his way up to the most advanced of the riflemen and told him to move forward. The young soldier shouted in a rage, "So the whole goddamned Army wants to kill me, does it? Okay, Lieutenant, here I go, but watch what happens." The soldier sprang up and was cut down before he took two steps. The effect on the other men was shattering.

For those who had the capacity for it, leading G.I.s in battle had its satisfactions and its rewards. These are clearly reflected in a letter an officer named Morton Eustis addressed to his mother—one of the last letters he wrote before he was killed in France in the summer of 1944:

> It also means a lot to know that you have the enlisted men of an outfit behind you, as without their cooperation you are lost. And I really think, without in any sense blowing my own trumpet,

that the men do like, and what is far more important, respect me. Quite a number of them told me so when they were a bit intoxicated at the company party, but it's more something you can sense and feel.

Actually, in one humble opinion there's a good deal of plain unadulterated nonsense in the theory so widely expounded in the officer's guide that an officer must be so remote from his men and live on another plane from them altogether; otherwise that familiarity will breed contempt. That's all very well in garrison, maybe, but in combat, where you live, eat and sleep with the men and are on terms of the most complete intimacy, it all breaks down. And they respect you then, if they do, not because you wear bars, but because you can lead them—if you can.

Neither good leadership nor any of the other "incentives" measured by opinion surveys tell the whole story of how the G.I. coped with the dangers he faced at the front. Diaries and letters hint at a variety of expedients to gain at least temporary release from the tensions and the exhaustion of combat. One of these was alcohol. An observer in the Pacific reported that "the issue of small 2 oz. bottles of brandy to individuals to counteract shock and fatigue has been of great recuperative benefit." When soldiers had taken and "secured" a town or hamlet in France or Germany, they frequently sought out a cache of cognac or schnapps to finish the day's fighting with celebrating, relaxing, or just putting the war out of their minds for a little while. The bouts of ransacking fields and houses for "souvenirs," common to all armies, may also have been a kind of release after the tensions of battle.

Humor, too, was a kind of safety valve, though things that were hilarious on the battlefield might not be very funny in another setting. In his semiautobiographical *WWII*, James Jones recalled that his outfit had just taken a hill from the Japanese after token resistance when it suffered a bizarre casualty. One of the men was stunned by a spent bullet; it came out of nowhere, rapped him solidly on the forehead, and caromed away, leaving only a superficial cut. The man's eyes slowly crossed; he sat down, then fell on his back. Another soldier who had been talking to him at the instant he was struck opened his mouth to call for a medic when he was suddenly overcome by the comic side of his friend's mishap.

He, too, fell to the ground, gripping his sides and roaring with laughter. Between guffaws he managed to tell Jones and the others who gathered around what he had seen:

> If we could only have seen those eyes going crossed, he groaned, breaking out again and hugging himself. The medic had come up now, and looked at the slight tear on the hit man's forehead with disgust. "Christ, is this what you guys got me up here for?" He got the casualty on his feet, "Come on, I'll take you to battalion. They'll give you some aspirin." By now there were six or eight of us roaring and paralyzed, on our knees or squirming on the ground or holding on to each other, as the medic led the stunned man off. "You sons of bitches, I coulda been killed," he called back irately at us. And we all broke out afresh.

Sometimes a soldier found it easier to bear the strain of combat with a kind of self-delusion, usually a belief that if he performed some ritual act or observed some taboo, he would survive. There was the infantryman in Italy who took—and kept—a vow never to fire his rifle in anger; there was the G.I. Ernie Pyle met who planned to wear a black silk opera hat into battle with this rationale: "The Germans will think I'm crazy, and they're afraid of crazy people." Then there was the most dangerous delusion of all, the belief that one was invulnerable. A soldier who had been in the Pacific told Arthur Miller, "I started taking chances and got the name 'The Ridge Runner.' It got so I didn't believe any more that I would get killed." Then one day the Ridge Runner got miraculous news: He had been selected for OCS and was to leave immediately for the United States. He instantly lost his mantle of invulnerability. He told Miller: "Well, I had to go back two miles through jungle alone. That was the first time I was really scared. I knew I was going to get killed now, just when I was getting home. I tell you I fired over eighty rounds in those two miles, and it took me nearly a whole day to make it. Every leaf that moved got a bullet through it."

James Jones spoke of another state of mind—no less dangerous in the long run—that enabled a soldier to bear up and keep going through the worst the jungle had to offer. He called it "Combat Numbness," a somnambulist state produced by fear, fatigue, and disbelief in what was happening. A veteran of the fighting in Europe described the same state of mind among the men of his outfit: "They're scared all right, but they don't care. When they're running they run about fifteen yards and then start walking—don't give a damn." Any G.I. who fought long enough would probably reach this state. But he would not simply stabilize there; sooner or later fear, fatigue, and harsh field conditions would get the better of him and he would be classified as suffering from combat exhaustion. William C. Menninger, who was the Army's chief consultant in neuropsychiatry, described the soldier who had had all he could take: "Typically he appeared as a dejected, dirty, weary man. His facial expression was one of depression, sometimes of tearfulness. Frequently his hands were trembling or jerking. Occasionally he would display varying degrees of confusion, perhaps to the extent of being mute or staring into space. Very occasionally he might present classically hysterical symptoms."

In ascribing a medical condition to men who broke down or became ineffective in battle, and in sending them to a rest area rather than to the stockade, the Army's leadership was in a sense redefining the concepts of bravery and cowardice. But as the evidence mounted, it could hardly do otherwise. A study of NP cases in the Mediterranean indicated that the infantryman in combat with little or no relief ceased being an effective soldier in about two hundred days on the average. And there was no such thing as the "battle-hardened veteran," so inured to combat that he could go on endlessly. "Old sergeant's syndrome" would claim him after six to fourteen months in the lines; one day he, too, would break down and say he could take no more. Eli Ginzberg pointed out the inescapable conclusion to be drawn from the findings: "There has been a striking change from the formerly held belief that a clear-cut distinction can be made between 'the weak and the strong' to the current opinion that 'every man has his breaking point.' "

Not everyone accepted this interpretation. The Army's leaders were themselves divided. General Omar Bradley subscribed to the view that every man did indeed have his breaking point. General Patton, on the other hand, issued a memorandum branding the men in his command who were "nervously incapable of combat" as "cowards." General Eichelberger spoke of getting rid of the "weaklings," and the commander of the Americal Division, then fighting on Guadalcanal, told his chief surgeon he wanted every neuropsychiatric case court-martialed (the surgeon was able to talk him out of it).

Even after combat exhaustion was recognized as a treatable condition, treatment was a particularly difficult problem in the U.S. Army. In other armies, divisions were pulled out of the line from time to time and given the period of rest that was the essential element in preventing and treating combat exhaustion. But American divisions were limited in number and virtually all committed in one theater or another. As casualties and other losses occurred, they would be made good with individual replacements. This scheme had a number of advantages, but it created severe morale problems. First of all, the veteran soldiers in a division had no prospect of relief. They were destined to remain in the line until they became casualties; their best hope was the "million-dollar wound"—one that would get them out of combat without being disfigured or permanently disabled. Only in 1944 did the Army devise a rotation system to offer the combat soldier a better chance. Tardy and inadequate though such efforts were, they could work wonders in the morale of a fighting unit. Orval Faubus noted in his diary for December 1944: "Lt. Sperl-is here to get the list of 20 men and·one officer who can go to the states on 30 day furlough. My God! What a hope! What a chance for the men in the lines."

Another bad feature of the individual replacement system was the unhappy lot of the replacement soldiers. Turned out by the training camps in great numbers in the latter part of the war, these men had neither hearth nor home for much of their career in the Army. No bands played when they sailed for the overseas theater in anonymous lots. Stocked like living "spare parts" in the "repple depple" (replacement depot), they awaited orders to a combat unit, where they found themselves friendless and alone, coping with strange surroundings and danger at the same time. Not surprisingly, a significant number of replacements fell victim to combat exhaustion in their very first engagement.

Making the best of a bad situation, many combat outfits devised their own makeshift rest and rehabilitation centers whose main purpose was to give relief to a jittery G.I. and perhaps forestall his breakdown. An observer in the European Theater of Operations described rest camps he found in Germany early in 1945 as little more than artillery-proof dugouts with a stove and hot coffee: "But to a soldier on the verge of exhaustion, an opportunity to dry out in a safe place for a few hours is a haven of refuge that will revive his will to fight." A scheme used in the XIX Corps area in France worked as follows: "Each company commander endeavored to have an officer see each enlisted man on the front line at least once each day, and if any enlisted man appeared nervous, restless, or on the point of breaking, his name would be turned in to the first sergeant, who would pull him out of the line and send him on a fatigue detail to the service company. While in service company area they were used on various chores and soon, never longer than two days, men would request to be returned to their own front line unit."

There were persistent complaints in the Army's command structure about such facilities and about the "coddling" and "catering to malingerers" they supposedly represented. But the American soldier continued to be told in battle indoctrination lectures that he had a breaking point, that he might reach it, and that such a breakdown was not cowardly or disgraceful. It is doubtful that such an enlightened policy was an open invitation to malinger— most psychiatrists said that combat exhaustion in its various forms was almost impossible to simulate, and they reported few attempts. And the stress the G.I. knew in combat tended to be a passing thing. Nine soldiers out of ten came through battles without any serious mental damage.

If the trauma was temporary, it was no less real. Sometimes what a soldier said or wrote while under the impress of that trauma has a special value, for it may provide a privileged view of war in its elemental and unadulterated horror—and also a glimpse of that mysterious substance called courage. Such is the case with a letter written by a G.I. named Sandford Africk. He had had a particularly bad experience: Severely wounded during heavy fighting on the Italian front, he was being evacuated when his stretcher-bearers blundered into the German lines; since Africk was Jewish, he was more than a little concerned about how the Germans would treat him. But before long both captives and captors had to move hurriedly, and in the confusion Africk's stretcher-bearers were able to carry him back to the American lines. Shortly afterward, he wrote home from the hospital, recounting his adventure matter-of-factly, praising the medical staff and expressing hope for a thirty-day furlough. But two months later, still in the hospital, he wrote a different kind of letter. This time he was reliving the trauma of battle in all its intensity, and that intensity is captured in a letter whose lines are possessed of an extraordinary power:

My whole company was replaced except for a handful of lucky men. All my buddies were killed or wounded. At one place I and my squad leader were the only two that were alive and unwounded after the squad was caught in a mortar fire trap. That fellow that I wrote you about that used to hunt chickens and rabbits with me was killed lying next to me. My heart almost broke as I looked at him, but what could I do?

So many buddies gone and so many wounded! My lieutenant got off easy with a scratch on the arm. He is the only officer alive except for the company commander who will have a stiff arm for the rest of his life. Oh, darling, it was hell having my friends falling all around me and all we could do was say goodbye with a salute, and kill more Germans. We walked straight into death, not one man flinched or tried to save himself. I am proud to say, darling, that I was one of the brave lost children. We were only children after all. The dead boys were cuddled up, the wounded cried for dead friends. All children, after all.

The Variables
of Battle

ANY HISTORIAN who interviews combat veterans soon learns that World War II was many wars. For the soldier the key questions were always what sort of enemy he would meet, and in what conditions he would fight him; the answers to those questions could vary greatly from one theater of operations to another, or from one campaign to the next. One of the most important variables was climate. Under the North African sun, temperatures inside a "buttoned up" tank could go to 130 degrees. Though in general troops used to temperate climates adapted to heat without great problems, part of the adaptation consisted of changing the soldier's tempo of activity. At the other extreme, cold probably presented the more serious challenges on the battlefield. At extreme low temperature combat ceased altogether; even when it was less severe, in certain conditions cold could decimate combat troops. The fifteen thousand American troops who invaded Attu, in the Aleutians, beginning in May 1943, encountered a cold, wet climate for which they were poorly equipped. By the end of May they had suffered twelve hundred casualties from the cold, more than resulted from the fighting with the Japanese.

Not only could the conditions in which soldiers were forced to live produce more casualties than combat, there were cases of lonely overseas outposts in which the emotional stress was so great that combat would have been a relief. An Army psychiatrist wrote in this connection:

> I do not feel that combat was as likely to bring out psychoneurotic behavior as boredom and lack of purpose. I remember one island in the South Pacific which was never attacked by the Japanese and on which the executive officer was something of a martinet. The men developed an extraordinarily wide range of symptoms. I saw boys with hemianesthesia, anesthesia of a quarter of the body, gun barrel vision, legs in extension which could not be flexed—in short the richest collection of gross hysterical symptoms I have ever seen. I felt very certain at the time and feel more certain now that the number of neurotic individuals would have been greatly decreased either with good leadership or if the island had been attacked once in a while by the enemy.

Most G.I.s who saw combat did so either in the Pacific or in Europe, with the largest commitment of troops being to Europe, so the nature of battle in these two areas is of particular interest. (For our purposes here the Mediterranean Theater of Operations —essentially Italy—is included in Europe, and the Pacific includes both General MacArthur's Southwest Pacific area—including New Guinea and the Philippines—and the Pacific Ocean areas under the command of Admiral Chester Nimitz.) The fighting in both areas differed considerably from that seen in 1914 to 1918. Amphibious operations were a feature of the war in both theaters, where they were carried out with almost uniform success. The battlefield became three-dimensional as tactical air power came into its own. By the summer of 1944 Allied air superiority was such that the German Army could not use the roads of France with any safety until the sun went down; on the other hand, Allied armored columns advanced under a canopy of close support fighter-bombers. Another fundamental difference from the previous war lay in the nature of the front. In the First World War the front had been a continuous line, with each infantry division occupying about two miles of front. In the Second World War the "front lines" tended to be a network of outposts and strong points that were more lightly held, so that a division could hold a front of ten miles or more. Such a front was far more easily displaced, since the armies did not burrow into the earth as they had in 1914 to 1918. The soldier was up and moving, contenting himself generally with nothing more than a temporary foxhole. In open country it was possible to catch sight of the enemy; in the Pacific, where visibility was usually more limited but the opposing front lines closer to each other, the enemy could often be heard.

With the front more sketchily defined there could be a "mixing" of opposing units, especially when the front was flexible and one of the opponents was advancing. During the taking of Kwajalein, a company of the 32nd Regiment advanced too far one day, so when it bivouacked that evening it had Japanese in its front, rear, and on both flanks; moreover, it discovered inside its perimeter an air raid shelter occupied by an unknown number of Japanese. Bodies of opposing infantry would unexpectedly bump into each other; curiously, a number of instances were recorded in which groups of German and American soldiers passed within close proximity of each other, and though they saw and recognized each other, they continued on their way without firing (such episodes involving Americans and Japanese are very rare). Armor, too, could be involved in some odd accidental encounters. In July 1944 in northern France, two tank battalions of the 4th Armored Division mistook each other for the enemy and engaged in a brief shootout for possession of a night assembly area. Shortly after the fighting stopped, a German tank battalion arrived to share the area. Incredibly, the Germans parked unchallenged, and some time elapsed before someone realized what had occurred. Then once again the assembly area was filled with the sound of frantically revving engines and the roar of cannon as tanks dueled at ranges of less than twenty-five feet.

But there were also some very important differences in the nature of combat in the two major theaters. First of all, the tempo of operations was different. In Europe, amphibious operations, while important, were less frequent; in the Pacific the island-hopping strategy made the war cyclical, with landing, conquest, then staging for the next invasion. The soldier who fought in the Pacific thus got at least a chance to catch his breath between islands, while the soldier fighting in Europe continued to fight until the sizable landmass of Western Europe was all taken. In general, troops in the Pacific had been committed in larger numbers earlier; the largest mass of G.I.s in Europe did not get into battle until 1944.

The rate of killed and wounded was on the whole lower in the Pacific than in Europe. The explanation probably lies in the higher quantity and quality of German artillery, since fragmentation devices, artillery and mortar shells for the most part, produced some 60 percent of the battlefield casualties in World War II; the G.I. was right to respect the German 88. But there was one type of casualty in which the Southwest Pacific area led all others, and that was the neuropsychiatric variety. There were a number of factors that made the Pacific a particularly bad place to fight a war, and these will become evident as we continue our comparison of the two theaters.

The G.I. who campaigned through Europe did his fighting in a temperate climate (though veterans who spent the bitter winter of 1944/45 in the field might challenge this assertion). The terrain over which he fought was generally comparable to the fields and woods he was accustomed to, though he occasionally encountered truly alien topography: The hedgerow country of Normandy, the *bocage*, is perhaps the best-known example, though the mountainous terrain in Italy presented an equally severe challenge. Then, too, in Europe the G.I. found himself in an area with cities, paved roads, electricity, and a culture not too dissimilar to his own. He could often find a bottle to help him relax, a chicken or a couple of eggs to vary his diet, and a roof to shelter him on a cold night. When lines were stationary, fixed affairs, as they were for a time in Italy, the soldier could settle in and create for himself a surprisingly comfortable dugout. Armored troops even electrified theirs, running wires from their tanks nearby. Ernie Pyle visited a dugout in Italy that had a writing desk with a table lamp, a washstand with a big mirror, porcelain lamp shades with little Dutch girls painted on them—"and best of all, hidden on a shelf, I noticed two brown eggs." An officer with the 9th Division artillery said that surprise inspections revealed similar amenities, including a Beautyrest mattress, a four-poster bed, and a large bird cage containing two canaries.

Soldiers were also tempted to linger in the towns and villages they passed through for "gratifying contacts with women," as *The American Soldier* decorously put it, or simply to take a break. In some cases the AWOL G.I. thought of himself as simply taking a self-prescribed treatment for combat exhaustion. Short-term AWOL was a serious problem in 1944; it is said that when the First and Third U.S. armies crossed the Seine near Paris that summer, no fewer than ten thousand G.I.s took off to see the city. Though the punishment could be draconian, in most cases the Army was content to see the offenders returned to their units for punishment there. The Military Police often had difficulty distinguishing between AWOLs and stragglers—the latter being men separated from their outfits through no fault of their own; in such cases the authorities would often give a man the benefit of the doubt.

The soldier who fought in the Pacific found himself in a strange and forbidding region inhabited by primitive people with a culture that had little or no attraction for him. Ultimately, beer began to reach troops in the Pacific combat areas, but for much of the war the only alcoholic relief was offered by the occasional availability of "jungle juice," a surreptitiously brewed concoction made from raisins, canned peaches, or whatever else the soldiers thought could be fermented. The low venereal disease rates—a fraction of those in Europe—are eloquent testimony to the cultural isolation of the G.I.s in the Pacific. For a generation that believed sexual abstinence was unhealthy, this deprivation was a matter of genuine concern. If the VD rate was low, so was the AWOL rate. Elliott Thorpe recalled: "The problem of men going absent without leave was practically nonexistent for the simple reason there was no place to go." The best the men could do was attempt to slip aboard supply ships or aircraft; Thorpe remembered one G.I. who made it all the way to San Francisco. (More enterprising were four men from Merrill's Marauders: Evacuated to a hospital in India, they used forged furlough papers to get flights from Calcutta to Karachi, then on to Casablanca and finally Miami. From there they hitchhiked to their homes in New Jersey.)

The tropical jungles of the Pacific had hot-season temperatures that ranged from 92 to 112 degrees; humidity stayed between 65 and 100 percent. In addition to their enervating climate, the jungles harbored a variety of exotic and disabling diseases, of which the best known was malaria, which claimed more victims than the Japanese. The 25th Infantry Division, which was sent to Guadalcanal early in 1943, had 46 percent of its men come down with malaria one or more times. So widespread was the disease on Guadalcanal that at one time there were standing orders not to evacuate any soldier from the lines until his temperature went over 103 degrees. The disease could be treated with Atabrine, but the drug was not popular with the men. It was said to produce impotence and insanity, and it did in fact give a sickly yellow color to the skin of many who took it. (It also could trigger "Atabrine dermatitis," but the Army's Medical Department kept the cause of the malady a secret for fear it would erode "Atabrine discipline"; as it was, the men usually took their Atabrine under close supervision.)

But malaria was only the most prominent health hazard. There was dengue fever, also spread by mosquitoes; it appeared in epidemic form on Espíritu Santo in 1943 and in New Guinea in 1944. There was filariasis, which had monstrously swollen the limbs of natives, and there was scrub typhus, transmitted by mites that lived in the kunai grass. And there were swimmer's itch, tree sap dermatitus, miliaria, and "blue nail"—a vague disorder the doctors never quite figured out. An outbreak of one or more of these disorders, coupled with normal battle losses and a high NP rate, could cripple a body of troops. During three months of operations on New Georgia in 1943, a force of thirty thousand U.S. troops had thirteen thousand admissions for disease and injury, nearly half the force. Of the admissions, 27 percent were men wounded in action and 11 percent otherwise injured, 21 percent for malaria, 19 percent for neuropsychiatric disorders, 18 percent for diarrheal disease, and 4 percent for various other diseases.

Though the jungle was dangerous because of the diseases it harbored, it was in itself an extremely uncomfortable place in which to live and fight. A report made on morale in New Guinea early in 1943 said that troops new to the combat zone there experienced "violent shock" at first: "The conditions confronting them were difficult and cruel beyond expectations." And the same report noted that among troops who had been in the lines for some time, "the Japs are described as tough, resourceful, treacherous and inhumanly cruel, but hated equally as much as the enemy are heat, mosquitoes, rain, canned food and warm chlorinated water." No one ever became truly acclimated to the jungle; when the I and E questionnaires invited free comments, Pacific veterans made this clear. "It is hell living here in the Pacific," wrote one. "God damn it, get me out of these jungles."

If we turn from considerations of temperature and terrain to the nature of the enemy—real or perceived—and the kind of "dialogue of violence" the G.I. carried on with him, then World War II becomes two emphatically different conflicts: the one carried on against the Germans and the one against the Japanese. Despite all the denunciations of Nazi "barbarism" and the oft-heard theme on German radio that the Americans were all "gangsters," each army tacitly acknowledged that the other was fighting in basic conformity with the rules of civilized warfare; on the battlefield this meant that as a rule neither side tried to exterminate without quarter, that there was a sort of mutual respect, and that, as one ex-G.I. put it, "It was something of a gentleman's war." Such was the basic attitude on both sides, though as we will see, that attitude could be swept away in a moment and replaced by the deepest animosity and the most burning desire of revenge.

Wehrmacht officers who interrogated American prisoners of war reported that the men expressed no strong negative feelings about their German opponents—hardly surprising, given the circumstances. But bitter denunciations of the Germans are also the exception in G.I. letters. The I and E Division probed the G.I.'s attitude toward his German counterpart and found essentially the same lack of deep hatred. When soldiers of two veteran divisions that had fought in North Africa and Sicily were asked what effect the sight of German prisoners had on them, 54 percent subscribed to the statement: "They are men just like us, it's too bad we have to be fighting them."

The G.I. would generally admit that his German counterpart was a first-rate soldier; according to an I and E poll cited earlier, he was rated second only to the Russian, and considerably better than the Tommy. The American would also admit that in the technological aspects of war—the "hardware"—the German was a keen competitor. The reputation of the German 88, quite possibly exaggerated, survived the war intact. The German light machine gun, the MG42, was probably the best such weapon of the war. G.I.s were impressed by its lightness and its high rate of fire. As one G.I. put it: "Our gun sounds like a slow motorboat, theirs like a buzz saw." (From time to time American troops would "liberate" these weapons and use them themselves. Unfortunately, this practice had a disquieting effect on other American units when they heard the telltale chatter of an MG42 on their flank.) For most of the war the Americans could not match the Germans in superheavy artillery. This was graphically demonstrated in Italy, where the Germans bombarded the Anzio beaches with the fearsome "Anzio Annie," a monster 280-mm cannon firing from a distance of thirty-six miles. Finally, no one could quite appreciate the German heavy tank as much as a man facing it in an American medium tank.

If German matériel inspired respect, and sometimes admiration, the German soldier inspired no strong detestation. There was nothing particularly pejorative in the terms "Jerry" and "Kraut." G.I.s rarely referred to German soldiers as Nazis, and the World War I appellation "Hun" was also rarely heard. (In Italy some

American soldiers picked up the habit of calling the Germans "*tedeschi*.") Ernie Pyle, who had a good sense of how G.I.s felt about things, wrote that they had little real dislike of German soldiers who fought an honest fight and lost. On occasion they protected German prisoners from the anger of liberated populations and were often accused of treating the Germans "too well," especially in France. The prevailing attitude among G.I.s was probably well represented by John Roche, an infantryman in Italy who found himself with four German prisoners—men who only a few minutes before had manned a machine-gun nest and killed one of his comrades and wounded another: "I stood over them as they sat on the ground. For a while I simply stared at them. But their expressions were guileless and their faces not those of wanton or dedicated killers. I mused on what had actually happened; Aiken died at the head of the column they had been ordered to halt, and Oliver and I were shot at because we made the only aggressive moves thereafter. De Hojos was not fired upon, because it was plain he only went to Oliver's aid." In Roche's judgment, then, the Germans had fought a fair fight. He got them up and headed back with them toward the POW collection point.

The story did not end there. As the party of eight—four G.I.s and four prisoners—headed back, Roche, who spoke good German, struck up a conversation with one of the prisoners, a man he called "Stalingrad." Before long "Stalingrad" was carrying Roche's broken M1. The party stopped for a meal and ended by exchanging rations. "They were tickled to get our cans of meat instead of fish to eat," Roche recalled, "and we liked the fish paste for a change." As the men were sitting around eating, a body of American replacements resting nearby began to shout, "Why feed them? Shoot them! Don't take them back, kill them." Roche reassured his prisoners, " '*Furchtet nicht* (Don't worry),' I said, '*diese sind nur Rückenhelden* (they are only heroes of the backside).' Our prisoners laughed and kept on savoring my invented word, *Rückenhelden*, after that."

It was rare that fraternization developed to such a degree, but there are numerous examples of contacts under conditions of truce, especially regarding the wounded. A journalist named Ed

Ball, who was with Patton's troops in the summer of 1944, described a remarkable instance of this sort of humanitarian ceasefire:

On a Sunday after Patton got cracking AP artist Howell Dodd and I came upon a dramatic situation, as moving as any encountered before or after. A 90th Infantry Division unit had gotten itself mousetrapped the night before in a broad marsh with high hedgerow-like embankments on either side.

The action continued on Sunday while from the marsh below could be heard the moans of the wounded. In midafternoon three chaplains—Catholic, Salvation Army, Church of God—could bear it no longer. They hoisted a big white flag with a red cross in the center and clambered down into the marsh. Shooting died away on both sides. Medics went in and began returning the wounded. While this went on a German lieutenant emerged from his side and joined the chaplains. He told them he had several American wounded behind his line but had run out of morphine. The medics produced the needed syrettes. The German also told the Catholic chaplain he too was a Catholic but had lost his crucifix somewhere in the war. The chaplain removed his own and blessed it and handed it over.

The group saluted, shook hands, wished each other well and started their separate ways. Just then another German farther down the line appeared, pointing into the marsh. The medics found a soldier they'd missed.

As this marshy tableau dissolved it once more was no-man's-land, the unofficial armistice ended and the war was on again.

The censor gutted the story because it "put the Germans in a chivalrous light."

On a static front, such as the one that prevailed in Italy for a while, soldiers on opposing sides sometimes observed certain "living arrangements" that made life easier for everyone. Not only did the firing stop when ambulances appeared and medics brandished Red Cross flags, but by mutual consent no one fired while food was being brought forward. The historian of the 88th Infantry Division related a truce of a different nature:

Perhaps the most spectacular single instance of tacit rules of conduct was the Easter Service of the 349th Infantry Regiment (1944). For nearly an hour all firing ceased while the division chaplain conducted services in English and German. Loudspeakers carried Protestant services, Catholic Mass, and nondenominational female vocal accompaniment along the length of the front. Services concluded with notification that troops on both sides should return to cover, after which the firing resumed.

The same front saw an even more curious display. In what was billed as a "colossal" feat, a tiny American observation plane flew along the front while a passenger "strafed" the German lines with a .45 caliber automatic pistol. The Germans responded: A daredevil motorcyclist rode the length of their lines while artillery roared and both sides cheered.

The truces and tacit agreements were always tenuous, fragile affairs. Near Monte Cassino, the 350th Infantry Regiment and its German counterpart observed a cease-fire while food was being distributed, and the 350th tried to extend the agreement to cover the evacuation of the dead between the lines; but the Germans, perhaps misunderstanding American intentions, laid down a hail of mortar and machine-gun fire. And when, at Christmas 1944, men of the 350th in forward positions reported hearing the German troops singing "Silent Night," after some discussion "it was agreed to throw a few rounds of artillery around the spot to remind them that we weren't buying any propaganda to relax our readiness to receive German visitors."

No one lost sight of the soldier's basic goal, which was to best his enemy in combat, and some soldiers did it with an apparent relish. In the poll cited earlier, some 18 percent of G.I.s questioned claimed that the sight of German prisoners made them like killing Germans "all the more." It is also possible to find in G.I. letters a pride and sense of accomplishment in killing enemy soldiers, though it is not a common theme. A G.I. wrote his mother in October 1944 that he had just killed two Germans: "The first one I got was for Papa's brother, that was killed in Poland. The second was for a boy in our outfit who was killed. . . . The next ones are for me. Do I sound blood-thirsty? I'm not really." Something of the same tone can be found in the entry a German soldier in France made in his diary in July 1944: "I killed my first American today. Three at one time. One had his hands up. I shot him first.

I think he had a pistol in his hand. Then I shot the other two. They really are gangsters, these Americans."

As a rule, the Germans tended to be more formalistic and punctilious about the rules of warfare than the Americans. Ernie Pyle related to Arthur Miller a story he had heard about a pair of American medics who were carrying a wounded man along a road. One medic saw a grenade in a hole and picked it up and put it in his pocket for a souvenir. The men were captured by the Germans, who found the grenade. Since by international agreement medics were noncombat personnel and barred from carrying weapons, the Germans shot the offending man and sent back word with the surviving medic that the Americans had better play by the rules. By the same token, the Germans believed that a sniper who killed one of a party of advancing American troops could then drop from a tree with his hands up and receive the honors of war; but often the Americans would not see it that way, and they would shoot him. The same fate could befall the crew of a German artillery piece who fought too long. The historian of the 88th Division recorded that "American troops acting on their own initiative frequently elected not to accept the surrender of men who used their guns to the last second and then threw up their hands."

Snipers galled American soldiers so much that they were sometimes tempted to take out their feelings on any handy German. Orval Faubus recalled that two men in his outfit who were charged with taking back prisoners had been fired upon by a German sniper who had already killed one of their comrades: " 'We shoot the next prisoners,' they remark, the iron creeping into their blood." Hated almost as much as the sniper was the German S mine or Bouncing Betty. When tripped it bounded into the air, then exploded at chest height, scattering steel balls in all directions. Walter Bernstein and several buddies were escorting German prisoners in Sicily when they came upon a pile of empty S mine boxes. "The dirty bastards," said one man; another said he'd like to shoot the four prisoners, who were smoking nervously. "I think that's what we all felt," wrote Bernstein, "but nobody did anything about it; there would have been no satisfaction in doing anything to them once you had them. There was only the impotent hatred, the inability even to say, 'See where you are now.' "

The G.I. was also less inclined to accord the honors of war to troops of the German SS. In the fall of 1944 Faubus recorded: "We are fighting SS troops today, Hitler's Bad Boys. Co K had 10 PWs. They asked them about Hitler and if they were still for him. Four said 'yes' and 'Heil Hitler!' So only six ever got back to regimental PW point. I have not confirmed the story but it has been generally accepted." Accounts of German atrocities had definite though generally temporary effects on the G.I.'s view of the enemy. After the massacre of American prisoners at Malmédy in December 1944, Faubus found in the G.I.s "a hatred such as I have never seen." In another outfit the men refused to take any prisoners for ten days. The historian of the 3rd Armored Division wrote that after having seen the concentration camps at Nordhausen and Dora, "The tankers of the 3rd were in a savage mood as they went on to the final battles."

Toward the end of the war there were numerous cases of enemy "treachery," or what seemed to be so in the excitement of the moment, as German troops attempted to surrender. Combat "tips" passed along in one American unit included this advice: "If a Heinie begins to holler after his hands are raised in surrender give him the works as he is trying to warn others." This recommendation virtually condemned to death any German soldier who spoke as he came forward to surrender. Sometimes as Germans came forward with their hands up and Americans went out to escort them in, someone would fire a shot. Immediately, this would trigger a fusillade, and those caught in the open would sometimes be cut down before they could take cover. In an American infantry company that lost a popular sergeant this way, the men decided it was a "trick" of the enemy, and they resolved to take no more prisoners. But the knife cut both ways, as is clear from this unmailed letter found on a German paratrooper in August 1944:

I have just been informed that two of my pals have been killed in a most treacherous way. It was like this: Red Cross ambulances came towards our lines; soldiers with Red Cross brassards get out, take the brassards off and are being shot at and surrender, but when they advance they get shot by the Americans. That is what they call American humanity, that is what they call the country with the most freedom. . . . I pity the Americans who get within range of my rifle, the damn crooks.

Once a German decided to quit fighting and allow himself to become a prisoner—as increasing numbers did toward the end of the war—finding the right opportunity was a considerable challenge. While the German Army instructed its men in their rights and duties as prisoners of war, it did not give them information on how to surrender—nor did any army, for that matter. Perhaps for that reason American soldiers found themselves accepting surrender in some unusual situations. A pair of medics sleeping in an ambulance in Italy were awakened in the middle of the night by two German soldiers who opened the ambulance door and called in *"Kamerad."* In another case a German officer clambered up onto a Sherman tank, rapped on the turret, and called, "Gentlemen, gentlemen, please let me in." An even more unusual episode was related by an officer of the U.S. 88th Division. One morning he was heading to the command post when he was astounded to see a German soldier standing just outside the entrance. The German was in full battle dress, with rifle and potato masher grenades, and was smoking a cigarette. Shaking off his surprise, the officer tackled the German, whom he soon disarmed. The German told a strange story. He had decided to desert and had managed to get through both the German and American lines. He had held on to his weapons so that if he encountered a German patrol he would say he had gotten lost. Daylight found him outside the command post and unsure exactly how he should give himself up. In the meantime, Americans passing by had simply taken him for one of their sentries. A soldier coming out of the command post had even stopped and offered him the cigarette he was smoking before he was finally recognized.

The correct protocol for surrender was not a matter of much concern in the "other war," the one that pitted the G.I. against the Japanese soldier. There the dialogue of violence was carried on at a different level; in the Pacific it was war to the knife hilt.

The mood that prevailed among American troops there can be judged by a controversy that took place in the pages of *Yank* in 1944. The magazine had carried an article on the fighting on Makin, in which the author related the tactic of throwing grenades into caves in which Japanese might be hiding and of then shooting any who came out whether they were armed or not. One of *Yank's* readers wrote in to say he thought the practice was inhuman, since it gave the Japanese no chance to surrender. *Yank* printed the letter and was soon deluged with replies. Of the hundreds of letters *Yank* received, only one took the humanitarian's side; all of the others rejected his argument, often violently: "Have that guy locked up!" "No mercy for murderers!" "We are fighting back-stabbers!" "The motto in the Southwest Pacific is 'Kill the bastards.'"

This attitude was not one that the G.I. had picked up in the course of fighting the Japanese; polls revealed that soldiers in Europe and those still in stateside training camps were just as strong in their feeling against the Japanese, and sometimes even more so. The way the Japanese initiated the war may help explain this generalized animosity: Getting revenge for Pearl Harbor was a war aim that everyone endorsed. But the detestation in which the Japanese were held also had roots in a sense of cultural superiority, with certain racial overtones. When an Army corporal and amateur poet addressed the following lines to the Japanese, he was not just speaking for the G.I.s in the Pacific:

> Your code is the code of assassins
> Who stalk in the shadow of night.
> You learned a lot from the white man
> But—*you didn't learn how to be white.*

What most effectively stopped any argument for scrupulous observance of the rules of war in the Pacific was the universal belief that the Japanese themselves violated such rules constantly. The stories of prisoners of war being beheaded or bayoneted were legion—and they had some basis in fact. By the middle of the war some details of the Bataan Death March had come out, and likewise the news that the Japanese had executed some of the airmen who participated in the Doolittle raid on Tokyo in April 1942. In truth, the Japanese military took a dim view of surrender and of anyone who gave himself up. Interrogation of Japanese prisoners revealed that they had never been instructed about the Geneva Convention or their rights under it. To be sure, nowhere in any of the many theaters of operations of World War II could a soldier throw down his weapons, put up his hands, and walk toward the enemy with any assurance that he would spend the rest of the war in a well-appointed POW camp. But with the Japanese one had the least chance of all, and the G.I.s who fought against them never forgot that.

The idea that the Japanese used wounded Americans to bait ambushes gained official credence. The issue of *Yank* for November 5, 1943, cited a War Department intelligence bulletin when it explained in an article on jungle warfare: "Another favorite Japanese trick is to capture a wounded man and place him near a trail or perimeter and cover him with machine gun fire. They will torture him until he screams and yells for help, but it is absolute suicide to send in help for him."

In Europe, if a G.I. disappeared during a firefight or vanished while on a patrol, his buddies could hope that in a few weeks they would hear that he was a prisoner of war in Germany. When that sort of thing happened in the Pacific it was a calamity. An observer there wrote early in 1945: "Foremost in the minds of men going on patrol against the Japanese is the thought 'what is going to happen if I am hit.' Patrol leaders of all ranks should have it ingrained into them that they must never leave a wounded man behind. If each man who goes on patrol knows that the patrol leader will get him out someway, he becomes more confident; when a patrol leader, captain or corporal, returns from a patrol with a man missing, none of the other men want to go on patrol with that leader again. Men know that unlike the Germans, the Japs kill our wounded men."

If a man was wounded, his buddies would make superhuman efforts to get him back. In Norman Mailer's *The Naked and the Dead* two G.I.s stagger for miles over unbelievably difficult terrain, trying to evacuate their wounded comrade. After he dies, they struggle doggedly on with his corpse. And if a man were missing, his friends did what they could to find him again. When two soldiers of the Americal Division failed to return after a patrol clash, their friends combed the area where the incident had occurred and found the rifle one of the missing men had been carrying. After further searching they came upon two pairs of combat boots; subsequently they found on the body of a Japanese soldier a diary with the notation, dated the same day their friends had vanished, that two Americans had been captured. The next entry in the diary read, "Two PW taken yesterday were executed."

There were American outfits in the Pacific that almost as a matter of policy took no Japanese prisoners, and to justify their action they cited Japanese atrocities. The troops of the 112th Cavalry Regiment "did not believe in taking Japanese prisoners." If asked why not, they would answer that the Japanese had used men of the 112th for bayonet practice. It was common practice all over the Pacific to shoot any Japanese soldier one encountered, whether or not he was armed. Japanese soldiers caught bathing in streams were gunned down, and wounded enemy soldiers were routinely "finished off." The practice caused considerable unhappiness among American intelligence officers, who thus missed out on information that would have been gained by prisoner interrogation. When men of the 112th Cavalry killed an unarmed Japanese soldier, an officer noted on the report: "Another prisoner that could have told us if the 41st [Division] had arrived, what effect our bombing had had, possibly when the attack was expected, where were what units; these troops seem to want to fight the war the hard way, they won't take prisoners."

G.I.s did not always shoot potential prisoners from a sense of reprisal or retribution; many said they did it from the simple motive of self-preservation. When Myles Babcock approached a wounded Japanese Marine, the wounded man rolled over. Babcock instantly threw his rifle to his shoulder. "Fearing treachery, I killed him by placing a bullet in his stomach and another in his face," Babcock related. Japanese soldiers had, in fact, been told to sell their lives dearly and to take as many of the enemy with them as possible. Thus, there was some danger in approaching a Japanese soldier with the intention of making him a prisoner, and many G.I.s declined to run the risk.

To many G.I.s it was this treachery that made the Japanese soldier a dangerous opponent. In purely military qualities the G.I. did not rate him highly in I and E polls (though there was an important qualification here regarding jungle warfare, as we will see). Soldiers in the Pacific agreed with those in Europe that the German fighting man was the one to beat: Generally, the G.I. rated the Japanese soldiers below the British but above the Italians. The belief in Japanese treachery no doubt owed a great deal to Pearl Harbor, but once sprouted, it grew prodigiously in the field. If American artillery fired short, the story would run that the Japanese had tapped into American telephone lines and given the artillery coordinates that would drop the shells into American positions. If a Japanese was killed wearing a poncho or some other item of American clothing, it was always assumed that he was masquerading for some sinister purpose. The Australians, who had early experience with the Japanese in New Guinea, passed on "tips" about Japanese practices in which they warned that the enemy would also try on occasion to disguise himself as a native. It was said that the Japanese signaled each other by imitating the calls of wild birds.

It was also believed that Japanese were operating far behind the American lines. They were sometimes suicide volunteers, like the Japanese soldier who was supposed to have concealed himself inside a water bag and sprung out to kill two G.I.s before he was himself cut down. Then there were Japanese spies and agents, who were presumably active everywhere. G.I.s liked to attribute an almost demonic ability to Japanese intelligence, and they were sure that when Tokyo Rose and other Japanese radio propagandists mentioned the location or movements of American units, the information had been fed in by spies watching those units. Army Intelligence, which monitored the broadcasts, determined that the data had been taken from everyday sources such as American newspapers—but the G.I.s in the jungles preferred the spy version.

A fair number of Japanese who served in the Pacific had some knowledge of English, and it was widely believed that they would call to American soldiers whose names they had learned. There were verbal exchanges between the two sides, though probably fewer than was claimed by Pacific theater folklore. It may be true that the Japanese shouted, "American, you die!" the stock phrase attributed to them in Hollywood's version of the war. As for the Americans, they contented themselves with unsophisticated taunts such as "Tojo eats shit."

There was another element in the duel fought in the Pacific, and that was the belief—widely disseminated among American troops —that the Japanese were somehow peculiarly suited to the distinctive style of warfare that prevailed in the Pacific. Just why this should be so was a subject of speculation in the foxholes. The Australians believed the enemy had the gifts of patience and cunning supplemented by excellent training in jungle craft. Some felt they did not have the "white man's feelings" and so were less sensitive to heat and other forms of discomfort. But for whatever reason, their reputed advantages in jungle warfare created some severe morale problems for the Americans. A colonel reporting on combat in the Southwest Pacific reported: "Troops have been told so much about the trickery, deception, stamina and fighting ability of the enemy that in their minds the Japanese were little short of 'supermen.'" And Myles Babcock spoke for many when he wrote: "We cannot compete with the Japs in jungle conditions. Truly a white man's graveyard."

One manifestation of the supposed Japanese superiority was the inordinate time and preoccupation given to enemy snipers. Snipers there were, and a number of victims who fell to their fire, but the efforts expended against them seemed excessive to many observers of combat in the Pacific. Some units deployed special contingents of "squirrel hunters," others followed the practice of blasting any suspect tree, bringing down palm fronds, coconuts, and monkeys. An observer of the fighting in Guadalcanal concluded that "the Jap sniper tied in a tree is not an effective killer of anything but time and morale." But the men who stayed in the jungles could not take such a detached view. A veteran of the Pacific fighting recalled that his unit was dug in near a mass of trees and that a Japanese sniper would take position there and fire on the first man to come out of his foxhole after daylight. A sniper was not there every morning, and even when he was, he often missed his target; but the danger was sufficient that there was considerable apprehension for the first man who left his foxhole each morning. When a replacement arrived in the unit, the men did not tell him about the sniper. If a man had to be lost, better a stranger than a buddy.

Then, too, the night belonged to the Japanese. A combat analyst wrote that the men in the Pacific had to wage three separate wars at once: one against the Japanese, one against the jungle, and one against the night—"the night that in itself is bad, but when added to the jungle, produces fear that makes unaccustomed men forget all the military wisdom they have acquired." The Japanese would often infiltrate at night, so American troops would form a defensive perimeter composed of a chain of outposts. The men along the perimeter would be two, three, or four to a foxhole, taking turns staying awake. A veteran told Myles Babcock that a man by himself had no chance, for "if a soldier sleeps he never wakens." Babcock wrote from Bougainville: "When I was on guard at night I had a hand grenade in my left hand, a hunting knife in my right hand, and a rifle across my knees."

As they listened and stared into the darkness, the men along the perimeter could see the enemy in their mind's eye—silent, cunning, a relentless and single-minded predator. They never saw the Japanese as being in any sense akin to themselves in feelings and emotions. American intelligence officers who read the letters and diaries taken from the Japanese knew differently. In those letters and diaries the jungle appeared as a sinister and alien place; there were complaints about American snipers, and some writers claimed the Americans signaled each other by imitating bird calls. Army intelligence drew from the captured papers an analysis of the morale of the Japanese soldier. The three most common gripes have a familiar ring: the food, the privileges of officers, and the men who had soft jobs at home.

German and Japanese intelligence services made similar studies of the G.I. and his battle performance. From combat reports, prisoner interrogations, and other sources, they sketched out a fairly complete "portrait" of the American soldier. Interestingly enough, many of the same traits are attributed to the G.I. in both German and Japanese versions. Japanese evaluations obtained and translated by ATIS (Allied Translation and Interpreter Service) and those formulated by the German Army General Staff's Abteilung Fremde Heere West agree on two specific points: The American soldier was not adept at night fighting and he appeared to dislike hand-to-hand combat. There was also evidence in both theaters of the war that he was not strongly motivated. A Japanese report of 1943 noted: "With the enemy there is little idea of dying for one's country." The German verdict was similar: "The American soldier lacks feeling for the iron necessity of battle and a practical war aim in Europe."

In his advance the American was characteristically slow and methodical rather than impetuous. "The enemy absolutely will not charge," declared one Japanese study of American combat behavior. Another Japanese analysis of fighting on Guadalcanal noted: "So long as even one of our men remains in a position and resists, they do not break through. Even though they realize that the position is completely demolished, they concentrate their trench mortars, and then penetrate, yelling loudly. . . . They penetrate little by little, most cautiously but very steadily." German observers found that the American foot soldier's advance depended upon support from such weapons as tanks and artillery, and that when that support was not forthcoming, the American faltered. In truth, American observers sometimes noted the same tendency. An officer in the Southwest Pacific recorded: "In too many instances, either due to lack of training or poor leadership, or to a combination of both, our troops did not have the will to close with and kill the enemy. Troops seemed to think they should be able to stand off at a distance and kill the enemy, or have our aircraft, tanks, artillery, mortars, or machine guns do the killing for them, and were reluctant to believe that it was their duty to personally go forward and kill the Japs themselves."

Many conclusions the Germans and Japanese reached about the American soldier seem to have been rooted in nothing more substantial than wishful thinking or the observer's prejudices. Thus, German intelligence estimated that as much as 15 percent of American manpower was useless for war because it was composed of blacks and "poor whites." Japanese analysts felt that "because of the simplicity of the American people," surprise attacks would be very successful against them. Elaborating on this theme, another Japanese observer explained: "In line with their national characteristics, they will sometimes act unexpectedly, without considering the advantages and disadvantages at stake." Japanese tactics should be adjusted accordingly, with an emphasis on bold, spirited attacks: "Right up against the guns of the enemy, our hand-to-hand fighting ability still has decisive power, and the enemy greatly fears it."

Such was not the testimony of American observers. One of them wrote: "The Jap bayonet attack has been reported as a terrifying onslaught. All units on Guadalcanal loved them. The Jap practice of singing his Banzai song for about five minutes prior to his assault has simply been a signal for our troops to load a fresh belt of ammunition in the machine guns, new clips in rifles and B.A.R.s and to call for the Tommy gunners to get into position."

Both German and Japanese analysts recognized the American strength in matériel and logistics. The American soldier seemed to have inexhaustible supplies of ammunition, for example (there was some speculation among Japanese soldiers that their American counterparts were paid according to how much they fired their weapons). The Japanese believed that American "material power" could be effectively counteracted by Japanese "spiritual power." The Germans tended to attribute American victories over them to overwhelming material resources and manpower, which more than made up for the indifferent fighting qualities of the G.I. Hugh Cole recalled that many of the German generals he interviewed claimed that the American soldier was "spoiled" with chocolate rations and clean underwear; deprived of such things, he would suffer a decline in morale. The analysts of Fremde Heere West shared this view; they argued further that if the German Army could meet the U.S. Army on terms of rough equality, the German superiority would be telling. This line of thought persisted until the German Ardennes offensive of December 1944; thereafter, Hugh Cole noted, "You begin to get a different story."

What has come to be called the Battle of the Bulge gave the Germans a chance to test their notions of qualitative superiority. They had roughly equal numbers, the element of surprise, and overcast skies that robbed the Allies of air support. Charles MacDonald, who fought in the battle and then wrote perhaps the best history of it forty years later, described the American soldier caught up in the German offensive as "surprised, stunned, unbelieving, incredulous, not understanding what was hitting him." Yet generally he stood fast, fought tenaciously, and bought precious time for Allied commanders to take countermeasures. The analysts in Fremde Heere West acknowledged as much. In a report on the Ardennes fighting dated January 20, 1945, they called the American soldier a "first-rate, well trained, and often physically superior opponent." The bitter cold in which the American had fought, often without adequate clothing, had had "no decisive effect on his morale." American defense of villages in the Ardennes had been stubborn and effective: "Often units inside strongpoints had to be wiped out in hand-to-hand fighting." When they attacked, American troops showed themselves to be "tough fighters in close quarters," able to carry the fight despite the lack of air or armor support. If there was a single battle in which the G.I. Army demonstrated its purely human qualities, to friend and foe alike, it was the Battle of the Bulge. Charles MacDonald was right to argue that it was "a story to be told to the sound of trumpets."

·9·

Their Luck Ran Out

ANY MAN who put on an Army uniform after 1941 gave thought at some time to the possibility he might be wounded or killed. The inductee thought about it when he filled out the papers for his ten-thousand-dollar life insurance policy. The trainee thought about it when he received instruction in how to give himself first aid. And when a man entered the combat zone he had to face the possibility of death or injury in a more immediate way. Most men seem to have taken the optimistic view: Somehow nothing would happen to them and they would return no worse for the experience. But some, curiously, armed themselves with the conviction that they were doomed, hence they did not have to worry about survival. James Jones was apparently one of these. Each soldier must have a compact with fate or with himself that he is lost, Jones wrote. "Only then can he function as he ought to function under fire. He knows and accepts beforehand that he is dead, although he may still be walking around for a while."

Many men concerned themselves fully as much with how others would be affected if something happened to them. If a man were wounded, often his first thought was to send an airmail letter home, hoping it would arrive before the government's terse telegram. Some men avoided any reference to being in combat in their letters home, so that when the telegram arrived the shock was all the greater. Still others wrote after the danger was over. "I have been in some combat," wrote a private from the Pacific, "coming out without a scratch, or being in the hospital for any sickness at all, and I am now safe and well in Australia again." Sometimes when a soldier had been killed, his family would find a "last letter" that he had placed among his papers. Occasionally, the soldier carried his last letter with him. Such was the case with a twenty-one-year-old private who was struck by a sniper's bullet in the fighting for Hill 609 in Tunisia. His captain reported that "before he died he managed to get his last letter to his parents out of his pocket, and when we recovered his body the letter was grasped firmly in his hand."

A man was bound to speculate on the odds. Not until the war was over and the casualty statistics were all collected could those odds be known. Armywide they were surprisingly favorable. In 1946, total battle casualties were placed at 949,000, including 175,000 killed in action; with something over ten million men in the Army between 1941 and 1945, the odds that a soldier would appear on a casualty list were something less than one out of ten. The chances that he would be killed in battle were close to one in one hundred. It was known of course that some arms of the service were more prone to casualties than others, and that risks were greater in the arms than in the services. Once again postwar computations told the full story. Fatalities in the arms were ten times those of the services, and the nonfatal wound rate was twelve times higher, though two categories of ASF personnel had notably high casualty rates: combat engineers and medical aid men. Of the arms, infantry was the most hazardous, suffering 264 cases of wounds per thousand enlisted men per year. But armor was a close second with 228 cases, while field artillery trailed considerably with fifty wounded per thousand per year.

Even within each arm there were different specialties, and casualty rates that varied from one to the next. The British established that gunners had higher casualties than other members of tank crews, presumably because when they evacuated the tank the gunner got out last. These calculations were apparently not made on the American side, but the soldiers themselves had a good idea of which jobs were more dangerous. Taking "the point" on an infantry patrol was taking the position of greatest danger. Many felt radio men faced special hazards because their antennae revealed their positions. Handling the flamethrower was also risky. S. L. A. Marshall recorded a case in the Pacific where a man was so detested by everyone else in his outfit that they gave him the flamethrower to get rid of him.

The longer the war continued, the greater the chance a man would become a casualty; this was so because the United States Army did its heaviest fighting in the last fourteen months of the conflict. The Army Medical Department's *Medical Statistics in World War II*, a twelve-hundred-page compilation that appeared in 1975, has an arresting chart as its frontispiece. It shows admission rates "per 1000 average strength per year," that is to say, the rate per thousand at which men were treated during the years 1942 to 1945 for three categories of illness: disease, nonbattle injury, and "wounded in action." Both disease and nonbattle injury are essentially horizontal lines: Thus, nonbattle injuries ran at a rate of from fifty to one hundred per thousand for month after month. But the "wounded in action" line is anything but straight. From February to October 1942 it is not even on the chart since it was less than one admission per thousand. In November there is a jump to four per thousand, corresponding to commitments of troops to North Africa, New Guinea, and Guadalcanal. For the next year and a half the line is a gradually ascending series of peaks and valleys, at one point reaching just under twenty per thousand. Then, in June 1944, the line shoots up dramatically, hitting fifty per thousand and staying in the fifty-to-one-hundred-per-thousand range until May 1945.

From D-Day to VE Day, then, the G.I. Army paid the heaviest blood price. For the last six months of 1944 between twelve and eighteen thousand G.I.s were killed in battle each month, and forty to sixty thousand more were wounded. In the months of June, July, and August of 1944, infantry casualties alone totaled a hundred thousand. The Army had made casualty estimates for planning purposes, but in 1944 the plans went awry, producing a grave shortage of fighting men for the rest of the year. This was the era when thousands of former ASTP "quiz kids" went into the line in France, as did hastily created platoons of black G.I.s and levies of ASF "typewriter commandos."

Postwar casualty statistics are also useful in confirming that some types of military operations were far more hazardous than others. Two wartime medical officers, Gilbert Beebe and Michael DeBakey, offered some striking evidence in this regard in their postwar study *Battle Casualties*. According to their calculations, defensive fighting was the least costly, producing about 3.73 wounded in action (WIA) per thousand combatants per day. Crossing rivers, taking towns, and assaulting fortified lines cost between five and six WIA, while offensive breakthrough operations yielded 7.14. Most costly of all were beachhead operations, with a WIA rate of 11.04.

Battle Casualties recorded another characteristic of beachhead operations: Troops wounded in seaborne assaults received a higher proportion of wounds to the upper body. Soldiers who fought in the mechanized forces also had a characteristic injury—burns. For infantrymen, the head was the portion of the body most frequently hit, accounting for almost a third of all wounds. Beebe and DeBakey credited the M1 helmet with saving any number of lives. They also found that most men were not standing erect when hit, but were crouching, kneeling, or prone.

A very special type of casualty, and one that was little spoken of during the war, was that resulting from friendly fire, a phenomenon sometimes referred to as amicicide. Artillery rounds that landed among friendly troops were perhaps the most common mistake of this type, but attacks on American troops by American aircraft were sufficiently frequent for G.I.s in Europe to dub the U.S. Ninth Air Force "the American Luftwaffe." The most spectacular episode of this kind occurred during Operation Cobra, a massive air strike against German positions in the Saint-Lô area in July 1944. Bombing errors on July 24 and 25 resulted in over eight hundred American casualties; there were 131 dead, among them General McNair.

Ground amicicide was an all-too-common occurrence in the Pacific, especially when the Americans used perimeter defense against Japanese infiltration, and green or edgy G.I.s fired at anything they saw or heard in any direction, including the interior of their own perimeter. In some cases men were killed by their comrades in arms while they slept in their hammocks. After one such shoot-out on Bougainville, an investigation determined that 12 percent of the wounds suffered by American soldiers and 16 percent of the deaths had been caused by American weapons.

Investigators researching casualties found that wounded G.I.s could tell them disappointingly little about how they had been hit. Sometimes a man would say he did not even know he had been wounded "until I saw the blood." And occasionally a man might think he had been hit, then discover otherwise. One G.I. in a foxhole on New Guinea felt a soft blow on his buttocks, then a telltale trickling down his thighs. His panicky efforts to find and treat his wound attracted the attention of his buddies, then provoked them to gales of laughter: A Japanese bullet had passed harmlessly through his full canteen.

A wound of any consequence brought shock, of course, but with it there was sometimes a sense of relief as well. If the man had been in the line a long time, and if he saw no chance of being relieved, he might be glad to receive his "million-dollar wound." Myles Babcock wrote of his unit in the Pacific: "Most fellows pray they will at least be wounded mildly, thereby enjoying a hospital convalescence and perhaps shipment home." There were cases in which the wounded man's buddies would congratulate him, shouting "You lucky dog" as he was evacuated. From time to time an ex-G.I. would candidly admit that he had even sought a wound by holding up his arm as bullets whistled overhead. More disturbing was the S.I.W., or self-inflicted wound, usually a bullet fired through one's foot or lower leg. This became a serious problem in France in the early summer of 1944, but tended to appear wherever a major offensive was planned. A medical historian for the First Army noted: "With self-inflicted wounds the patient usually recovered rather quickly, but in each instance a thorough investigation was conducted. Approximately 300 such cases were investigated at the 4th Convalescent Hospital, but in only fifteen instances were charges brought. . . . The general attitude was that these men should be given a chance to return to combat and have the opportunity to vindicate themselves before further steps were taken."

For the man who was wounded in battle, the odds for survival were favorable. Armywide there were 3.4 cases of nonfatal wounds for each KIA or DOW. (The Army used the term KIA only for those who succumbed before admission to a treatment facility, usually the battalion aid station. Those who died subsequently were classified as DOW, died of wounds.) Curiously, the ratio between killed and wounded had not changed in a century, despite vast changes in weaponry. There were a number of variables that increased or lowered the chances of survival in each man's case. Where a soldier was struck was one of these; wounds to the abdomen were considered the most dangerous, for example. Then the "agent" that caused the wound made a difference. About one of four bullet wounds was fatal, a ratio that held for both the European and Pacific theaters. But the "lethality rate" for shell fragments was not the same in the two theaters: In Europe it was 25 percent; in the Pacific, 16 percent. This discrepancy reflected an inferiority in Japanese artillery, and particularly in their mortars. The Japanese hand grenade was a notoriously ineffective weapon, with only one wound out of twenty proving fatal. Stories were told of Japanese soldiers who attempted suicide by grenade and survived with nothing more serious than bruises.

The soldier himself was the first line of defense when wounded. The men were trained to give themselves first aid and carried the necessary dressings as part of their battle gear, but if a buddy was nearby they would rely on him; medics also reported that wounded men preferred them to treat even minor wounds, perhaps in the belief that the "professional" would do a better job. When left to their own resources, wounded men often showed great presence of mind. Orval Faubus once watched a badly injured G.I. caught in the middle of a mine field. One foot and part of the leg were blown completely off, and the other leg was badly shattered, the foot pointing crazily in the wrong direction. Two medics tried to reach the man, but had to wait until the engineers cleared a path to him. The wounded G.I. waited in the field for six and a half hours, remaining fully conscious all the time. He applied a tourniquet to the stump and succeeded in stopping the bleeding; he was able to bandage his other wounds after a fashion, and even managed to dig himself in. Faubus recorded that "he appeared quite happy when his rescuers reached him."

But the chief factor in determining whether a wounded man lived or died was the quality of treatment he received and the speed with which he obtained it. The Army's Medical Department, like its logistical service, was the envy of the other belligerents. According to James Jones, "No nation ever laid out such enormous sums and went to such great lengths to patch up, repair and take care of its wounded and its injured as the United States did in the Second World War." (Jones was a privileged observer since he spent most of 1943 in one Army medical facility or another.) But the most eloquent tribute to the Army's medical service is not in words but in figures: Of those wounded men who survived to reach a battalion aid station or other medical facility, only 3.5 percent subsequently died of their wounds. Nearly three soldiers in four were returned to duty, while 23.5 percent received disability separations. The rate for DOWs was half that of the previous war, and reflected better treatment of shock and infection by means of transfusions and penicillin. Though initially Army doctors had put their faith in plasma, by the end of the war large quantities of refrigerated whole blood were being routinely airlifted to the major theaters.

The medical aid man who accompanied the soldier into battle was the first link in the Army's medical support system. As a group the medics seem to have been almost universally held in high esteem. Very occasionally one can hear a story of a medic who hesitated to go to the aid of a wounded man lying exposed in a field of fire and was threatened with shooting by the wounded man's buddies. But for every such story there are a thousand more testifying to courage and dedication. Men in the 124th Cavalry Regiment, fighting in Burma, remembered a medic named Green who continued to treat a fallen soldier though badly wounded himself: "His patient told him that he should stop to give himself aid because blood was flowing down his trouser leg. Green finished his first-aid job before he would help himself. By that time he·had lost too much blood. Before his buddies could apply a tourniquet, he was dead."

From the battlefield the wounded soldier moved to the battalion aid station, manned by two physicians and three dozen enlisted men. From there the more serious cases were sent to the rear, to divisional clearing stations, evacuation hospitals, and on to more permanent facilities well behind the front or in the United States. The speed with which the men were treated and evacuated was critical. A surgical consultant for the Third Army felt many men on the battlefield died of exsanguination, simply bleeding to death before anyone could reach them; there was some talk of equipping soldiers with individual radios so they could summon help more easily. Surgeons believed the first, excisional surgery needed to be done within six hours of wounding, during what they called "the golden period," but one study showed that fewer than a fourth of the cases reached them within that period of time.

The most seriously injured were carried to the battalion aid station by litter bearer, while the "walking wounded" went under their own power; from there the most seriously wounded went on by ambulance, sustained by morphine and transfusions, and those classified as "sitters" rode in the back of trucks. Such were the prescribed procedures, but in practice they could be difficult or impossible to carry out. Terrain and the tactical situation could hamper evacuation; in the Pacific litter hauls tended to be long, while in the mountains of Italy they were slow and arduous. The Pacific theater had a slightly higher DOW rate, in part because the wounded could not be moved as easily through the medical echelon: Often they had to be held in beachhead surgical hospitals with limited facilities, and occasionally they were wounded a second time while waiting for evacuation.

In all the theaters of the war there was considerable experimentation in ways to evacuate the wounded more rapidly. Small observation planes were mobilized for the purpose (the helicopter, which would perform such work so well in later wars, was still in its infancy). The jeep was also converted for moving wounded. A British officer visiting the American Army in Italy was not enthusiastic about a "Double Decker Jeep Ambulance" he was shown: "A wounded man lying on the top tier of one of these vehicles travelling along narrow and dangerous mountain roads with a 2,000-foot drop beside him cannot but feel a sense of profound insecurity."

Inevitably, some men in the evacuation channels were making their final trip. When Ernie Pyle visited a field hospital in Italy, he was struck by the custom observed in the case of dying men: "When a man was almost gone, the surgeon would put a piece of gauze over his face. He could breathe through it but we couldn't see his face well." But when a man died in his own unit, there was no way to shield his buddies from his death, and the impact on them could be wrenching (NP rates were closely tied to casualty rates). Those who were with dying men in their last moments were strongly affected. A friend of Orval Faubus told him about trying to comfort a soldier who had been almost ripped in two by a burst of machine-gun fire: "He said, 'Lieutenant, can't you do anything for me?' There was nothing I could do. Then he began to say his prayers and died there beside me. Faubus, when you hear a man say his prayers like that and die, you can't forget it."

For the family a man left behind, the first news was often the telegram, followed shortly by a letter of sympathy from General Marshall. Word also came from someone in the man's outfit, usually the chaplain or a company officer, offering some details about the death and the disposition that had been made of the body. Orval Faubus often had this task. In August 1944 he wrote the widow of a sergeant: "He was leading his squad in the attack on the morning of our first assault on enemy lines. He was struck by small arms fire and killed. There was no suffering. His body was recovered and is now buried in an American cemetery on the northern coast of Normandy." To symbolize its sacrifice, the family would place a gold star in the window; in the normal course of events a package would arrive containing the dead soldier's personal effects. Later, family members would have to decide whether they wanted his body brought home at government expense or interred in one of the fourteen overseas military cemeteries (more than half the remains were brought back, though the recovery operation did not begin until 1947).

The recovery, identification, interment, and eventual repatriation of the remains of Army personnel were functions of the Graves Registration Service, which recovered some 280,000 bodies (from both battle and nonbattle deaths). Many of the recoveries were made after the war by "sweeps" over former battlefields and by querying local officials and inhabitants. The highest proportion of unfound remains involved airmen, but the proportion was also higher where there had been airborne operations or battles of withdrawal, as in the Ardennes, when the dead could not be evacuated. The search was diligent and thorough: The service even reopened caves in which Japanese defenders had been sealed up during the fighting, in the belief that they might also contain American remains. But some bodies they did not even try to recover; among them were those of the crews of "duplex-drive" Shermans lost off Omaha Beach (the tanks had been fitted with propellers and flotation collars to enable them to come ashore with the assault troops, but a good many swamped and went down in deep water).

In Europe the task of locating and identifying remains was easier because the two sides generally observed the conventions in handling each other's dead. American Graves Registration men thus followed Wehrmacht regulations and broke the German identification disc in two, burying half with the corpse. The Germans were just as scrupulous. "General Patton advised me," one Graves Registration officer wrote another, "that the enemy does one thing exceptionally well—and that is giving proper and adequate burial to his own dead, and that he extends the same courtesy to our dead, and to the dead of our allies." Such was not the case in the Pacific War. The Japanese disposed of corpses by cremation when they could; the Americans buried their fallen enemies with bulldozers.

Identification of American dead sometimes presented problems.

According to a grim piece of G.I. folklore, one of a dead man's dog tags was always driven firmly between his teeth—that's why the notch was there. (Actually, it was there to help align the tag in the stamping machine.) In fact, correct procedure was to leave one tag around the man's neck and attach the other to the temporary grave marker. But all too often the tags were missing, as an observer's report indicates: "Men lose their identification tags, leave them in bath houses or when washing in the field, and do not report the loss. Laundry marks were formerly of value but the bathing system in use in most units where men exchange dirty clothing for clean makes that unreliable. Some units require the men to carry a piece of paper in their pockets with their name, rank and serial number on it, but again these papers get lost. In the final analysis, personal identification is the surest way to identify the man."

Identification sometimes required all the techniques of police science, including the use of fingerprints and dental charts. In one case, a body recovered in France bore only one clue to its identity, a class ring with the inscription "S.V.H.S., Spring Valley 1944 D.T." It proved to be a high school ring that Dorothy Thomas of Spring Valley, Michigan, had given to Don Peters, a soldier in the 90th Division. By one means or another, the Graves Registration Service achieved an identification rate of 96.5 percent. Ten years after the war the number of unidentified remains stood at just under nine thousand. Oddly, the figures change slightly almost every year as bodies turn up or identifications are made. As recently as October 1984, an American airman whose remains had been discovered in Sicily was reinterred—with full military honors—in the Ardennes Military Cemetery.

Sometimes the War Department telegram announced a third type of casualty—"Missing in Action." In many cases these were fatalities whose bodies had yet to be recovered, but there was another possibility, and that was the one families clung to: These soldiers had been taken prisoner and would eventually be heard from. A form letter that the War Department sent to the families of missing men encouraged them in this regard: "Experience has shown that many persons reported missing in action are subsequently reported as prisoners of war, but as this information is furnished by countries with which we are at war, the War Department is helpless to expedite such reports."

As for the men in the combat zone, while they could envisage injury or even death, they rarely gave thought to the idea that they might be captured. Nor did they get much warning before it happened, save in cases of negotiated collective surrender, such as on Bataan and Corregidor in 1942. So when it came it was an emotional body blow. "Being taken prisoner is a terrific nervous shock," recalled a man captured by the Germans, "in the first place because it involves extreme personal danger during the minutes before the enemy decides to take you instead of keep shooting at you, and in the second place because you suddenly realize that by passing from the right side of the front to the wrong, you have become a nonentity in the huge business of war."

The first moments as prisoner were the most perilous. The captors were usually in a state of excitement as well, and things could happen. After one group of American soldiers surrendered in Belgium during the Battle of the Bulge, a German soldier inexplicably threw his rifle to his shoulder and shot one of the Americans point blank; this provoked general firing by the Germans and a massacre of the prisoners. The captors could also be provoked by something they found while searching their prisoners. (Some G.I.s never carried war souvenirs since doing so suggested that they had looted the enemy dead.) On Bataan some American soldiers who were found to have Japanese coins in their pockets were killed on the spot.

The road to the prisoner of war camp could also be hazardous in the extreme. On the Bataan Death March many hundreds died or were killed, though the exact number will never be known. Traveling though German-held Europe could also be hazardous late in the war, since Allied aircraft roamed the skies at will and attacked trains and troop convoys wherever they found them. But sooner or later the prisoner was evacuated and "processed." He was interviewed and his name recorded (interrogations of enlisted men in the ground forces tended to be perfunctory), and German authorities even issued him a new identification tag. He was assigned to a camp whose routine he learned as he adjusted to a new way of life.

In the meantime, he could only hope that his captors had relayed his name to the International Red Cross, so that his family and friends would know he had survived.

In this fashion some 120,000 Army personnel became prisoners of war. Approximately ninety-five thousand were taken prisoner in the European theater and about twenty-five thousand in the Pacific. In several ways they were two distinct groups. The prisoners of the Japanese were a bit older (an average age of 26.7 years as against 25 for POWs in Europe); and the men taken prisoner in the Pacific were 70 percent Regular Army men, while the vast majority of those captured in Europe were draftees. The great majority of POWs in the Pacific were taken in 1941 and 1942 (most prisoners subsequently taken by the Japanese were airmen), while most of the G.I.s who fell into German hands did so in 1944 and 1945. As a consequence, prisoners of the Japanese averaged thirty-eight months of confinement, those of the Germans ten months. Finally —and this is the most telling distinction—about 1 percent of the G.I.s in German hands died in captivity, a figure in the "normal" range; for the prisoners of the Japanese the figure was 35 percent.

Nominally the existence of an American POW was regulated by the 1929 Geneva Convention on Prisoners of War. Germany had ratified the Convention and formally announced that she would apply its provisions to prisoners taken from the Western Allies (though not to the Russians, who never recovered more than a minority of some five million prisoners taken by the Wehrmacht). While the Japanese government had not ratified the Geneva accord, in February 1942 it sent word through the Swiss government that it would apply its provisions whenever they were not in conflict with existing laws and regulations. The Convention laid down rules for the health, welfare, and right of communication of those held prisoner; it limited the ways in which they could be disciplined and punished, and it stipulated that while they could be required to work, their labor should be of a nonmilitary nature and they should be paid for it.

In practice both the Germans and the Japanese violated various provisions of the Convention, though the record of the Germans was distinctly better. Hitler issued orders that all prisoners taken in commando raids were to be shot out of hand, and the Nuremberg trials turned up evidence of many executions of Allied prisoners (Field Marshal Keitel's involvement in such episodes helped send him to the scaffold). In the German system each branch of the service was responsible for POW camps for that branch, thus Luftwaffe personnel had control of prisoners belonging to the Army Air Forces. This probably helped shield prisoners from the harsh proposals sometimes made in Nazi party circles; when some of those around Hitler wanted to renounce the Geneva Convention in the case of Allied airmen and put them on trial for the murder of German civilians, the Luftwaffe successfully opposed the plan.

Though the Japanese record was far worse, the most appalling violations do not seem to have sprung from any high policy decisions. The Japanese Army's *Regulations for Handling Prisoners of War* stipulated that they were to be treated "with a spirit of good will and . . . never be subjected to cruelties or humiliation." A guide for *Procedure in Interrogating and Handling Prisoners of War*, issued late in 1944, prohibited "senseless countermeasures against POWs such as useless murder caused merely by anger toward the enemy, or cruelty caused by a man seized by emotion." But the Japanese authorities did not seem to give much thought to what to do with prisoners of war until after they had acquired a considerable number of them. The administrative structure they set up was a ramshackle affair with a low priority. It also had a low priority in personnel, for those who staffed it seem to have been inefficient or downright inept. A year after Pearl Harbor the Japanese had not supplied a list of prisoners taken in the Philippines; and prisoners in one camp were never reported, so that they were carried as missing in action during the entire war.

The shortcomings of the Japanese administration had their most tragic effects at the level of the camps. Prisoners in some camps never received the life-sustaining Red Cross food packages; at others they were distributed in erratic or arbitrary fashion. At Camp Cabanatuan, in the Philippines, some twenty-five thousand letters from home—equally life-sustaining in their way—lay undistributed because the single camp censor would process only a hundred a day. Japanese camp personnel were often of low quality.

"All our guards were misfits," one prisoner recalled, "deformed, alcoholic, insane. Depravities of all types stood guard around us, hating us and hating the world because of themselves." Sometimes guard duty was turned over to Koreans or Formosans; they were mistreated by the Japanese, and they mistreated the Americans in turn.

While all American prisoners, even officers, were under the humiliating obligation to salute and bow to all Japanese military personnel, they were also subjected to the discipline of the Japanese Army; this subjection, sanctioned by the Geneva Convention, was to have evil consequences for many prisoners. Within the Japanese Army the custom of "personal punishment" still survived. According to it any Japanese officer or noncom could slap, punch, or beat into insensibility any man under his authority whenever he felt it was a good idea. The policy was naturally extended to prisoners, so that one of them might be clubbed to the ground with a rifle butt for failing to execute an order given in Japanese, a language that he did not understand. (Some Japanese guards learned to give commands in an approximate English; their word for "hurry up" was "speedo.") In a postwar survey, 90 percent of former POWs from the Pacific said they had been beaten. And should the beating of an ill and undernourished prisoner result in his death, the perpetrator was not held responsible—at least not until the war crimes trials began some time after the conflict ended.

The Japanese had other habits that their prisoners would remember. When Red Cross recreational equipment arrived in one camp, the guards appropriated the baseball bats for use on prisoners. In another camp near Tokyo, the prisoners were made to shout "banzai" three times, raising their arms in salute in the direction of the Imperial Palace; in still another camp they were forbidden to smile or sing for three days following the death of Admiral Yamamoto. And they remembered the practice Japanese camp authorities used to discourage malingering: the already insufficient ration was cut for those too ill to work. Some who survived imprisonment said that despite their ordeal they had seen a good side to their captors, and evidence of sympathy and humanity. But others brought back with them a hatred that only death would extinguish. When a group of ex-prisoners published an account of their prison life shortly after the war, they refused to capitalize the word "Jap." Their explanation: "We feel that japs and formosans are sub-human and therefore should be common—and contemptible—nouns."

The conditions of life varied greatly from one camp to the next. The Germans had separate facilities for officers (*Oflag*) and enlisted men (*Stalag*); as a rule American airmen in Germany lived in better conditions than prisoners from the Army Ground Forces. Of the Japanese camps, Camp O'Donnell was a charnel house—a sixth of its inhabitants died in the few weeks it operated. On the other hand, men who were confined to the Bicycle Camp in Java lived relatively well. Food was the most critical element in a prisoner's life, and rarely did he have enough of it. The prisoner's diet in Germany was largely composed of a coarse bread called *Kriegsbrot*, potatoes, occasional sausage, and random vegetables. Fortunately, most prisoners in German camps received fairly regular dietary supplements in the form of Red Cross packages. Even so, a postwar survey indicated that on the average the "Kriegie" (for *Kriegsgefangener*, prisoner of war) had lost thirty-eight pounds during his captivity.

The same survey indicated that the prisoner in Japanese hands lost sixty-one pounds. The basic ration was rice, and in an amount less than that the Japanese soldier received. The diet was 80 percent starch and almost devoid of vitamins or minerals, so that even when the prisoner received enough calories, he suffered from malnutrition. While the prisoners who returned from Germany were restored to their former health fairly quickly, those who came from Japanese prison camps often suffered permanent impairment, such as optic atrophy (half of the surviving ex-POWs from the Pacific receive V.A. disability). This might have been averted had prisoners in the Pacific received food packages on a regular basis, but the Japanese government steadfastly refused to allow ships to bring them. Only when the liner *Gripsholm* entered Japanese-controlled waters for an exchange of diplomatic personnel in 1942 and again in 1943 was it possible to get packages through. At the very end of the war some relief also reached Japan through the Soviet Union.

Here and there, prisoners of the Japanese fared better in nourishing themselves. Prisoners in the Philippines were often able to buy extra food—if they had any money. American prisoners held in Manchuria nourished themselves with a food source that was still largely unknown outside that corner of the world—soybeans.

Poor diet contributed to health problems, and most camps were poorly equipped to deal with these. Almost none of the German installations met the medical standards of the Geneva Convention, and in many Japanese camps health facilities were nonexistent. In camps in both Europe and the Pacific there were instances of heroic surgery with a sharpened spoon handle as a scalpel. Diphtheria was one of the most common illnesses among Stalag inmates, while dysentery was a problem for prisoners everywhere. Prisoners of the Japanese often suffered the agonies of "dry" beri-beri, in which their feet became so painful they slept holding them in the air or in buckets of water.

Prisoners in German camps had their morale lifted by letters and packages from home, the flow being fairly regular. The Germans permitted each prisoner to receive an eleven-pound box every two months, and in addition families of prisoners could arrange for American cigarette companies to ship them a monthly supply directly. Families sending items to prisoners in Germany were counseled not to send books by Jewish authors or objects that carried slogans referring to victory. Unfortunately, there was no such line of communications with prisoners of the Japanese. When the prison authorities let the men write home, they sometimes insisted that it be a laconic Japanese Army postcard, with a few blanks to be filled in. The card carried no dateline, and the men were prohibited from adding one.

The prisoners worked at a variety of tasks assigned them by their captors, and some of these were clearly "military," in contravention of the Geneva rules; thus, in the Philippines they built airfields and fortifications. "Kriegie" Kurt Vonnegut worked at clearing away the rubble after the bombing of Dresden, an activity he described in his semiautobiographical *Slaughterhouse Five*. Other American prisoners labored to construct the Burma–Thailand

Railway, the line depicted in the film *The Bridge on the River Kwai*. For their labor they received ten cents a day (part of the prisoner's wage was invested for him in Japanese postal savings). Some American prisoners in the Philippines were employed briefly as extras in the Japanese war film *Down with the Stars and Stripes*. While POWs in one location were worked many hours each day, others found that time hung heavily on their hands. Most camps maintained libraries of sorts, and where the men had the energy and the facilities they organized courses of instruction, skits, and musical programs. And they talked about escape, though far more plans were made than were carried out (a man who contemplated escape from a Japanese camp could be almost certain that nine or ten of his fellow prisoners would be executed as a consequence).

But everywhere the chief preoccupation was simply survival; after the war a number of studies were made to determine just what factors led some men to make it through, while others succumbed. A study of former prisoners at Cabanatuan found the key factor was "a very strong motivation to return home, sometimes for very contrasting reasons." A recent V.A. study found the survivor to be "possessed of high morale even under the most trying circumstances, as having a never failing hope of rescue, able to repress hostility, physically adaptable to a strange environment, and willing to eat anything."

Survival meant, among other things, not provoking those who held the prisoners' lives in their hands. While in some German camps there was a subtle form of "goon baiting," such as making the prisoner counts come out wrong, the endless lighthearted capers and pranks occurred only in the later American television version of Stalag life. Prisoners of the Japanese gave their guards grim, hilarious names such as Webfoot, the Beast of the East, and Little Speedo—but took care the guards never learned of their nicknames. The camps were no place for noisy heroics, particularly the Japanese camps. Still, one could find courage there. One day when the Japanese learned that a corporal had escaped from camp they dragged out ten men who happened to have bunked near him and lined them up for execution. All the prisoners were assembled to watch. One of the condemned men refused the blindfold, and men remembered him for it: Private First Class Percival H. Holleyman of Laramie, Wyoming.

Late 1943 was a grim time for prisoners in the Philippines. The end of the war was nowhere in sight; Christmas was approaching, but for them it would be no holiday. A detail from the camp at Davao was forced to work in a rice paddy far into the night. A prisoner in the detail remembered that it was nearly midnight when the men were ordered out of the paddies and assembled in four columns for the long march back to camp:

> Very softly, before we had gone a mile, someone began to hum, then sing. Gradually it was taken up by the rest of us. The Japanese sentries ran in among us, beating us on the backs, kicking us in the shins, and screaming. But we would not stop. The jungle rang with our singing all the long black miles back to camp. And the song we sang was "God Bless America."
>
> Only when the prison gates were thrown back and we entered the compound did the voices stop. But when we went to our little huts and lay down for the night, each man felt stronger. I was proud of the unbeaten spirit of those who were with me. Nothing the Japanese could do would shake our faith in ourselves and our land.

Within a few months hope replaced despair. On clandestine radios the prisoners followed the progress of the Allied armies. Americans held in the Philippines knew what it meant when they were hastily evacuated toward Japan, jammed into the holds of merchant ships with insufficient air, food, or water. (Some of these ships were hit by American aircraft and submarines, and went down; the scenes aboard them came as close to hell as anything man could devise.) The men in the Stalags knew what it meant when their captors forced them to leave their camps and take to the roads. And everywhere prisoners knew what it meant when they spotted more and more American aircraft overhead: Their liberators were coming.

★ 10 ★

The Liberators

IN THE THIRD WEEK of August 1944, as Allied armies were pushing across northern France, two French teenagers decided they would go "see the Americans." Félix Mazure, age seventeen, and his fifteen-year-old brother, Hubert, got on their bicycles and set out along country roads, inquiring about the Americans at every village. Then they came upon an American armored car sitting along the side of the road. In schoolboy English they offered their assistance to the G.I.s who were clustered around the vehicle. The men were part of a reconnaissance unit with Patton's Third Army, and they had lost their way. By a coincidence, the village they were trying to reach was the very one in which the Mazure brothers lived. Félix and his brother offered their services as guides and the Americans accepted on the spot; the boys clambered up onto the armored car, to ride home in martial triumph. The story did not end there. After the stir and excitement had died down in the liberated village, the Americans asked if the boys could continue with them as guides and interpreters. Their father told them they could go, provided they were back by midnight. They rode off with the Americans again and did not return for three months.

That summer a great many people were waiting anxiously to "see the Americans," whose arrival would signal the end of German domination. They waited in Belgium and the Netherlands—where it was often the British Tommy they would see—and also in Italy, where the Germans had been overbearing allies at one moment and an occupying enemy the next. For every town or village over which the moving front passed, the transition from the Germans to the Americans was also a transition from conflict to peace; as each community was liberated, for it the war was over. Small wonder, then, that the moment of transition—the "liberation"—was often a stirring, emotional time. Sometimes it was also a surprisingly peaceable affair. The Germans would roll off to the north or the east, then later the first Americans would appear, probing cautiously along the outskirts of the town until they sensed the enemy had gone. At other times the Germans were waiting, with charges set to blow the bridges and tanks concealed in the side streets—then the liberation was violent and costly.

If there were partisans or resistance fighters in the vicinity, they made contact with advancing Allied forces, offering aid and information about enemy strength up ahead. To the G.I.s they often seemed more comical than heroic, carrying weapons from half a dozen armies and dressed in tatterdemalion fashion with an armband their only item of uniform. Quite often, too, advancing American troops ran into "delegations," local officials, sometimes wearing their Sunday best and sashes of office, accompanied by a schoolteacher or whoever else from the town knew some English. In the French town of Mayenne, local representatives waited anxiously to tell the Americans that the Germans had wired their bridge for demolition when the first American troops appeared there on August 5, 1944. An anonymous G.I. dashed across the bridge, severed the detonating wires, and saved the structure before German fire killed him. Later, the municipal authorities tried to find out his name; they wanted to name a street for him.

The arrival of American troops in the French town of Lagny-sur-Marne has been described in detail by one of its inhabitants, Georges Leduc. The first sign of the American approach was an artillery duel that brought a number of shells into the town late in the morning of August 27, 1944. At noon townspeople spotted the first Americans in an armored car that came to the outskirts. At 12:30 came the first contacts between leaders of the local resistance movement and a handful of G.I.s; a student from a nearby boarding school served as interpreter. Shells were still falling in the area. The Frenchmen tried to get the G.I.s to go further into town and attack a party of German soldiers who were preparing to blow up a bridge; the Americans refused and withdrew to await reinforcements, while the Germans finished their work and blew the bridge in question. But soon the Americans were back in greater number, an entire company. Two contingents of G.I.s were detailed to guard the remaining bridge, with resistance fighters assigned to each "to avoid the possibility of errors." Other G.I.s worked their way through the town. Though there was some firing, many of the inhabitants stood at doors or windows to watch the deliverance of their town. As Monsieur Leduc put it, "We wanted to see them in action, these 'ricains! We'd been waiting for them for such a long time." Apparently it was a fairly common occurrence for G.I.s to fight their way through a town under the eyes of an appreciative audience. A corporal who campaigned in France that summer wrote home: "Even when we meet 'slight resistance,' as it's called, and bullets are flying overhead, the people refuse to leave the streets and take shelter. They want to see Americans in action, and they cheer and clap continuously."

Soon the last Germans pulled out of Lagny-sur-Marne and the town was secured. Then, said Monsieur Leduc, the celebration began:

For four years Lagny had been awaiting this moment. A strange sound arose throughout the town. We were free again! In the streets and in all the houses there were cries of joy and excited shouts. People broke out bottles they'd carefully hoarded for the day of victory, and they offered drinks all around. Church bells began to ring frantically, filling the town with their joyous music. We poured into the streets, into the squares. We laughed, we sang, we acclaimed the F.F.I. [French Forces of the Interior], General de Gaulle, the Allies, the Americans. Clusters of men, women and children submerged the jeeps and the GMC trucks. Hugged and kissed and tugged at, the Americans took it all as best they could. . . . We offered them tomatoes and wine, and they passed to us chewing gum and all sorts of little packages of chocolate and candy and Camel cigarettes—how good they were! They were tired, those poor devils, covered in the dust and sweat and week-old beards, but happiness shone in their eyes.

Those were heady and exhilarating times for the liberators. Orval Faubus was profoundly moved. He wrote in his diary: "If ever I have seen a sincerely happy and grateful people, it is these liberated French." And for a black G.I. the reception he got from the French was a revelation: "They hugged and embraced us. It was the feeling of acceptance. I seriously considered not returning to the United States." In their zeal to show their appreciation, the French would sometimes display homemade American flags in which the number of stars varied and the stripes ran vertically. They even decorated the Army's filled-in latrines with flowers, no doubt thinking them graves. The differences in language sometimes produced hilarious results—as when a G.I. stopped the first Frenchman he encountered in a newly liberated town and read painstakingly from his Army-supplied phrase book, "*Où est la toilette?*" The Frenchman, mustering his best English, said with a sweep of the hand, "Monsieur, all of France is at your disposal." And a G.I. from New Canaan, Connecticut, recalled: "We'd yell 'Vive la France.' Then we got so tired of that we'd yell anything we could think of. I remember yelling 'Vote for Dewey,' and they'd cheer and yell back at us."

In Italy the reception was much the same. Most G.I.s seem to have found the Italians appealing after their previous contacts with the French and Moslems of North Africa; as for the Italians, who were in the direst of straits, the arrival of the Americans somehow represented the coming of better days. Then, too, there was an "Italian connection." In every outfit in the Army there was a sprinkling—and often a strong seasoning—of soldiers with Italian names and backgrounds, some of whom had kept fluency in the language of the old country. Many Italians had relatives somewhere in the United States; the mayor of one Italian town told every American soldier he met, "I was a big bootlegger in Rochester, New York."

From south to north, then, Italians tended to give the American soldier a warm welcome. Ernie Pyle noted in Sicily that the inhabitants of villages American troops passed through pressed on them as gifts small embroidered pillows from their parlors for the soldiers to sit on when they rested: "It was funny to march with a sweating infantry company and see grimy doughboys with pink and white lacy cushions tucked under their harness among grenades, shovels and canteens." A Neapolitan named Maria Luisa d'Aquino remembered that when American troops marched into Naples in October 1943, her two oldest children ran off to "see the Americans": "I found them in the middle of a circle of people who were pressing around two Americans, two tall, blond youths who were smiling as only victors can smile. But it was a youthful, healthy smile, that banished all rancor. A refugee went up and hugged and kissed one of them. It was the gesture of a man who had been freed."

When he found himself welcome in French or Belgian or Italian towns, and when he had a few hours, or even a few minutes he could call his own, the G.I. became a tourist of sorts. He already had some notions about the country he was visiting, and there were certain things he wanted to see or to do. Thus, when Louis Rossetti, newly arrived in France, visited the town of Soissons, he had two immediate goals: "The first place to go was to a café to get a taste of that French cognac we had heard so much about. Then to a *boulangerie* for a loaf of delicious French bread. One baker wanted a ration coupon which of course I did not have. But one other *boulanger* was good enough to give me part of a loaf."

In fact, it was illegal for Rossetti to buy bread in Soissons, and throughout much of liberated Europe there were restrictions or outright prohibitions on food purchases. In Brussels, for example, any G.I. who bought an ice-cream cone from a street vendor would be fined ten dollars if caught. The prohibitions were imposed for a very good reason. There was so little by way of foodstuffs—or anything else for that matter—in the shattered economies of the liberated areas, that G.I. purchases could have disastrous consequences. As it was, the Allied governments knew they would have to funnel considerable aid to the destitute populations.

In truth, the G.I. was doomed to see Europe at her worst. There was, of course, the physical destruction wrought by the war and a general dilapidated look caused by years of neglect of all but the most essential services. Tourist sites such as Versailles or the Guildhall in Brussels exuded an air of neglect and decay. There were streets and roads without any cars on them, and shops with near-empty windows. The populations lived with rationing and malnutrition. In Paris, where the food ration totaled 1,219 calories a day in December 1944, the French Ministry of Public Health estimated that between 60 and 70 percent of the French population was seriously underweight. It noted an increase in such diseases as rickets and tuberculosis and speculated on the effect long-term deprivation of milk would have on a generation of children. Then there were several million displaced persons scattered around Europe who had neither hearth nor home. In the bitter winter of 1944 the population of Western Europe was severely tried by lack of adequate heat and clothing.

There was room for real concern over what effect the G.I. and his free-spending ways might have on a bleak, post-liberation Europe, so the Army undertook a number of measures to reduce the impact of his purchasing power. In order to avoid currency speculation, the Army usually paid its men in the currency of the country they were in, rather than dollars. The soldier's purchasing power was further reduced by paying him at a rate that overvalued the foreign currency; thus, in France he was given fifty French francs for every dollar the government owed him, though on the open market a dollar was worth nearly two hundred francs. As a rule, the soldiers tended to run through their foreign currency quickly. When the soldier ran out of francs he soon discovered he could get more by selling his cigarette or candy ration, or he could simply switch to barter.

As a general rule, American troops were not very scrupulous in observing the various limitations and prohibitions. Many G.I.s considered them an unwarranted interference with what they did in their leisure rather than "on Army time," and such infringements were always resented. Nor could the average G.I. believe that his purchase of an ice-cream cone would disturb the local economy. His point of view was considerably different from that of the British soldier, as an observer for the British Foreign Office noted: "The ordinary British soldier observes meticulously the orders given to him not to buy up needed supplies and lives on his rations, whereas the Americans, who in any event have more money, do not observe this and make considerable purchases. This contributes to an impression that the Americans are the people of the future who are going to take care of France while the British are a poor country doing their best."

No G.I. who passed through Europe in 1944 or 1945 could have failed to notice the plight of its inhabitants, and there is a wealth of information to indicate that he was anything but indifferent to the things he saw around him. Almost every bivouac of the Army in Europe would draw some local inhabitants anxious to have the leftover food. Eventually, a sort of ritual became established. A crowd of locals, mostly women and children, assembled silently at mealtime. They placed before them rows of pots and tin cans, and then they waited patiently and silently until soldiers scraped into those containers any food left in mess tins. It was a scene that struck the soldiers, for they often described it in their letters. A soldier in the Netherlands recalled that G.I.s would sometimes go through the chow line a second or even a third time for the benefit of the Dutch families with whom they were billeted.

In northern France in the winter of 1944/45, thefts from Army coal depots were attributed indirectly to Army guards, who simply turned their backs and refused to see the locals filling their pails with the precious fuel. By the same token, Army authorities in Austria found that thefts from food warehouses in Salzburg were reduced when G.I. guards were removed and replaced by "off limits" signs. Though the food was intended for eventual distribution to the Austrians, the G.I.s had been passing it out on their own initiative. When a soldier had occasion to visit a European household, he could see firsthand the consequences of years of war and privation. Louis Rossetti particularly remembered visiting the home of a Frenchwoman near Laon who had contracted to do his laundry: "The kitchen was the only room she could use, because it was the only one with heat. Beside the stove her sick child lay under worn blankets. Before returning next day for our laundry, Chuck and I gathered up everything we could in the line of soap, canned foods, and candy and brought them to her as payment for her labor. She was amazed at all we offered, exclaiming her delight by gestures of her hands."

The Army made considerable and generally successful efforts to ensure that its presence in a liberated area would have beneficial effects; to that end a special corps of civil affairs officers had been trained to assist in getting local government and essential services back into operation, and in supplying the most pressing needs of the population. Army engineers were called in to help get the local water works back into operation, and the Medical Corps might supply assistance to a municipal hospital. The Army also gave employment to considerable numbers of locals. Within the Communications Zone in France alone, about a quarter-million people found jobs at one time or another as "static" and "mobile" workers with the Army Service Forces. Untold thousands of others contracted individually with G.I.s to provide certain services, especially cooking and laundering, in exchange for money, and more often for goods—above all, food. Ernie Pyle noticed that in the Anzio area, "practically every inhabited farm house had gigantic brown washing hanging in the back yard." Almost as common were the cooking arrangements, *cucine volanti*, or flying kitchens, as they were called in Italy. The G.I. brought the food, the woman of the house prepared it, and often the children served it.

While many Europeans thus worked for the Army in some capacity or other, there were a number who joined it in a certain fashion. Among these were the Italians who staffed the mess halls and took over KP work in North Africa, and their compatriots who worked in large numbers for Delta Base Section in Marseilles (they were so numerous there that they had their own mess). Displaced persons also attached themselves to various Army units. Louis Rossetti recalled: "On our return from an ammo run we found a stranger serving us chow. He was a Yugoslav D.P. who volunteered to help the cooks in payment for his meals. We named him Joe and for the next six weeks he remained with us." There were Polish DPs serving with a number of Army medical units in France, usually in the capacity of stretcherbearers. They wore discarded uniforms and helmet liners with "Poland" painted on them. Then there were a number of young resistance fighters, especially in France, who unofficially joined American combat units passing through. Given uniforms and weapons, they fought in the ranks all across France and in some cases on into Germany; a number were killed fighting under the American colors.

Boys in their midteens and younger who "joined" were a special case; often they would hang around American encampments until the G.I.s adopted them. They picked up English almost overnight, and acquired American names and cut-down uniforms; sometimes the G.I.s supplied them with dog tags and weapons as well. The practice was especially common in Italy, where swarms of homeless, threadbare waifs were drawn to American bivouacs; at least two Italian "mascots" made the Anzio landing with their outfits. Adoptions also took place in France. A corporal wrote from there in September 1944: "We have a very sweet kid with us here who has become a part of us. Everyone is crazy about him and we are thinking of smuggling him into the United States after the war." For the French or Italian teenager, integration into G.I. society was amazingly swift. The Mazure brothers, who had gone looking for the Americans in August 1944, were full-fledged members of their reconnaissance unit within a matter of days. Félix inherited the clothing and equipment of a G.I. who had recently been killed; he carried a light M3 "grease gun" in combat, while his fifteen-year-old brother manned a jeep-mounted machine gun. Félix related that they enriched their English considerably. The G.I.s taught them one term that was somewhat strong but extremely useful, since you could use it to designate anything you didn't know the name of. The term was "son of a bitch."

If some were attracted to the Americans, others were attracted by their opulence, by the infinity of things they carried with them and then casually discarded. It was possible to nourish oneself—

monotonously, it is true—on the K and C ration items G.I.s disdained to eat and left behind them. A man could reconstitute his wardrobe with the items of clothing the American soldiers seemed to discard at every turn. The G.I.'s habit of shedding encumbering items—and obtaining more from an understanding supply sergeant later on—was so widespread that the Quartermasters occasionally put Burma Shave–type signs along the roads the Army traveled: "If you leave—good clothes behind—you may need them—another time." The G.I.'s tendency to get rid of excess clothing was particularly pronounced in the jungles of the Pacific, where every ounce seemed to weigh a pound and the men went shirtless whenever possible. General Eichelberger complained that "men threw away their packs with food and ammunition within two miles of the enemy, and the natives are now wearing our uniforms." This last phenomenon was even more rampant in Europe. Not long after the end of the war, General Eisenhower proposed to the War Department that American troops stationed in Europe be issued blue uniforms. One of his main arguments for the change was that so many Europeans were wearing the Army khaki that it was hard to distinguish between the American military and the locals.

Even when Americans did not discard items, they kept them in such negligent fashion that spiriting them away was child's play. The Army was ill prepared for the widespread, consummate thievery it encountered in North Africa, and it paid a high price for its negligence. Graves Registration units reported that recently buried corpses were unearthed and robbed; surveying parties claimed their range poles were stolen the moment they turned their backs (the poles made excellent shepherd's staffs). One surveyor said he had just lined up his transit on a marker flag three thousand yards away when the figure of an Arab suddenly appeared in his field of vision; the next moment both Arab and flag had vanished. During the North African landings, when truck drivers were scarce, beach authorities engaged native drivers, who were given loaded trucks and directions for delivery. In many cases they were never seen again, though tons of munitions and rations were later discovered on native fishing boats. Opportunities for theft—and theft itself—no doubt increased when the Army moved massive quantities of supplies to the European continent. There were too few undamaged warehouses available; stocks were placed in open fields or rail yards and were insufficiently guarded and poorly lit at night. At one time eight million gallons of gasoline in jerricans were stacked along the banks of the Meuse at Liège for a distance of two miles.

It was also in North Africa that the G.I. first realized that items that belonged to him (or that belonged to the Army) had considerable value to the locals. A soldier wrote from Algeria: "I was offered 1000 francs for a G.I. mattress cover. I believe that the cost to us was $1.60 when they were issued." (The covers were in demand by Arabs, who cut neck and arm holes and wore them.) The same correspondent continues: "They will give you 50 francs for a bar of candy or 25 francs for a package of chewing gum. The boys have sold them so much stuff of their issue equipment and of their rations from the P.X. there is now a directive out to the effect that no item of any kind that has been purchased from the Army will be sold to any civilian and if you are caught doing it they will really burn you for it."

Neither the directive issued in Algeria nor any issued subsequently put an end to the mutually profitable traffic between G.I.s and Europeans. The soldiers sold or traded their possessions, and quite often they trafficked in the Army's possessions as well, and the traffic increased as the European war came to an end. (Postal inspectors discovered that G.I.s were also sending Army property home in considerable quantities; incredibly, they even sent home K rations.)

John Roche recalled how two of his buddies replenished their supply of "trade goods" from an Army depot: "Walt had affixed a 'US' brass button to the front of his helmet liner and Buck had his staff sergeant's stripes painted on his. When they approached a supply depot, the guard, and others after him, thought Walt was a major, so gave him all he asked for."

Louis Rossetti was a frequent participant in the black market, as everyone called it, and he had a similar technique. He and a buddy wanted some coffee to take to two girls they knew; the only way to get it was to stand guard at the rations tent. Rossetti stood guard while his buddy carried off a case of 10-in-1 rations. Later they sorted the contents; they decided to take coffee and some bacon, but to hold back on the candy and gum until they got to know the girls better. Another time, Rossetti tried to sell a Frenchman a pack of gum, but instead the man expressed an interest in his shirt. "I refused at first," Rossetti recalled, "but when he quoted me a fair price I rushed to the truck for my field jacket, took off my shirt, gave it to the Frenchman, and wore the jacket for the remainder of the evening." Like most G.I.s, Rossetti learned only a few words of French, which he did not pronounce very well—yet this rarely handicapped him in his operations: "I asked a farmer who was driving his horse and wagon whether he had eggs to trade for soap. I mentioned the French word for eggs 'oeuf.' He didn't know what I was talking about. I repeated the word over and over, gesturing with my hands the shape of an egg. Still he did not understand. Finally I cackled like a hen. The attempt was not a failure. The farmer raised his eyebrows. 'Oeuf,' he repeated. 'Oui, that's what I said.' I gave him soap in return for a dozen eggs."

Some G.I.s, like Rossetti, sold items for spending money; others saw them as a way to alcohol, women, and good times. There was also a considerable traffic in war souvenirs, especially in German Luger pistols and Iron Crosses. The G.I.'s tendency to acquire weapons caused considerable concern to General Marshall. He dictated a memo on the subject after actress Marlene Dietrich arrived in the States from Europe with eleven pistols offered to her by G.I.s, while the ship she came on carried thirty-five thousand other "trophy weapons" sent home by American soldiers.

Where G.I.s and locals mixed in great numbers, as they did in a large city, the amount of commercial contact—the volume of "beezness," as it was called—could be very great. If that city was Naples, site of the vast Army depots that constituted Peninsula Base Section, then the "beezness" could become a whole illicit economy of vast proportions.

The Wehrmacht had used the city as a recuperation site for convalescents; they had kept apart, avoiding much contact with the local population. The Germans took what they needed in foodstuffs from the local economy, which could scarcely maintain the city's population. The German authorities blamed food shortages on the black market, against which they conducted a heavy-handed, fruitless campaign. They suppressed food riots with force, though Neapolitans had some justification for taking to the streets. The daily ration was around a thousand calories; bread was limited to a hundred grams—about four ounces—per person per day; pea pods were common fare, and the only high-protein food was to be found on the black market.

American troops who arrived by ship were appalled at the sight of the stunted, malnourished Neapolitans, dressed in rags, who clambered over the docks, picking little scraps of garbage from crevices in the pier. They received another shock when they discovered the price of a prostitute in Naples—twenty-five cents in the first days after liberation. Even more shocking, though few G.I.s may have realized it, the vast mass of girls and young women on the streets had been driven there by sheer economic necessity. According to Sergio Lambiase and G. Battista Nazzaro, historians of wartime Naples, "The women prostituted themselves because they had to earn money to spend on the black market. Prostitution in Naples was always related to this economic necessity." Whatever the origins of this particular commerce, it grew apace, even after prices increased twenty or thirty times over. In April 1944, the British Bureau of Psychological Warfare estimated that some forty-two thousand women in Naples were practicing prostitution. By then the venereal disease rate had begun to soar. The Army found that the VD rate assumed major importance for the first time in the European campaign; as for the Neapolitans, no fewer than four thousand showed up for treatment at one Naples hospital in a two-week period in August 1944.

Other Neapolitans worked for the Americans in more conventional ways. The port of Naples became a linchpin in the supply system, and so did the vast depots of Peninsula Base Section, scattered around the city. Army Service Forces became an important employer of Italian labor, hiring thousands of Neapolitans for jobs ranging from stevedore to stenographer. Some went to work for the British as well, but according to Lambiase and Nazzaro they found them less satisfactory as employers:

> The British were hard and rigid in the application of labor agreements, conceding nothing that was not specified in the contracts. They were generally haughty in their relations with the workers, keeping their distance and carefully avoiding any semblance of fraternization. . . . In general people preferred to work for the Americans; there it was easier to avoid the severity of discipline, either because they were more tolerant, or because in the long run a climate of comradeship with the troops developed. In some cases the Americans even set up messes for the workers and distributed gifts in food and money on special occasions, or gave "bonuses" to the most meritorious and efficient workers.

With the liberation the Neapolitan black market took on new life. First of all, certain stocks and supplies abandoned by the Germans found their way into the marketplace, as did items of all sorts looted from private houses whose owners departed with the Germans. And the G.I.s and Tommies brought still another flood of goods onto the market: Clothing merchants acquired great mounds of khaki garments, and C ration cans appeared in incredible numbers—a can of meat and vegetable hash sold for about twenty-five cents. G.I.s were interested in cameras, linens, Neapolitan cameos, and of course, the usual war trophies; Neapolitans were interested chiefly in food and clothing, and the trafficking between them went on endlessly throughout the city. According to Lambiase and Nazzaro, the black market was composed of "continuous currents and counter-currents, apparently subterranean and invisible whenever the authorities were around, but then welling up out of the ground again into the streets and alleys, into the squares and to the thresholds of houses and the gates of military camps."

The black market spawned a number of satellite activities. A man who bought an American uniform could take it to a tailor, where the pieces would be taken apart, dyed, recut, and assembled into a civilian suit. The tailors could also perform wonders working with G.I. blankets—one dressmaker's shop raided by Italian police had thirty blankets waiting for "alterations." There was also a cigarette industry of sorts. Cigarette butts discarded by American and British troops were collected and "processed"; that is to say, the tobacco was removed and then rolled into new cigarettes. There were those who even preferred the new brand, claiming it had a richness of flavor lacking in Luckies and Camels.

Theft was an increasingly important element in Naples' underground economy. The siphoning of gasoline from Army trucks was a highly developed art. The Signal Corps lost miles of wire; cut from telephone poles, it appeared again as merchandise on the Via Forcella, along with other purloined items of Army hardware. Then there were whole gangs of small boys who climbed into the backs of Army trucks stopped in traffic and threw out items to accomplices in the streets. But these were nickel-and-dime operations compared with the widespread thefts from Army stocks arranged by Army personnel working in collaboration with locals. Such thefts tended to be massive, smoothly executed, and "covered" by officials on the take. There were fortunes to be made in such undertakings; certainly they had radiating effects throughout the local economy. The British estimated that 65 percent of the income of Neapolitans derived from transactions in stolen Allied supplies; they also calculated that about a third of everything coming into the port of Naples ended up on the black market. The illicit traffic had its violent side. There were stories—never quite documented—of an entire freight train seized by hijackers who subsequently found a market for their booty—cargo, railway cars, locomotive, and all. What is indisputable is that armed gangs, including American deserters and local mafiosi, became a serious menace in and around Naples.

The plain fact is that for all the enthusiasm it engendered, and for all the real benefit it brought, liberation was not without its difficulties. Whether it be Naples or another town the Americans moved into, the community's problems did not go away with the Germans; sometimes in the short term they were intensified, and sometimes they were joined by other difficulties stemming from the presence of the liberator. While the welcome the local population offered its deliverers was genuine, after the first euphoria passed the liberator seemed less heroic in stature, less altruistic in his motives, and as time passed less easy to get along with. By the same token the G.I., or the Tommy for that matter, quickly developed a different, less charitable, view of the locals. There was usually a "honeymoon," followed by a period of sometimes painful adjustment; ultimately, in the best of cases, an accommodation was reached. In other cases the soldier wore out his welcome and became part of an "army of occupation," disliked almost as much as the enemy garrison he replaced. This is the perennial problem of all armies that linger among those they have freed. It was a problem for the G.I. everywhere he went in Europe; but more than anywhere else it was a problem in France.

The fact that the American military presence created so many problems in France seems paradoxical, and yet at the same time not unexpected; somehow it fits into the customary pattern of relations with our oldest and most baffling ally. And at bottom the difficulties of 1944/45 stem from the same mutual incomprehensions, the same stereotypes, and the same nuances of difference in looking at things that have always divided us.

The G.I. probably expected too much of France, and so was bound to be disappointed. It was a country that he already had some fairly precise notions about—precise, but not necessarily accurate. Hollywood, popular literature, and the sometimes highly colored reminiscences of World War I veterans all contributed to the G.I.'s image of France. To him it was the land of *l'amour*, of cognac and truffles, of the Folies Bergères, and the silk-hatted elegance of Maurice Chevalier—in short a collage of images suggesting lighthearted fun and racy good times—and bearing little relationship to the distracted and destitute country the G.I. saw in 1944.

There were little shocks as the G.I. observed French manners. The French were casual in matters of hygiene. Encouraged by their mothers, small children relieved themselves in the gutters or along the roadsides. G.I.s wrote home that they had had their attention attracted to some historic building or monument—and then to a Frenchman casually urinating against it. There were no color barriers in France, a discovery that shocked many white G.I.s as much as it delighted black ones. Not only would Frenchwomen dance with black men, they would also dance with each other; Frenchmen would likewise embrace and kiss each other—to many G.I.s such habits suggested a looseness in morals that hinted of degeneracy. Even more noticed by G.I.s was the way young French couples behaved in public. They kissed and caressed each other, paying no attention to those around them, who in turn ignored their intimacies—something that could not have happened in the America of the 1940s. For the red-blooded G.I., tantalized by such scenes, it was easy to conclude that the Frenchwoman was casual and uninhibited in her sexuality. But when he acted on this assumption and approached a Frenchwoman, he was coldly rebuffed.

On the other hand, he always seemed to be well received in brothels and nightclubs, at least so long as his money lasted (the Army operated four nightclubs in Paris, partly to prevent price gouging). In Paris, which G.I.s visited by the thousands, overcharging and other sharp practices were common enough for many servicemen to leave the city shorn and resentful, convinced—as doughboys had been in 1918—that the French were an ungrateful, rapacious lot. It didn't always work that way, of course. A soldier might go to Paris on a forty-eight-hour pass and come back with memories that would warm his heart forty years later. The city would work her magic on him, and then he would meet a girl. An American officer stationed in Paris saw it happen many times: ". . . the uninhibited girl in the metro, standing on tiptoe to kiss an embarrassed G.I. partner fresh from the Ozarks, where it wasn't being done that way when he left town. Our soldiers were devastated by aphrodisiac dreams who curled like kittens against their shoulders and tickled their cheeks with kisses—oblivious to the crowds around them."

There is no doubt that everywhere he went, the G.I. made difficulties for himself and for others by excessive drinking. An Army psychiatrist who had extensive experience with the alcohol problem overseas concluded: "While living among the Allies drunkenness has been the greatest ambassador of ill will." And an Army study of criminal offenses by soldiers in the European theater stated flatly: "Intoxication was the largest contributing factor to crime in the European Theater of Operations." And in truth, nowhere were the temptations placed before the G.I. greater than in France; alcohol seemed to permeate French society in endless forms, indeed sometimes it was virtually forced upon him. Officers soon learned the perils of letting their men linger too long in towns whose inhabitants wanted to drink a toast with them or offer them "one for the road." Combat troops tended to limit themselves out of a sense of obligation to their buddies, especially if more fighting seemed imminent, but Orval Faubus noted from time to time that some of his men were drinking more than they should; he did nothing about it, though, for if it helped the men bear up, he felt it was justified.

The men who landed in Normandy had been accustomed to Britain's watered-down wartime scotch and to beer. In the towns and villages of Normandy they were offered Calvados, distilled from apples. The distilling was often done by peasants who produced a drink of great potency—140 proof and above. Some G.I.s burned it in their cigarette lighters, and Orval Faubus wrote that his outfit used Calvados as lantern fuel. Calvados soon acquired a formidable reputation. Some said it was made from ground-up grenades. Louis Rossetti called it "truly the devil's fluid." He went on: "Even small amounts made soldiers go on rampages. Whenever there was a melee involving a soldier and a Frenchman, it was almost certain the G.I. had had more than his share of Calvados."

The French did not object to the G.I.'s drinking, or even to his drinking to excess. What angered them was the kind of drunk he made: loud, belligerent, and when he had his weapons with him, downright dangerous. A civil affairs officer named John Maginnis encountered this problem in the town of Carentan, which had been liberated by the 101st Airborne Division. Maginnis recorded on June 19, 1944, what could be called "the second battle of Carentan": "It stemmed from a basic resentment by the paratroopers towards the First Army military police who patrolled the town. Their philosophy was: 'The 101st took Carentan, it's our town, and no outsiders are going to tell us how to act here.' Wine and Calvados stirred things more. There was shooting, physical contact, and some property destruction, but fortunately no-one was killed or seriously wounded."

Officers of the 101st were instrumental in getting the fighting stopped. Army authorities imposed a 10:00 P.M. curfew and curbed Calvados sales. Paratroopers took over the maintenance of order in Carentan—not efficiently enough, however, to spare Maginnis another serious problem two nights later. A soldier of the 101st went into the "out of bounds" area of the town to drink with one of the locals. The soldier tried to teach his host English, but the Frenchman was a poor pupil. The drunken soldier pronounced him "too dumb to live" and shot him. Fortunately, the Frenchman did not die, but Maginnis had to arrange for his care and also the upkeep of his wife and five children. The soldier was arrested and held for court-martial.

Even when he was not drunk, the American had some irritating habits. He was casual about property rights—if he was generous with what he had, he did not hesitate to make free with the property of others. He shot game out of season, fished with hand grenades, and took shortcuts across cultivated fields. He was casual about the amenities; he would speak to anyone whenever he felt like it, even to complete strangers. His approach to women was sometimes crudely direct, consisting of a blunt question delivered without the slightest preliminaries: *"Voulez-vous coucher avec moi?"* In this regard he seemed unable to tell the difference between a prostitute and a housewife. Even when he kept to himself, the American seemed to some Frenchmen to make a vulgar parade of his affluence, trying to buy the best seats and the best bottles, leaving behind him unfinished meals and half-smoked cigarettes.

In May 1985 there was a colloquium in Reims to commemorate the German capitulation there four decades before. The first sessions were dedicated to questions of high policy and strategy, but on the final day the participants talked about how life had been for the Rémois, as the city's inhabitants call themselves. The Rémois had seen a lot of Americans by the time the war ended. Eisenhower's headquarters had been there, of course, and Reims was also a class II depot, which meant it had its share of ASF people; then, too, large numbers of combat troops who passed through the nearby camps at Mourmelon and Suippes came to Reims on pass.

A historian named Georges Clause had lived in Reims at the end of the war and he evoked the era in a talk that was followed by lively discussion. For two years, Rémois had bathed and shaved with soap and razor blades originally issued to U.S. troops; the American presence had been a major stimulant to the economy. Some Rémois said they had formed fast friendships with American servicemen, with whom they still exchanged letters. Others spoke of downtown brawls, and of an apparent "contest" among U.S. airborne troops to see how many windows they could punch out with their fists (the Army paid for the damage, but because of a shortage of glass, many of the windows remained boarded up for some time). A woman got up to say that when the Germans occupied Reims she had been able to go about the city in complete freedom, but that when the Americans moved in she could scarcely go across the street to the bakery without being approached by a libidinous G.I. Another woman rose to speak in defense of the Americans. She, too, had spent the war years in Reims and not once had she been propositioned by an American soldier. Everybody laughed.

The inhabitants of Reims probably saw more Americans, and for a longer period, than most Frenchmen. They were immensely relieved to see the Germans leave—as a reminder of their presence the headquarters of the Gestapo still stands in the center of town, a grim, dark fortress of a place that has stood empty for forty years —and it follows that the Rémois were delighted to see the Americans arrive. It diminishes nothing of their gratitude to acknowledge—as the historian must—that when it came time for the American soldier to depart in his turn, the Rémois were, for the most part, quite content to see him go. And as for the G.I., he was probably ready to leave. For he had discovered another people among whom he felt more at ease, more at home—across the Rhine, in Germany.

★ 11 ★

The Conquerors

On the evening of September 11, 1944, a U.S. First Army patrol that was reconnoitering in northern Luxembourg crossed the Our River; in doing so it became the first American unit to set foot on German soil. Though the event got prominent play in the American press, it did not catch the country's military and political leaders unprepared; they and the British had already made plans for the German population and territories their armies would conquer. Now these plans, which covered almost every aspect of German life, would be put into effect as the Allied armies progressed.

The G.I. who fought his way into Germany had little to do with most of these projects. But one measure that went into effect in "occupied" Germany affected him directly; this was the non-fraternization order that governed—or rather circumscribed—his relations with German civilians. He was to have nothing to do with them, save in the line of duty. There was to be no trading of goods, no convivial drinking or visiting in German homes or other social contact under penalty of severe punishment. Just speaking to a German girl, for example, could cost a G.I. a sixty-five-dollar fine. Thus began the controversial policy that, in the words of *Yank*, produced "the loudest and most engaging international discussion of sex since Adam discovered that Eve had not been placed in the Garden purely for decorative purposes."

The origins of the nonfraternization policy went all the way back to 1918, when American soldiers who briefly occupied German towns along the Rhine were ordered to avoid contact with the local population. The policy adopted in 1944 was given to General Eisenhower by the Combined Chiefs of Staff, who apparently saw nonfraternization as the right approach for several reasons. First of all, it would be easier to govern the conquered population if the occupiers kept their distance and maintained only "official" relations; also, the Germans would be held in a kind of moral quarantine, and this, it was argued, would bring home to them the enormity of the crimes their government had committed. Finally, and most important, nonfraternization seemed an indispensable security measure.

Allied leaders were fearful that behind their advancing armies a German resistance movement might spring up, just as such movements had appeared in countries Hitler's armies had overrun. And the Nazi regime gave credence to this notion, first by its highly publicized effort to arm the general population and form Volkssturm units for defense of the Reich, then by its talk—and little more than that—of a Werewolf organization specifically charged with carrying on the war behind enemy lines. These concerns were passed on to Allied troops. At the German frontier there were large signs announcing: GERMANY. YOU ARE ENTERING AN ENEMY COUNTRY, KEEP ALERT. American troops received a *Pocket Guide to Germany*, which reminded them that Hitler had recruited some half a million fanatical followers in the Gestapo alone, and that "with the defeat of Germany what are left of these 500,000 will discard their uniforms and disappear into the anonymity of civilian clothes." To the G.I. the warning was clear: "Your life may be in greater danger than it was during the battles."

Both *Yank* and *Stars and Stripes* carried stories that highlighted the enemy's perfidy, even if they involved nothing more sinister than German soldiers who were wearing parts of American uniforms when killed or captured. And everywhere the G.I. heard the slogan, "Don't fraternize." It was on a special label pasted to the cover of his *Pocket Guide*, and it was heard in a frequently repeated "spot" announcement, on the Allied Forces Network, which stressed the danger a German girl could represent to the unwary soldier: "Don't play Samson to her Delilah. . . . She'd like to cut your hair off—off at the neck. Don't fraternize."

These warnings had their effect on the G.I.s who fought their way into Germany, and they seemed in part confirmed in the early days of the American advance. The G.I.s occupied half-empty towns, for much of their populations had fled. Aachen, the first major city to fall, contained only a fraction of its normal population. To the G.I. this flight was evidence of complicity with the Hitlerian regime. (Actually, the partial evacuations had been done at the insistence of the regime.) The G.I.'s suspicions were easily roused: When Louis Rossetti and his buddies came upon a house whose occupants had hastily fled, they did not dare touch the food they found on the dining room table. "It was possible that the food had been placed there and treated with the hope that a pair of invading and hungry Americans might devour it and suffer fatally," Rossetti recalled. Rumors ran through American units: a German boy had picked up a G.I.'s M1 and shot him with it; a *fräulein* had smiled at a passing soldier and beckoned him into a farmhouse from which he never returned. And when there were incidents—a G.I. killed by a Wehrmacht straggler or blown up by a booby trap—the soldiers often assumed the local population was somehow involved. A G.I. in an antiaircraft unit recorded: "One of our finest soldiers, Walter A. Kasten of Btry 'C,' was ambushed and killed in Biedenkopf, 29 March, two hours after the treacherous population had hung out surrender flags following the passage of nearly a hundred tanks."

The wariness and the suspicion of the G.I. were matched by the fear and the uncertainty the average German civilian felt in those final months of the war. The writer Ernst Jünger recalled that a neighbor had been approached by an American soldier who tried to hand him a glass of water and make him drink it. The neighbor threw up his hands in refusal, thinking the water was poisoned. The G.I. then led him to a pump, where he refilled the glass and thrust it on the German again. At that point Jünger's neighbor understood: The American was afraid the water system had been poisoned.

The German people had been led to expect a saturnalia of slaughter, rapine, and plunder when the American "gangsters" came, so they were quite understandably apprehensive over the arrival of their conquerors. Here and there people were so distraught that they took their own lives. In one village, father, mother, and teenage daughter hanged themselves after strangling their pet dog; troops of G.I.s passing through stopped to stare at the macabre scene. In the town of Marburg, where there were two suicides, an unsettling rumor ran through the streets: The Americans would open all the jail cells and unleash criminals on the townspeople. When the Americans appeared, few townspeople came out to greet them; most stayed out of sight, watching from behind windows or hiding their possessions. Occasionally, a skirmish in a village would flush them from their homes—old men, women, and children, their hands in the air and their faces contorted with fear, captured on film by Signal Corps photographers who happened to be there.

The first days and weeks of the occupation were particularly harsh. Mutual suspicion effectively prevented much fraternization, and the American authorities tended to enforce regulations to the letter. All German civilians were ordered to turn in any arms, ammunition, or explosives in their possession, and while they came forward with sizable quantities of weapons, the Army conducted searches of houses and from time to time turned up forbidden items. Patrols and checkpoint personnel carefully scrutinized credentials; curfews further restricted the movement of the local population, and a prohibition against gathering in groups of more than five curbed their social activities. The occupying troops were braced for trouble. Convoys on German roads were escorted by fearsome "meatchoppers," M16 half-tracks carrying quadruple-mounted .50-caliber machine guns. In Cologne and some other places, searchlights were used to illuminate the streets at night and facilitate patrols. And when the Germans broke the rules they got harsh treatment. Some troops fresh from combat no doubt transferred their hostility to German civilians, and the revelations about concentration camps created a wave of resentment in the Army.

It was soon apparent that the conquered population was not giving the Allies any problem and was not going to. The occupation troops moved through the conquered areas in complete safety; the Werewolves proved to be a fable. The acts of sabotage the authorities had feared never occurred. Telephone lines that were vital to Allied communications stretched for miles over country roads without attracting saboteurs. In fact, the only damage was caused by American troops; they used insulators for target practice to such an extent that the Army had to put out a stern warning against the practice.

As the occupation proceeded, as troops settled down in their billets, relations between the conquerors and the conquered began to change. First of all, occupation policy called for the troops to be disseminated throughout the American zone, so their presence in every village or hamlet would nip disorders in the bud. This put them in daily contact with the local population, and at the same time out of the sight and the control of higher levels of command—a situation almost guaranteed to erode the nonfraternization policy. The Germans, of course, detested the nonfraternization policy from the start, since it carried a stigma. The G.I. resented it first of all because it represented another intrusion of the Army into off-duty time he considered his own. It robbed him of the diversion, the good time to which he felt he was entitled (there were those who believed nonfraternization was a scheme to keep men from competing with officers for German girls). Then, too, fraternization offered certain practical benefits: It would permit them to vary their diet, trade for more souvenirs, and get their laundry done.

Some men later claimed that nonfraternization was like prohibition, massively violated from the outset and doomed to eventual repeal. Ultimately the Army agreed, but not before the issue had stirred immense debate, not only within the occupation force, but also in the American press and among the public. Injected into the discussion at different times were the Army's rising venereal disease rate—from fifty cases per thousand at the beginning of 1945 to five times that by the end of the year—and the story that American women at home were dating Italian prisoners of war. The nonfraternization order was not uniformly enforced; in one place a violation was simply ignored, in another it might earn a soldier six months' confinement. General Eisenhower said at a press conference in March 1945 that he "would be the last one to deny that soldiers don't get in the back door and get Rhine wine and whatever else they are after." Journalist Ed Ball was present when General Patton offered his solution to the problem: "Copulation without conversation is not fraternization." Succeeding orders from General Eisenhower's headquarters increased the scope of authorized contacts. In June fraternization with young children was authorized; in July contacts with adult Germans were permitted in public places. But as an Army historian put it, "Nonfraternization did not end, it disintegrated."

There was one basic consideration that hastened the demise of nonfraternization more than anything else: Once the G.I. had a chance to take a close look at the Germans, he decided that he liked what he saw. If he had expected the country to be peopled with fanatics and heel-clicking automatons, he was in for a pleasant surprise. An observer for the Psychological Warfare Division of SHAEF wrote a tongue-in-cheek account of this "discovery": "The crossing of the German frontier is something of a shock. Even in Nazi Germany the cows have four legs, the grass is green, and children in pigtails stand around the tanks." Historians of the occupation have written that fraternization began with the children, which is scarcely surprising; nor is it much of a revelation to learn that it was quickly extended to German women. *Yank* reporters could scarcely hide their enthusiasm for the young women they saw in Germany; they described them as looking somehow out of place, neatly and attractively dressed in the midst of ruins. (The reporters also wrote more than once that the women liked to stand in the sunlight, wearing thin cotton dresses and no slips.) A G.I. spoke for many of his fellow soldiers when he said simply, "They looked healthy. They looked good."

Any number of G.I.s commented in their letters home that the Germans were industrious and knew how to work. In September, a *Yank* article on "Germany's Steep Road" claimed: "In a matter of weeks, or sometimes days, they bring order, even neatness to cities that were twisted masses of rubble." The reportage also echoed the average G.I.'s observations on the cleanliness of the Germans: "Somehow, despite living in cellars and bombed out buildings, the German civilians have kept clean." And there was the general acknowledgment that somehow Germans seemed remarkably like Americans. "Put them in Trenton, N.J., and you wouldn't know they were German," concluded *Yank*. A G.I. who wrote to the magazine in that same month, when nonfraternization was a dead letter, asserted, "The German women are so much like American women that it is hard to pass one without talking to her when she speaks to you in English."

And inevitably, the G.I. compared the Germans with other people he had encountered. "Observations of how the Germans lived, worked, ate, and thought led the typical American soldier to make many comparisons which were adverse to the people of other European nations through which he had passed." Such was the conclusion of one historian of the American occupation. The comparison most frequently made was with the French; in the fall of 1945 an I and E poll revealed that the G.I. liked the Germans better by a clear margin. A G.I. summed up the prevailing attitude in these words: "Hell, these people are cleaner and a damn sight friendlier than the Frogs. They're our kind of people."

The Germans were not quite so enthusiastic about the G.I. One could eat best under the Americans, the saying went, for their abundance of everything had a way of percolating down, but one lived most tranquilly under the British. Living under the Russians was to be avoided, for there one knew neither peace nor plenty. The G.I. discovered schnapps, which had on him the same unfortunate effect that Calvados had had in France. There was also a disturbing pattern of rape in occupied Germany in the spring of

1945: 402 cases in March, 501 in April. A high proportion of the cases were proved in court, and authorities suspected they were seeing the tip of an iceberg. Instances of pillage rose when the Army moved into Germany. Some soldiers said they felt that if they'd conquered the country they had also conquered its contents; others reasoned that if they came upon an unoccupied house its owner must have fled because he was a Nazi, so his possessions could be taken with impunity. All the armies looted in World War II, but in Germany the Americans seem to have been more aggressive about it than the British, though less so than the Russians. In Austria, the G.I.s apparently gave the Russians keen competition. A riddle that went the rounds in postwar Austria asked, "What's the difference between an American soldier and a Russian soldier?" Answer: "The American bathes."

Yet on balance the American occupation was a success, in part because the Germans had no choice but to accept it, and in part because the American presence proved in the end to be a beneficent one. Eisenhower's orders were to be "just and humane" in treatment of the German people, and by and large the G.I.s he commanded adhered to that policy. The long-nurtured vengefulness, the desire to humiliate, which found expression in the zones controlled by the Soviets and by the French, were not part of the G.I. character. As one veteran put it, defeating the Germans was "like beating a good football team," and the winners shouldn't celebrate their victory by roughing up the losers.

For both the conquerors and the defeated the reality of the occupation was probably something of a relief, since it did not conform to the grim and bloody scenarios they had imagined beforehand. If this was true in Germany, it was doubly true in Japan. Well into the summer of 1945, that scenario called for the most bitter fighting into 1946 or even into 1947; the Japanese authorities had begun to mobilize and arm virtually the entire adult population to resist the invaders, and Allied planners were preparing what everyone conceded would be the most costly seaborne invasion of all time. Even when the Japanese government signaled its willingness to surrender, there was some doubt as to whether or not it would be able to restrain the more fanatic elements in the Japanese military, or even the urban masses, which had been so savagely punished by American bombing raids. This concern was very real for the first Americans who went into Japan at the end of August. Though an American fleet of awesome size and power was anchored in Tokyo Bay, the first ground troops were to be flown into Atsugi Naval Air Station some twenty miles away. General Eichelberger was not enthusiastic about the idea: "It will be very easy for the Japs to become hysterical. They must have suffered terribly in the bombing of their cities. . . . Personally I am no great proponent of flying troops in there."

An advance party of 154 understandably nervous Signal Corps men flew into Atsugi on August 28; they made preparations for the more massive flights of the next few days. MacArthur flew in on August 30. When the instrument of surrender was signed three days later, American troops were only a microscopic force in a nation that had never before been defeated in war or occupied. The Americans remained on the *qui vive*. They went armed, though this would have done them little good, for there were between three and four million Japanese still under arms. G.I.s arriving in Japan speculated on what their reception would be in Hiroshima or Nagasaki; some pup tent analysts claimed that for the next twenty years any American who showed himself there would be torn to pieces by the inhabitants.

In fact, carrying out the occupation of Japan proved to be surprisingly easy. The Japanese met the first planes with flawless courtesy. Japanese troops lining the roads from the air base stood with their backs to the passing convoys of Americans as a sign of respect—so did farmers in the fields. There were no attacks on American troops, save by one obviously demented Japanese who assaulted an American sentry. What other incidents occurred in the early days were minor—on August 30 a Japanese woman reported that a G.I. had taken her wristwatch, for example. The lack of trouble was itself almost troubling. One soldier complained: "It's too damned quiet here." Late in September a *Yank* article on the occupation announced, "Things are going so well it's monotonous."

For a considerable length of time, G.I.s and Japanese were destined to live in close proximity but with very little contact. Both American and Japanese authorities made efforts to keep those contacts limited. The Metropolitan Police Board of Tokyo gave the city's women their marching orders: "Women will never be sloppily dressed nor bare their breast in public. If hailed by foreign soldiers with 'hello' or 'hey' or in broken Japanese the women must pay no attention to them." Among other taboos were heavy makeup, smiling at G.I.s, or accepting cigarettes from them. *Yank*'s "Occupation" article said that "the average Japanese girl is unapproachable and never on the make." There were the geishas, of course, but *Yank* warned that they would not respond to "the quick slap and tickle fondly imagined by the G.I.s." Later there would be other girls at the entrance to Tokyo's Hibiya Park who had learned to say to passing soldiers, "Very good, Joe, very cheap."

It was not just the girls who were unapproachable. A *Yank* reportage on "Three Beaten Cities" concluded: "Nobody here seems to want to have much to do with us. It looks as if there will be no fraternization problem in Japan." There was an initial reticence on both sides, no doubt, but there were also major problems that stood in the way of much contact. The first was the barrier of language. The G.I., who could pick up a smattering of French or German, found Japanese impenetrable. And then there were far fewer incentives for "beezness" in the early days. The Japanese economy had been pretty thoroughly wrecked at the consumer level. The terrible air raids, in particular, had destroyed a fifth of the furniture and household goods in the country. There was little available by way of tourist goods, and the G.I. did not find anything interesting with which to vary his diet. In any case, the Japanese had no food to spare. So critical was the shortage of foodstuffs at the end of the war that Japanese authorities asked for the garbage from the American fleet. The situation did not improve for some time. (Though the occupying authorities began importing goods for the German population as early as June 1945, such aid for the Japanese was much slower in coming.) An American officer in Tokyo noted at the end of 1945, "This city now is a world of scarcity in which every nail, every rag, and even

a tangerine peel has market value. A cupful of rice, three cigarettes, or four matches are all a day's ration. Men pick every grain
of rice out of their tin lunch boxes; there are too few to be wasted."

In the early days of the occupation, the G.I.s kept largely to
themselves, eating and living in Army facilities, spending leisure
time watching American movies. Their forays into Japanese society took them to geisha houses or to huge mountains of metal
objects the Japanese had collected in Tokyo to be melted down
for the war effort—picking through them would sometimes yield
a candlestick or other souvenir. The best souvenirs were, of course,
military items, and the Army consented to share with G.I.s some
of the countless Japanese guns and swords it had acquired; sometimes the men lined up for the privilege of picking a rifle from a
mound of them as large as a house. There was some traffic with
the Japanese in these commodities, with the best trade goods
being American cigarettes. (There was a desperate shortage of
tobacco in Japan, and one of the less-admirable customs G.I.s
developed was the practice of throwing a half-smoked cigarette
into the street and watching Japanese scramble for it.)

Only in the fall of 1945 was there evidence that the American
presence was beginning to stimulate certain segments of the local
economy. The Ginza was still mostly lined with empty storefronts,
though some of the department stores had partially reopened.
Most of the trading was with curbside merchants. Kimonos were
the item most sought by Americans, but other goods were appearing, frequently advertised in bizarre English, such as the curios
"from the backside of Japan." Cheap pottery and ceramics were
beginning to appear also, bearing the "Made in occupied Japan"
stamp that would be eagerly sought by American collectors forty
years later.

Americans still stuck together most of the time, carousing and
fighting among themselves. Racial confrontations occurred in
Japan, as they had everywhere else the Army had gone. A historian
of the occupation recently described a common weekend scene:
"Off base, fueled with Saturday-night booze, white and black
would go after each other before crowds of interested Japanese
bystanders." But by October there was clear evidence that some-

thing of a cultural thaw had begun in everyday Japanese-American relations. *Yank* reported: "The kids in the Yokohama-Tokyo area now wave and make the V sign with their fingers when American trucks drive by." And the same reporter saw an even more promising sign: A couple of teenage Japanese girls in a railway station had looked at American soldiers and then giggled to each other. For American soldiers and Japanese the era of mutual discovery had barely begun in an occupation that was to last some eighty months. For the historian John Curtis Perry the essential feature of that occupation was to be "the insignificance of the unpleasant" and the "essential benignity" of the American military presence. Much of the credit goes to that first wave of G.I.s who came in the late summer of 1945. Elliott Thorpe, who was there and saw them, paid them an eloquent tribute:

> I want to reiterate my great respect for the enlisted man who had fought the long hard road from Australia to Japan and had known the toughness and cruelty of the enemy in the field. Arriving in Japan fresh from the fighting field, these men showed a dignity and restraint that is hard to describe. Near illiterate hillbillies and sophisticated city lads alike showed in their demeanor and action this was not a time for revenge but one for a course of conduct that would help bring lasting peace to a worn-out people.

So to the Japanese as to the Germans, the American soldier came to symbolize a unique form of domination, one without any particular rancor or vengefulness. Yet it is doubtful that the G.I. gave much thought to what he symbolized. "He had only one thought," continued Thorpe. "He wanted to go home." This view was emphatically confirmed by the I and E Division, which had been keeping its finger on the G.I.'s pulse for over three years and had found an "all pervasive eagerness of the men overseas to get the job done and return home." Already in 1943, men fighting in the Pacific believed they had "done their share" and should be replaced and rotated home; by 1944, 75 percent of the men believed the Army could send home soldiers with two years overseas if it really wanted to. With the end of the fighting in 1945, the pressures built up very rapidly.

At the end of the European war, the Army put into effect its redeployment plan; part of its manpower in Europe was to be left there on occupation duty, part was to go to the Pacific for the anticipated invasion of Japan, and part would be sent home and discharged. It would have made sense militarily simply to send the best fighting units to the Pacific, but the Army's high command knew that neither the American public nor the soldiers themselves would accept such a plan. From 1943 on, the I and E Division had been asking G.I.s how the Army should determine who got to go home and who stayed in uniform (it knew from other opinion surveys that no more than 2 percent of the men in the Army planned to stay on for a career). By 1945 the division had polled over twenty thousand G.I.s, and the Army had created a point system for discharge based on the men's responses: A soldier got one point for every month in the service, one point for every month of service overseas, five points for each campaign star or combat decoration (including the Purple Heart), and twelve points for each child (up to three children). To qualify for discharge, a man had to amass eighty-five points.

Since the point system provided for the disposition of individuals rather than units, there was necessarily a massive shuffling of personnel. A division slated for service in the Pacific would thus lose all its high-point men and acquire replacements. This operation took time; it was not until July 15 that the first shipload of ETO troops bound for the Pacific sailed from Naples. Then came the Japanese surrender, which led to a massive revision in all theaters of operation. Now, in theory at least, most of the Army could be demobilized; but there were practical problems to be overcome—notably, arranging transportation for several million men. The American public let Congress know its feelings on the subject. Senators and representatives received hundreds of pairs of baby shoes in the mail, along with the message, "Please send my daddy home." By September, Congresswoman Clare Boothe Luce acknowledged that everyone on Capitol Hill was under "intense pressure" to get the men back from overseas. Congress in turn pressured the executive branch and the Army, which did its best to accelerate the movement—including bringing men home by air, several thousand each month. The number of points needed for discharge was dropped to eighty in September, to sixty in October, then to fifty at the end of December. In May 1945, the Army's strength stood at 8,300,000 men; by the end of the year half that number had returned to civilian life, and by mid-1946 the Army's strength had been halved again. Pentagon planners shook their heads at the precipitate haste with which the nation was liquidating its military might. When the Army tried to slow the demobilization process early in 1946, the soldiers who were still overseas took to the streets and demonstrated in a dozen countries.

To the men waiting overseas, the Army seemed to be taking forever. It was the last great opportunity for the G.I. to gripe, and he made the most of it. In billets and tent cities throughout Europe and Asia, "the Goddamn Army" was endlessly denounced. *Yank* and *Stars and Stripes* published streams of indignant letters. There were those who doubted the point system had ever been derived from the G.I.s themselves. Did anyone know a soldier who had actually been polled on the subject? Older men complained the system was weighted against them; single men who had been overseas for four years objected to the paternity provision: "How in the hell can we have children?" And a G.I. who couldn't find anything wrong with the point system still managed to complain in a letter *Stars and Stripes* published early in June: "This point system seems too easy on us guys. It ain't like the Army. I ain't planning nothing til I get that discharge."

The determination to "get the job done" had been the glue that held the G.I. Army together; now that the job was done, the glue was beginning to dissolve. Cohesion and discipline both suffered. Orval Faubus was appalled at the situation he found at Camp Pittsburgh, near Reims, in the fall of 1945: "Men took off without authorization for various places, mostly Paris, returning when they were ready or not at all. A guard detail list would be posted and only a few of the men would appear. . . . Those who had been the most responsible soldiers during combat in the finest American Army ever put together, now declined and often refused, to accept any responsibility or to perform properly any assigned duty."

Ennui and frustration told on the soldiers. Louis Rossetti wrote home from France: "I almost believe some of the boys are going crazy. They lie around on their bunks and make dizzy noises and tell nutty stories. One guy said he used to throw fits and he feels it coming back." The men got into trouble with the local population with alarming frequency; the men in Rossetti's camp could no longer go to the neighboring town of Sissonne. In Germany there were problems with men drinking "buzz bomb juice" containing methyl alcohol; thirty-one men died there of poisoning in a single week in May. In July, General Patton told General Marshall that in one week the Third Army had had fifty men killed and five hundred wounded in shooting accidents. His staff had first suspected a rash of self-inflicted wounds, but discovered that the casualties resulted from the indiscriminate shooting of captured German weapons. When the news of the Japanese surrender reached Okinawa, the men celebrated by firing into the air every weapon they could find, including antiaircraft guns; the hail of bullets and rain of shell fragments killed seven and wounded scores of others. Another common and sometimes dangerous diversion in Europe was "liberating" vehicles and taking to the roads in them. One G.I. drove around for a time in an immense Mercedes-Benz that Hitler had used for state appearances, another recalled that when his outfit moved, its procession of vehicles made it look "like the Ringling Brothers Circus." Road accidents were frequent.

Some officers were convinced that articles and letters printed in *Stars and Stripes* and *Yank* contributed to the impatience and malaise of the G.I. waiting to go home. *Yank* ran a series of pictures showing the main streets of towns across the country, and both journals dedicated articles to the demobilization and discharge procedures; in them a soldier could read what would happen to him when the lucky day came. Soldiers in Europe were processed through tent cities near ports of embarkation—places such as Camp Herbert Tareyton and other "cigarette camps" set up around Le Havre. Processing for embarkation could take two or three days and would include a physical (with the inevitable shortarm), exchanging money, and the recording of souvenirs—one ship left Le Havre carrying five thousand troops and twenty thousand souvenir weapons. This time the ocean crossing could be made without the vexing security procedures, and when the vessel arrived it would probably be at a pier decorated with bunting and Welcome Home signs. Often there was a victory arch to pass through. The men could look forward to a steak dinner, a hot shower, and a telephone call home; then after a day or two at the port of entry, they would move on to a separation center—and shortly thereafter home.

Such was the homecoming that men overseas looked forward to. *Yank* reporters who visited them as they waited wrote that they talked mostly of getting back. One reporter in Munich found G.I.s ensconced in the room in which Hitler had hosted the Munich Conference of 1938. They sat around in the overstuffed chairs and talked about how many points they had. In Tokyo, another reporter, Sergeant Knox Burger, visited a former barracks of the Imperial Guards Regiment. There G.I.s were waiting, too, but these men talked about the past, about the little part of the immense war they had fought together, as reported in the Tokyo edition of *Yank*:

> It was after midnight and the lights had just gone out. Someone moved restlessly in his bunk. "Damn fleas," he said.
>
> There was a short pause, and then someone else said, "Feed 'em, they're hungry." It was very dark; the voices sounded detached and impersonal. They seemed to echo in the big room.
>
> "Remember the last time we heard that?"
>
> "Yeah, Purple Heart Hill. That BAR man running up shooting."
>
> " 'Feed 'em, they're hungry,' he was yelling."
>
> There was a pause. "What was that kid's name?"
>
> "I don't know, some foreign-sounding name. Was he French?"
>
> "Was that the kid who was killed Christmas Day?" It was a new voice. The talk of people lying on their backs has a heavy, deliberate quality. The words came slowly.
>
> "No, I don't think he was killed at all. It was the kid who had the wave in the front of his hair and was always so careful how he combed it."
>
> "I remember."

"Remember the guys going up that hill being pushed from behind and yelling? Boy, that was a bitch." A match flared, and there was the glow of a cigarette.

"That was the place where the Jap yelled at us 'Come and get us, you souvenir-hunting sons of bitches!'"

"No, that was in the potato patch the day before. . . ."

They kept on talking, trying to remember the name of the kid who had led the way up the hill, discussing how various men had been killed, recalling the rain that had fallen six weeks, and the mail that had come just before they went up. The memory of the war, of that little war on the hillside almost a year ago, was getting rusty. They were trying hard to hold on to it.

★ 12 ★

Reunion

I STOOD near the door so I could watch them as they arrived. I knew that at these reunions there were sometimes moments of intense emotion; a man would recognize a buddy he had not seen in forty years and he would burst into tears or be incapable of speech. But I did not see anything like that. What I saw were men and women, in their sixties mostly, the men coatless, their wives in blouses and slacks (it was August, and Springfield, Illinois, was hot). They filtered in by twos and threes, and by late afternoon they had filled the motel lobby. Conversation groups grew or dwindled or split in two, amoebalike, in that ambience of easy sociability peculiar to Americans. They might have been members of a church congregation on holiday, or conventioneers of some fraternal organization. But this was the fortieth reunion of the "Railsplitters," the 84th Infantry Division, United States Army.

I had come to the Railsplitters' reunion because I believed that what I saw and heard there would help me flesh out the story of the

G.I. in the forty years since he returned from the war. The 84th Division proved to be a good choice. It was a "draftee division," one of those made up of Selective Service inductees from the outset. The division had been created in 1917 as the "Lincoln Division" and filled with men from the Illinois-Indiana-Kentucky region; sent to France a month before the Armistice, it never got into the line. The division came to life again in October 1942, when it was reactivated at Camp Howze, Texas. It did not reach Europe until two years later. It went into the line along the Dutch-German frontier in November 1944, took part in the Battle of the Bulge, and then in the final offensive into Germany. The 84th was selected for occupation duty, so it did not return to the United States until January 1946. Like other divisions fielded in a period of frantic mobilization, the 84th had no regional identity; the men it received came from the Selective Service quotas of many states. Judging from the accents I heard around me, the Army had seen fit to send to a division associated with Abraham Lincoln a sizable contingent of "good old boys" from the states of the former Confederacy. (In 1943 the Army also saw fit to give command of the division to a major general named Stonewall Jackson.)

I had been a practicing historian for twenty years, but never before had I had the subjects of my story before me in the flesh. I stayed with the Railsplitters for three days, and while I probably talked to no more than a small minority of them, I was considerably richer for the experience. They had furnished me with a name tag, and I moved among them easily, introducing myself and simply making talk rather than conducting interviews. But from time to time I would ask questions, trying to confirm impressions I had gained in my research. I asked one Railsplitter if mail from home had been that important to men overseas. He reflected a moment and then said earnestly, "It was more important than food and water."

For an old soldiers' meeting it had very little of the military about it. The only article of uniform was a white mesh bill-cap with the Railsplitter's patch on it. (I bought one but did not put it on; somehow it didn't seem right.) I noticed that the name tags made no mention of a man's former rank. Some men had tags with blue dots on them. These "blue-dotters" were men attending their first reunion, and I noticed a lot of them. The program of activities was leisurely and loosely structured; no one had to get up early except the participants in the golf tournament. The Railsplitters seemed to spend most of their time "socializing." There were little islands of people in conversation everywhere, and moving slowly around the islands were streams of white-capped conventioneers. Not until the third day would there be a business meeting.

The first afternoon I was content simply to watch them. In the "sociological" and statistical senses, I felt that I already knew them. I was not surprised, for example, to see almost as many women as men; the *Survey of Aging Veterans* that the Veterans Administration brought out in 1984 revealed that a very high proportion of veterans—84 percent—are married. I also knew that the median age of the World War II veteran was 63.2 years. In the V.A. *Survey*, nearly 60 percent of those polled pronounced themselves in good or excellent health, and the Railsplitters I saw around me seemed an especially vigorous group; I saw only one wheelchair and an occasional cane. (About one veteran in three is troubled by arthritis, while old wounds and injuries to the foot, leg, and back are among the most common service-connected disabilities.) But for the Railsplitters, as for their generation, time has become an enemy far more redoubtable than the Wehrmacht they faced forty years ago. The several hundred men who had come to Springfield were clearly holding their own, but the Railsplitter Association's newsletter told a sadder story; it carried death notices, letters from recent widows, and messages from men saying their physicians wouldn't let them come this time, and signing off with a jaunty "Proud to be a Railsplitter!"

As I watched these men in their sixties, I tried to imagine them in their twenties, when they came back from what was for most of them the greatest adventure of their lives. Just as the G.I.s looked forward to going home with great eagerness, so now they generally look back on the homecoming with fond memory: it was a golden time, when they had life and opportunity before them. In reality it was not that simple. While virtually everyone looked forward to the return, the soldiers' letters indicate some concern about what they would find and how they would fit in. Myles Babcock wrote: "The civilian political theorists would do well to remember the soldier lads are fighting for the way of life and the identical standards of living they abandoned when they left. Any radical changes will be condemned."

Yet Babcock also believed the returning veterans would be different men: "The exponents of 'live for the moment and damn the future' will acquire new disciples from the former men in khaki. . . . The smug, complacent, stilted life of a village shopkeeper or metropolitan haberdashery salesman is not for these." Some men were concerned that they would not be happy resuming their former existence. A *Yank* reporter detected this sentiment in an article entitled "Separation," which ran in September 1945. The reporter interviewed a corporal with a rural background who was particularly eloquent in this regard: "I never got much more than 15 miles from home. The Army's taken me through 15 countries from Brazil to Iceland and from Trinidad to Czechoslovakia. After where I've been and what I've seen, I couldn't settle down on any farm." When I asked a Railsplitter if he thought being in the Army had benefited him in any way, he answered instantly, "It got me out of the lumberyard."

The returning G.I. had some very specific concerns about earning a living. In June 1945, an I and E poll asked returning soldiers: "Do you worry about what kind of work you should go into after the war?" Of those responding, 21 percent said they worried "a lot" and another 49 percent acknowledged they worried "a little." Many feared they had fallen behind those who had stayed home. Then, too, no one knew how the nation's economy would fare after demobilization. Everywhere war plants were closing as the government canceled contracts. Some economists were forecasting a return to hard times; there were predictions that many communities in the South and West that had boomed during the war years would become ghost towns.

Experts in various fields spoke of the coming "veteran problem," as several million men tried to fit themselves back into civilian life. Some expressed concern over the return of mentally ill veterans who were "trained killers." A sociologist warned that ex-servicemen might have become so used to "an orderly world, of discipline from without, of paternalistic certainty," that they would have trouble coping when there was no one to tell them what to do. Some political analysts speculated that the ex-G.I.s might organize as a strong and possibly disruptive force in American politics. Significantly, as the war came to an end, both *Yank* and *Stars and Stripes* published numbers of letters whose authors called on G.I.s to organize and "stick together" after the war. Some political analysts believed the G.I.s would bring home a collective resentment against civilians; others felt they would be antimilitary. Anyone who listened to the conversations in the separation centers—and took them seriously—could only conclude that the returning soldiers had become militant pacifists. Men waiting for separation tried to outdo one another in vehemence: One man announced that if war came again he would hide in the Ozarks; a second swore that the next time no draft board would take him alive; a third would have his son jump off the barn roof carrying fifty-pound weights until his feet were too flat for the infantry. (When I related these stories to a couple of Railsplitters, they just grinned.)

These concerns over the veteran problem were all relayed to the American public by the media, chiefly the periodical press. Well-meaning authors sometimes stirred the very fears they were trying to allay. In April 1945, the *Saturday Evening Post* published an article with the reassuring title "They Won't All Be Psychoneurotics!" *Ladies' Home Journal* ran a series of articles on returning veterans and their problems; in its December 1945 issue it asked, "Has your husband come home to the right woman?" Any number of publications offered suggestions on how to treat the returning serviceman. Given this effort at indoctrination, it is not surprising that some veterans felt for a time they were under discreet surveillance by their own families. Sometimes a returning soldier's wife or mother would tell him in a flood of relief how glad she was that he had come back "normal."

In most cases coming home was attended by little shocks and adjustments. Often furlough syndrome appeared, only to fade after a few days or weeks. The returning soldier had changed in small ways that his family and friends could not fail to notice. He used words like "snafu," which he had to explain; initially he spent money a bit too freely, the way he had done in that other existence. He had learned to drink; his parents discovered this when he casually announced that he was going out for a beer. In most cases the shocks and adjustments were minor ones. The authors of *The American Soldier* talked of the G.I.'s return in their final chapter, and they guessed—correctly—that there would be no veteran problem: "Unless the data reviewed in this chapter are to be largely disregarded, there has seemed little reason for doubting the reabsorption of the vast majority of American soldiers into the normal patterns of American life."

The reabsorption was easy because in his heart and in his mind the G.I. had never left home; the military way of life mostly repelled him, and the foreign cultures he encountered did not appeal to him more than his own, so he returned pretty much as he had departed. Also, he came home to a genuine welcome, the sort any hometown accords to members of a winning team after a well-played game. In material terms his conversion to civilian life was made easier in the economic expansion and prosperity that continued a quarter-century after the war. Then, too, he enjoyed an unprecedented bounty of government programs to help him fit back into civilian society—everything from educational benefits and low-interest loans to medical care and the "52-20 Club" (twenty dollars a week unemployment benefits for fifty-two weeks).

Once they had plunged back into the civilian world, ex-G.I.s had little time or interest in organizing themselves for political or even fraternal ends. One of the Railsplitters' officials told me that for years just keeping the divisional association afloat was "mighty rough going." *The American Soldier* had been right in pinpointing "the absence of any pronounced tendency either for personal bitterness or for social action" among discharged soldiers. Nor did the ex-G.I. demonstrate pent-up bitterness in any other way: With one tragic exception—in Camden, New Jersey, just after the war—there were no cases of psychotic ex-soldiers running amok. Nor did the supposed wanderlust and restlessness of the ex-G.I. manifest itself in any marked degree in the aftermath of demobilization. A survey conducted in 1947 showed that in April of that year 85 percent of the discharged soldiers were living in their home state, while 72 percent of those aged eighteen to thirty-four—the most mobile group—were residing in their home county.

In 1951 a team of scholars headed by Robert J. Havighurst of the University of Chicago brought out a study entitled *The American Veteran Back Home*. It analyzed the lives of 416 veterans in a midwest community and compared them with men who had not been in the service; the study revealed "remarkably little difference in the adjustment of veterans and nonveterans four years after the close of the war." There was clear evidence that the veterans' fears of falling behind in the competition for jobs and careers had been groundless. By the time of the Havighurst study, ex-servicemen in large numbers were taking advantage of the educational and training benefits of the G.I. Bill—ultimately, almost eight million would make use of that program.

The Railsplitters are proud that they are an all-American mixture, that their members come from every walk of life. I was told more than once that some of the veterans in attendance were millionaires, while others, down on their luck, had been known to hitchhike to a reunion. One man told me to look in the motel parking lot if I wanted to see the variations in economic status among the Railsplitters. He was right; I saw everything from glistening Mercedes and sumptuous traveling homes to battered relics of the sixties. But statistics indicate that, as a whole, veterans of World War II have done well for themselves. The 1984 *Survey* revealed that nearly nine veterans out of ten owned their own homes, and that over half had paid off their mortgages (as often as not V.A.-financed mortgages). Using educational benefits as a springboard, a sizable number moved up into the professions. At the same time, sociologists found evidence that for ethnic minorities, notably blacks and Hispanics, military service was a "bridging environment," enabling them to move up the economic scale. Though by now about half of the World War II veterans have retired, 64 percent of those contacted in the 1984 *Survey* said they had "more than enough to get along on." The *Survey* concluded: "About thirty-five years after service, the average veteran appears to have a number of social and economic advantages over nonveterans of the same age. Compared to the population of similarly aged males, veterans have a somewhat higher educational level. They are less likely to be found at the lower end of the occupational scale than similarly aged non-veterans."

If the men ended by profiting materially from their time in service, it is only fair to ask if they also derived any cultural or intellectual benefit from their military experience. Travel, after all, is supposed to extend the mind's horizon, and the Army plucked countless young men from an isolated, provincial existence and sent them halfway around the world. Were they "broadened" thereby? The answer must be a very qualified yes. An officer writing in *New Republic* in 1943 predicted: "There will undoubtedly be a broader realization by millions of soldiers of the bigness and the wholeness of the United States." Soldiers' letters leave little doubt that this was the case: Any G.I. who traveled from New England to Fort Hood, Texas, or from Baltimore to Fort Lewis, Washington, on a wartime passenger train—usually jam-packed and behind schedule—had brought home to him the vastness of his country, and also its diversity. When the train entered Virginia the men would watch for cotton fields; when the conductor told them they were in Texas they would sometimes rush to the windows to look for cowboys. And if they saw places that had only been names in geography books, the Army threw them in with men from those places, and from every other corner of the country. They lived with them, they fought alongside them, and they often formed the deepest friendships with them. While most of the friendships were not kept up after the war, the memory of them is still very vivid. As I listened to the Railsplitters reminisce, I was struck by the frequent geographical references: "Hughie was a Georgia cracker, so he knew something about moonshine," "Me and this fellow from Wisconsin we called 'Moose' . . ."

In the Army, then, men discovered their own country, and a number of them promised themselves that once they were out of uniform they would explore it further. Typical of this feeling was a letter a corporal wrote home in 1944: "I intend getting that trailer I wrote you about, and going over the United States, taking pictures." Sometimes in his Army travels, a man discovered a part of the country he took a special liking to, and when he got his discharge he settled there. Today every southern city that was a World War II "camp town" has a sprinkling of male citizens in their sixties who have never quite shed their New England or Middle West patterns of speech. Most often they met and married local girls. An observer noted in the middle of the war: "The marriage records in county clerks' offices throughout the South tell the story of the ease in establishing cordial relations after the first shock of the invading Army has worn off."

A "mixing" of sorts also took place on an international scale; the opportunities here were extensive, since about two G.I.s out of three went abroad. During the war it was fashionable among social scientists to speculate on how the G.I.'s stay abroad would change his outlook, and some suggested that he might become a cosmopolite, "a citizen of the world." The I and E Division was intrigued by changes in the attitudes of the American soldier abroad, so much so, in fact, that it devised a very sophisticated survey of the readership of *Yank*: It was designed to show the subtle variation in readers' preferences between soldiers still in the United States and those overseas. To the surprise of its designers, the survey showed no variation at all: Wherever they were, G.I. readers liked the Sad Sack, sex, and humor. An I and E officer named M. B. Smith, writing in the *Harvard Education Review*, asked the essential question in an article entitled "Did War Service Produce International-Mindedness?" He answered his own question with a no. "The main effect," he concluded, "has been in the opposite direction." The Havighurst study of 1951 yielded essentially the same findings. The veteran seemed to regard the country's former allies "with tolerant contempt." As one ex-G.I. put it, "We haven't got it perfect here, by a long shot, but we're a damn sight better off than those poor bastards."

Here and there in letters from G.I.s, one can find a different view. The more educated and the more sophisticated, fortified by reading Dickens and Tennyson, would speak of England as a kind of spiritual home. Occasionally, if a man knew the language well enough and if he was persistent enough, he could begin to understand and savor the culture of France. But most G.I.s had neither the time nor the taste for such things. They looked around them as they passed through, they compared what they saw with what they already knew, and they were confirmed in their view that the American way of doing things was the right and the normal way. The final words of *The American Soldier* underscored this fundamental truth: "Though our armies crossed all the seas and lived on all the continents, the men whose attitudes provided the data for these volumes came home, as they went out, indubitably American."

This is not to say that the returning G.I. simply put his experience abroad out of mind. Many veterans of the European campaigns that I talked to said they would like to see those countries again (rather fewer indicated a desire to revisit the Pacific, though they often have fond memories of their days in Australia and the Philippines). And when he has the time and the means, the old soldier will often go back. The Railsplitters have organized two major expeditions to Germany in the past few years, and others have gone back on their own. Everyone I talked to who had made the trip was enthusiastic. Their itinerary is not the kind offered on the standard package tour. They go to places like Linnich and Geilenkirchen, and other little towns and villages that the 84th Division fought through in 1945. They will admire the cathedral at Aachen and the Rhine castles if they are part of the package, but what they really want to see is that little patch of woods where they were wounded, or the stone wall they leaned against as they sat in the sunshine and smoked a cigarette forty years ago.

This nostalgia for old battlefields is probably a by-product of the aging process; it certainly was not evident in the immediate postwar era. Then the G.I.'s desire was to reenter the mainstream of American life, to return to what he had known. This was true of most G.I.s but not all; one exception was the black veteran. While abroad he had often found an acceptance and had been accorded a dignity and respect he had never known before. This was particularly true of blacks from the South, and for many of them the return to the land of Jim Crow was no easy thing. It was not easy for one black G.I. who stopped in Americus, Georgia, on his way home: He made the mistake of reaching inside the white waiting room of the bus station to fill a cup with water. Local whites set upon him and beat him into unconsciousness. The soldier's name was Hosea Williams, and he would later march in the front ranks of the civil rights movement. In Williams's judgment, the conditions black servicemen returned to "engendered a bitterness that propelled many into the civil rights struggle."

Perhaps if I had attended the reunion of a black outfit I would have detected traces of that bitterness; but the Railsplitters were a "white" division, with a few American Indians and Chicanos as the only ethnic admixture, and among the conventioneers all was cordiality and fond reminiscences. They had no detectable animosity toward the Germans against whom they had waged war. They had no detectable animosity toward the United States Army, against whom they had also waged a war of sorts. Not once did I hear that epithet that once rang through barracks and bivouac— "the Goddamn Army." The Railsplitters—like all G.I.s—have long since made their peace with the Army, though for some the process must have been a long one.

When the men were mustered out forty years ago, most of them felt their service had harmed them more than it had helped them —such at least were the findings in I and E surveys. The men could not put the Army behind them fast enough. Though they were entitled to take a number of clothing items home with them, Orval Faubus noticed that at the separation center most men discarded everything but the uniform they would wear home, and some swore they would burn that. Every man was issued a gold lapel pin with the image of an eagle on it as a symbol of his service during the war; a few men who were discharged early found the pin useful to wear so that they would not be taken for draft dodgers; but soon the pin acquired an unflattering name—the "ruptured duck." The men would not wear it any more than they would have paraded their Bronze Stars or Purple Hearts—it was not the G.I. way.

G.I.s who published their memoirs in the years after the war often betrayed a lingering resentment. "I dreaded every day of Army life," wrote one. Another testified, "My strong aversion to militarism has remained intact." An ex-G.I. interviewed for the Havighurst study could see only a perverse sort of value in his years in uniform: "I've never given much thought to whether the war was worth fighting. I know the thing we were fighting for was democracy, and yet what they taught in the Army was just the opposite. So I guess in a way it accomplished its mission. The fellows who've been in the Army have learned to appreciate democracy just that much more."

Yet, deep down, there was in the ex-G.I. an impulsion not to forget, to somehow hold on to his Army days. He might have thrown his last remaining uniform in the garbage can, he might have spurned the "ruptured duck," but the most intimate, personal memento of his service he would probably keep. Ask any ex-G.I. where his dog tags are and the chances are nine out of ten that he will say, "In the desk upstairs," or "Somewhere around the house." Whether he fully realized it or not, there were other things—intangible ones—that the ex-soldier would have liked to hold on to, and when he could not, he felt a vague sense of loss. When Orval Faubus attended a reunion of the 35th Division some years after the war, he and an old buddy sat and talked about those lost intangibles: "We weren't homesick for the hardships of training or the dangers of battle, we concluded, but there were some things we missed in civilian life which we had known with our fellow soldiers. We were lonesome for the unequaled fellowship we had found in the ranks of our comrades. We missed the pleasure of the deep and abiding friendships."

This, I suspect, is what brings the Railsplitters together every year, though it is not the only thing; by now many have been friends for a half century, and when they're together they talk about many other things besides the war. But I also suspect that the blue-dotters, who seem to show up in increasing numbers every year, have come hoping to find something they have lost. I asked one of them if he had seen anyone from his old company, and he told me yes, he had recognized one man. I asked him if it had affected him. He said that it had, and I could tell as much from the way he said it. Most ex-G.I.s do not go looking for their past in this way—most do not belong to any veterans' organization—but somehow they must all commune with that past.

The third day I went to the business meeting. I had been wondering if somehow any privilege or distinction of rank survived among the Railsplitters. The meeting gave me the answer. The President was an ex-private; the Executive Secretary, whom I never heard called anything but "Buck," turned out to be a former major. The meeting followed the customary agenda for such things, with committee reports, announcements, and the like, but none of them seemed of great import or urgency; the Railsplitters had wound up their really important business forty years ago. Much of the program was ceremonial. They sang "The Star-Spangled Banner," then there was a scripture reading and prayer. There was the "Roll Call of the Departed." We listened as a voice slowly called the names of the Railsplitters who had died within the preceding year; occasionally the voice would hesitate or falter over a familiar name. Then a bugler played taps; here and there a Railsplitter dabbed at his eyes. Toward the end of the meeting we stood and sang "God Bless America." It is a song of the forties, not often heard these days. Whoever printed up the program had obligingly printed the words, but none of the Railsplitters needed them.

It was time for me to go. The reunion would go on for two more days; there would be an annual banquet, a bowling tournament, and the presentation of a Railsplitter of the Year award. But I had seen and heard enough. I shook a few hands, said good-bye to Buck, who had been my sponsor, and headed out of Springfield. As I drove out of town I reflected on the business meeting. It had been filled with God-and-country symbols, and the patriotic display had particularly struck me, because it was not the sort of thing the G.I. of 1945 would have felt comfortable with. In this respect the men had changed.

Then I began to think about something that I had looked for in the reunion but had not found. I had hoped to hear something quotable on the Railsplitters' role in the great struggle, something sincere and inspiring about their contributions and their sacrifices with which I could write finis to the book. Even without going back through my notes, I knew that I had taken down nothing of that nature. They had talked about everything but that. Here at least the men had not changed. They had scrupulously avoided that sort of self-advertisement. It was not the G.I. way.

Notes

Sources of text quotations not listed in the notes may be found in the bibliography.

1   The Draft

p. 3   "Every time they . . ." Gen. Louis B. Hershey, transcript of oral history interview, part II, p. 34, U.S. Army Military History Institute (USAMHI), Carlisle Barracks, Pennsylvania.

p. 8   "Nowhere in the . . ." J. A. Power, *You're in the Army Now!* (New York, 1940), p. 3.

p. 9   "My feelings were . . ." M. H. E. Marsden, *Khaki Is More than A Color* (Garden City, N.Y., 1943), p. 1.

p. 11   "We had a . . ." Quoted in Donald Dean Stewart, "Local Board: A Study of the Place of Volunteer Participation in a Bureaucratic Organization" (Dissertation, Columbia University, 1950), p. 182.

p. 11   "There was a . . ." Hershey interview, part II, p. 42.

p. 11   "We did not . . ." Holmes B. Springs, *Selective Service in South Carolina: An Historical Report* (Columbia, S.C., 1948), p. 3.

p. 12   "the boards were . . ." Raul Morin, *Among the Valiant: Mexican-Americans in World War II and Korea* (Los Angeles, 1963), p. 27.

p. 13   "What is the . . ." Quoted in Spencer B. King, *Selective Service in North Carolina in World War II* (Chapel Hill, N.C., 1949), p. 96.

p. 14   "a virtual blanket . . ." Selective Service System, *Problems of Selective Service (Special Monograph No. 16)*, 3 vols. (Washington, D.C., 1952), I, 207.

Notes

p. 15 "The War Department . . ." "History of the Office of the Director of Personnel, Army Service Forces," p. 47, typescript in the Office of the Chief of Military History, Washington, D.C.

p. 16 ". . . I noticed that . . ." Memorandum for General McNarney, December 27, 1943, George C. Marshall Papers, George C. Marshall Research Library, 65/41.

p. 17 "the most momentous . . ." George F. Jeffcott, *Dental Service in World War II* (Washington, D.C., 1955), p. 202.

p. 20 "the character of . . ." Robert R. Palmer, Bell I. Wiley, and William R. Keast, *The Procurement and Training of Ground Combat Troops (U.S. Army in World War II: The Army Ground Forces)* (Washington, D.C., 1948), p. 5.

p. 21 "the childlike greed . . ." Selective Service System, *Evaluation of Selective Service (Special Monograph No. 18)*, 3 vols. (Washington, D.C., 1967), I, 129.

p. 21 "I was in . . ." Ibid., p. 148.

2 Greetings . . .

p. 25 "There, for the . . ." Sergeant Don Robinson, *News of the Forty-fifth* (Norman, Oklahoma, 1944), p. 4.

p. 26 "the indulgence of . . ." Eli Ginzberg, James K. Anderson, Sol W. Ginsburg, M.D., and John L. Herma, *The Lost Divisions* (New York, 1955), p. 98.

p. 26 "The highest percentage . . ." Frederick R. Wulsin, "Manpower Contributions of Anthropology," in Leonard Carmichael and Leonard C. Meade, eds., *The Selection of Military Manpower: A Symposium* (Washington, D.C., 1951), pp. 174–75.

p. 27 "The number who . . ." Nicholas Michael, "The Psychoneurotic in the Armed Forces," in *The American Journal of Psychiatry*, March 1943, p. 652.

p. 27 "Many more are . . ." Sol S. Grossman, "The Psychiatric Screening Process for Selectees," in *Mental Hygiene*, April 1944, p. 228.

p. 27 "He taps the . . ." Arthur Miller, *Situation Normal . . .* (New York, 1943), p. 45.

p. 28 "an individual not . . ." Letter to State Directors of Selective Service, May 19, 1941, Hershey Papers, Box 58, USAMHI.

p. 30 "There were hectic . . ." Eli Ginzberg, John L. Herma, and Sol W. Ginsburg, M.D., *Psychiatry and Military Manpower: A Reappraisal of the Experience in World War II* (New York, 1953), p. 13.

p. 30 "Boys from the . . ." Ibid., 14

p. 31 "It was cold . . ." Marsden, *Khaki*, p. 6.

p. 33 "Our present social . . ." C. W. Wyckoff, "The Swing Age of Youth," in *Hygiene*, March 1940, p. 250.

p. 34 "We also had . . ." John S. Stradling, *Johnny* (Salt Lake City, 1946), p. 24.

p. 39 "a workable, practical . . ." William C. Porter, "What Has Psychiatry

Learned during the Present War?" *American Journal of Psychiatry*, May 1943, p. 551.

p. 40   "One hayshaker from . . ." Marsden, *Khaki*, pp. 14–15.

p. 40   "Tell all of . . ." Quoted in King, *Selective Service*, p. 308.

p. 41   "I just took . . ." Marsden, *Khaki*, p. 29.

3 The World of the Training Camps

p. 43   "demands for special . . ." Lenore Fine and Jesse A. Remington, *The Corps of Engineers: Construction in the United States (United States Army in World War II)* (Washington, D.C., 1972), p. 131.

p. 46   "the machine . . ." Quoted in E. J. Kahn, Jr., *McNair, Educator of an Army* (Washington, D.C., 1945), p. 24.

p. 48   "It is believed . . ." Typescript diary of General Paul S. Robinett, entry for August 6, 1941, Marshall Library.

p. 49   "It is doubtful . . ." John Sloan Brown, "Draftee Division: A Study of the 88th Infantry Division, First All Selective Service Division into Combat in World War II" (Ph.D. Dissertation in History, Indiana University), p. 57.

p. 50   "They picked up . . ." Report B-68, SWPA, June 8, 1944, p. 2, Collection of Observers' Reports, AGF, SWPA, USAMHI.

p. 50   "Training should be . . ." "Report of Col. Harry Knight concerning Observation in the S.W. Pacific Area during the Period October 16 to December 30, 1942," p. 10, Obs. Repts., SWPA, USAMHI.

p. 51   "The initiating of . . ." Col. Thomas J. Heavey, "Visit in England and North Africa, 13 October 1942–13 January 1943," p. 9, Obs. Repts., ETO, USAMHI.

p. 52   "as realistic as . . ." Boyd Shafer and H. Faber Underhill, "Military Training in World War II," typescript 2–3.7 AN (microfilm copy), USAMHI, p. 31.

p. 53   "The programs were . . ." Ibid., p. 557.

p. 54   "I cannot picture . . ." Quoted in Howard H. Peckham and Shirley A. Snyder, eds., *Letters from Fighting Hoosiers* (Bloomington, Indiana, 1948), p. 33.

p. 55   "The Northern boys . . ." George O. Marshall, Jr., *My World War II: The Home Letters of George O. Marshall, Jr., U.S. Army., 1943–1945* (Athens, Ga., 1983), p. 37.

p. 55   "The culmination of . . ." Brown, "Draftee Division," p. 68.

p. 58   "Frequently the choice . . ." Howard Brotz and Everett Wilson, "Characteristics of Military Society," in *American Journal of Sociology*, March 1946, p. 374.

p. 59   "The essential fact . . ." Ibid.

p. 59   "Most men attempt . . ." Kirson S. Weinberg, "Problems of Adjustment in an Army Unit," in *American Journal of Sociology*, January 1945, p. 273.

p. 61   "In the slack . . ." Larry A. Ingraham, *The Boys in the Barracks, Ob-*

p. 62   *servations on American Military Life* (Philadelphia, 1984), p. xvii.

p. 62   "a vital concern . . ." Henry Elkin, "Aggressive and Erotic Tendencies in Army Life," in *American Journal of Sociology*, March 1946, p. 411.

p. 62   "an aggression against . . ." Irving L. Janis, "Psychodynamics of Adjustment to Army Life," in *Psychiatry*, May 1945, p. 171.

p. 63   "Soldiers acquire some . . ." Brotz and Wilson, "Characteristics," p. 374.

p. 64   "He's scared to . . ." Brigadier General Elliott D. Cooke, "Racking Up the 8 Balls," in *Infantry Journal*, February 1946, p. 273.

4   The View from the Barracks

p. 67   "If you will . . ." Letter to Pvt. Melvin J. Stone, September 4, 1941, Marshall Papers 102/13.

p. 69   "An abiding faith . . ." Hilton H. Railey, "Morale in the U.S. Army: An Appreciation," written for *The New York Times*, 29 September 1941; this typescript is in the USAMHI Library.

p. 73   "The mail had . . ." Quoted in Studs Terkel, *"The Good War": An Oral History of World War II* (New York, 1984), p. 281.

p. 73   "We had a . . ." Ginzberg et al., *Lost Divisions*, p. 33.

p. 73   "Opinions written to . . ." Elliott R. Thorpe, BG, USA (Ret), *East Wind, Rain: The Intimate Account of an Intelligence Officer in the Pacific, 1939–49* (Boston, 1969), p. 112.

p. 73   "I read some . . ." Quoted in Terkel, *"The Good War,"* p. 372.

p. 74   "Life was so . . ." Quoted in Peckham and Snyder, *Letters*, p. 66.

p. 74   "a sentimental overvaluing . . ." Robert J. Havighurst et al., *The American Veteran Back Home: A Study of Veterans' Adjustment* (New York, 1951), p. 26.

p. 74   "For the American . . ." Meyer H. Maskin and Leon L. Altman, "Military Psychodynamics: Psychological Factors in the Transition from Civilian to Soldier," in *Psychiatry*, August 1943, p. 264.

p. 74   "In those last . . ." Robert H. Welker, *A Different Drummer: The Odyssey of a Home-Grown Rebel* (Boston, 1958), p. 123.

p. 75   "The older fellows . . ." Louis E. Rossetti, *APO 451* (New York, 1969), p. 9.

p. 76   "Even in the . . ." Alfred N. Mayers, "Dug-Out Psychiatry," in *Psychiatry*, November 1945, p. 386.

p. 76   "the sight of . . ." Maskin and Altman, "Military Psychodynamics," p. 265.

p. 77   "If animals could . . ." Elkin, "Aggressive," p. 412.

p. 78   "The principal industry . . ." Walter Bernstein, *Keep Your Head Down* (New York, 1945), p. 32.

p. 81   "The other evening . . ." Peckham and Snyder, *Letters*, p. 29.

p. 83   "There is an . . ." Heavey, "Visit," p. 7, Obs. Repts., ETO, USAMHI.

p. 89   "Tell the movie . . ." Extract of letter read by British censors, "Report of Field Censors, U.S. Soldiers' Mail, 1–31 December, 1943," FO 371/38504, PRO.

5 The Compleat Soldier

p. 93 "Any symbol or . . ." Maskin and Altman, "Military Psychodynamics," pp. 264–65.

p. 95 "I told him . . ." John J. Roche, First Squad, First Platoon, typescript in USAMHI Archives, p. 84.

p. 97 "They will endure . . ." William F. Ross and Charles F. Romanus, *The Quartermaster Corps: Operations in the War against Germany (United States Army in World War II)* (Washington, D.C., 1965), p. 35.

p. 101 "At three o'clock . . ." Letter to Gen. V. H. Peterson, January 19, 1943, reproduced in Jay Luvaas, ed., *Dear Miss Em: General Eichelberger's War in the Pacific, 1942–1945* (Westport, Conn., 1972), p. 37.

p. 102 "useless as a . . ." Lt. Col. Louis A. Walsh, Jr., "Report Concerning the Southwest Pacific Area, October–December 1942," p. 11, Obs. Repts., SWPA, USAMHI.

p. 103 "I wore a . . ." Rossetti, *APO*, p. 77.

p. 104 "There were men . . ." James C. Fry, *Combat Soldier* (Washington, D.C., 1968), p. 279.

p. 105 "virtually all items . . ." Brown, "Draftee Division," p. 103.

6 Aboard and Abroad

p. 112 "The current movements. . . ." HQ, Fourth Service Command, "Report to the Adjutant General, Subject, Absence without Leave of Enlisted Personnel, April 7, 1943," National Archives, RG 381, Box 66.

p. 112 "Psychoneurotics had a . . ." Ginzberg et al., *Lost Divisions*, p. 3.

p. 114 "Early the next . . ." Welker, *Different Drummer*, p. 112.

p. 117 "It seems hard . . ." Quoted in Yitzak E. Rontch, ed., *Jewish Youth at War: Letters from American Soldiers* (New York, 1945), p. 69.

p. 126 "The entire keynote . . ." Quoted in E. Daniel and Annette Potts, *Yanks Down Under 1941–45: The American Impact on Australia* (New York, 1985), p. 348.

7 The Challenge of Combat

p. 131 "for officers to . . ." Col. Robert O. Montgomery, "Report of Visit to 9th Division Artillery, 8–10 March, 1944," p. 2. Obs. Repts., ETO, USAMHI.

p. 131 "There was no . . ." Luvaas, *Dear Miss*, pp. 38–39.

p. 131 "There will be . . ." Letter to Gen. R. K. Sutherland, December 4, 1942, Eichelberger Papers, Carton 3, Duke University.

p. 136   "In some . . . the . . ." Lt. Col. Roy R. Grinker, M.C., and Capt. John P. Spiegel, *War Neuroses in North Africa: The Tunisian Campaign* (New York, 1943), p 32.

p. 137   "About ten percent . . ." Quoted in Walsh, "Report," p. 16, Obs. Repts., SWPA, USAMHI.

p. 138   "In civilian life . . ." Quoted in Rontch, *Jewish*, p. 147.

p. 145   "They're scared . . ." Quoted in Samuel Stouffer et al., *The American Soldier: Combat and Its Aftermath* (Princeton, N.J., 1949), p. 189.

p. 145   "Typically he appeared . . ." William C. Menninger, *Psychiatry in a Troubled World: Yesterday's War and Today's Challenge* (New York, 1948), p. 143.

p. 147   "But to a . . ." Report, "Subject: Battle Experiences, ETO, March 10, 1945," Obs. Repts., ETO, USAMHI.

p. 147   "Each company commander . . ." "Report on Operations of XIX Corps in Normandy and Comments Based upon Interviews and Personal Observations, September 17, 1944," p. 3, appended to "Interviews, Personal Observations, etc., in France, 12 August–15 September 1944," Obs. Repts., ETO, USAMHI.

p. 148   "My whole company . . ." Quoted in Rontch, *Jewish*, p. 216.

8   The Variables of Battle

p. 150   "I do not . . ." Ginzberg et al., *Psychiatry*, p. 26.

p. 155   "The conditions confronting . . ." "Operations of the Counterintelligence Corps, SWPA," p. 13, typescript in MacArthur Papers, MacArthur Memorial.

p. 157   "I stood over . . ." Roche, "First Squad," p. 59.

p. 158   "On a Sunday . . ." Patton Folder, Ed Ball Papers, University of Georgia Library, pp. 7–8.

p. 158   "Perhaps the most . . ." Brown, "Draftee Division," p. 203.

p. 159   "The first one . . ." Quoted in Rontch, *Jewish*, p. 140.

p. 159   "I killed my . . ." Appended to "Observations in France," Obs. Repts., ETO, USAMHI.

p. 160   "American troops acting . . ." Brown, "Draftee Division," pp. 337–38.

p. 161   "If a Heinie . . ." "Cavalry Notes," p. 1, December 23, 1944, Obs. Repts, ETO, USAMHI.

p. 161   "I have just . . ." Unmailed letter found on captured German paratrooper, appended to "Interviews, Personal Observations, etc.," Obs. Repts., ETO, USAMHI.

p. 163   "Your code is . . ." Corp. John Alexander, "So Sorry," in *Reveille: War Poems by Members of Our Armed Forces* (New York, 1944), p. 121.

p. 164   "Foremost in the . . ." "Comments of a Battalion S–3, Subject: Patrolling, February 20, 1945," p. 2, Obs. Repts., SWPA, USAMHI.

p. 165   "Another prisoner that . . ." Quoted in Edward J. Drea, *Defending the Driniumor: Covering Force Operations in New Guinea, 1944,*

Leavenworth Papers, no. 9 (Fort Leavenworth, Kansas, 1984), p. 58.

p. 167 "Troops have been . . ." Col. Harry Knight, "Report Concerning Observations in the Southwest Pacific Theater during the Period October 16 to December 30, 1942," Obs. Repts., SWDA, USAMHI.

p. 168 "the night that . . ." Walsh, "Report," p. 4, Obs. Repts., SWPA, USAMHI.

p. 169 "With the enemy . . ." "Characteristics of American Combat Methods on Guadalcanal, November 21, 1943," ATIS translation No. 56, pp. 2–3, MacArthur Memorial Archives.

p. 169 "The American soldier . . ." U.S.A. Heer, Kampfwert, Jan. 2, 1945, p. 20, RHD 18/168, Bundesarchiv-Militärarchiv.

p. 169 "So long as . . ." ATIS No. 56, p. 2.

p. 169 "In too many . . ." Col. Knight, "Report," p. 4, Obs. Repts., SWPA, USAMHI.

p. 170 "The Jap bayonet . . ." Lt. Col. Walsh, "Report," Appendix III, p. 3, Obs. Repts., SWPA, USAMHI.

p. 170 "You begin to . . ." Hugh Cole, "Observations of the German Military on U.S. Army Operations," speech delivered at USAMHI, August 1982, audio tape (Keycode 687097), USAMHI.

p. 171 "surprised, stunned, unbelieving . . ." Charles B. MacDonald, *A Time for Trumpets: The Untold Story of the Battle of the Bulge* (New York, 1985), p. 619.

p. 171 "first-rate, well . . ." Feindnachrichtenblatt Nr. 14 Besonderheiten des amerikanischen Kampfverfahren seit Beginn des deutschen Gegenangriffes am 16.12.44, January 20, 1945, RH 2/V 1838, #10, pp. 1–4, Bundesarchiv-Militärarchiv.

9   Their Luck Ran Out

p. 176 "With self inflicted . . ." Medical Department, United States Army, *Neurophychiatry in World War II*, vol. II., *Overseas Theatres* (Washington, D.C., 1973), p. 285.

p. 179 "His patient told . . ." John Randolph, *Marsmen in Burma* (Houston, Tex., 1946), pp. 152–53.

p. 180 "A wounded man . . ." 220 Military Mission Report (undated), WO 33/1820, PRO.

p. 181 "General Patton advised . . ." Maj. Gen. John M. Littlejohn to Col. Henry Bobrink, February 17, 1945, quoted in Edward Steere and Thayer M. Boardman, *Final Disposition of the World War II Dead* (QMC Historical Studies, Series II, No. 6) (Washington, D.C., 1957), p. 38.

p. 182 "Men lose their . . ." Col. Albert G. Wing, "Report on Graves Registration, January 1, 1945," p. 2, Obs. Repts., SWPA, USAMHI.

p. 183 "Being taken prisoner . . ." Edward W. Beattie, Jr., *Diary of a Kriegie* (New York, 1946), p. 12.

p. 186 "All our guards . . ." Sidney Stewart, *Give Us This Day* (New York, 1956), p. 84.

Notes

p. 187 "We feel that . . ." Calvin Ellsworth Chunn, ed., *Of Rice and Men* (Los Angeles, 1946), p. 223.

p. 189 "possessed of high . . ." Office of Planning and Program Evaluation, Veterans Administration, *Study of Former Prisoners of War* (Washington, D.C., 1982), p. 59.

p. 190 "Very softly, before . . ." Stewart, *Give*, p. 116.

10 The Liberators

p. 193 "Even when we . . ." Quoted in Rontch, *Jewish*, p. 138.

p. 194 "They hugged and . . ." Quoted in Terkel, *"Good War,"* p. 280.

p. 197 "The ordinary British . . ." Report of Mr. Tilea, WO 371/41864, PRO.

p. 200 "men threw away . . ." Letter to Maj. Gen. Horace H. Fuller, December 14, 1942, in Luvaas, *Dear Miss*, p. 25.

p. 207 ". . . the uninhibited girl . . ." Lt. Col. H. L. Welles, G–5, typescript memoirs dated 1946, USAMHI, p. 117.

p. 207 "While living among . . ." Mayers, "Dug-Out," p. 305.

11 The Conquerors

p. 213 "One of our . . ." Sayward H. Farnum, *"The Five by Five"*: *A History of the 555th Antiaircraft Artillery Automatic Weapons Battalion (Mobile)* (Boston, 1946), p. 37.

p. 216 "The crossing of . . ." Quoted in Earl F. Ziemke, *The U.S. Army in the Occupation of Germany, 1944–1946* (Washington, D.C., 1975), p. 139.

p. 217 "Observations of how . . ." Office of the Chief Historian, European Command, *Fraternization with the Germans in World War II* (Frankfurt am Main, 1947), p. 28.

p. 219 "It will be . . ." Quoted in Luvaas, *Dear Miss*, pp. 202–203.

p. 220 "Women will never . . ." Quoted in Harry Emerson Wildes, *Typhoon in Tokyo! The Occupation and its Aftermath* (New York, 1954), p. 21.

p. 220 "This city now . . ." Mark Gayn, *Japan Diary* (Rutland, Vt., and Tokyo, 1981), p. 47.

p. 221 "Off base, fueled . . ." John Curtis Perry, *Beneath the Eagle's Wings: Americans in Occupied Japan* (New York, 1980), p. 171.

Bibliography

Abbott, Harry P. *The Nazi "88" Made Believers* (Dayton, Ohio, 1946).

Ahrenfeldt, Robert H. *Psychiatry in the British Army in the Second World War* (London, 1958).

Augé, J. N., and Ferrier, P. M. *With the British and U.S. Forces at War: A Military Reader* (Paris, 1948).

Babcock, Myles. *A Guy Who Knows . . . Diary.* Edited, published, and copyrighted by A. E. Babcock and Norma McKee (n.p., 1946).

Baumer, William H., Jr. *He's in the Army Now* (New York, 1941).

Beattie, Edward. *Diary of a Kriegie* (New York, 1946).

Beebe, Gilbert, and DeBakey, Michael E. *Battle Casualties: Incidence, Mortality and Logistic Considerations* (Springfield, Ill., 1952).

Bernstein, Walter. *Keep Your Head Down* (New York, 1945).

Blum, Albert A. *Drafted or Referred: Practices Past and Present* (Ann Arbor, Mich., 1967).

Bolte, Charles Guy. *The New Veteran* (New York, 1945).

Bourget, Pierre. *Paris Année 44* (Paris, 1984).

Bowker, Benjamin C. *Out of Uniform* (New York, 1946).

Bradley, Omar N. *A Soldier's Story* (New York, 1951).

Breger, Dave. *Private Breger* (New York, 1942).

Carmichael, Leonard, and Meade, Leonard C., eds. *The Selection of Manpower: A Symposium* (Washington, D.C., 1951).

Bibliography

Chunn, Calvin Ellsworth, ed. *Of Rice and Men: The Story of Americans under the Rising Sun* (Los Angeles, 1946).

Chapman, Robert P. *Tell It to the Chaplain* (New York, 1952).

Cohen, Bernard M., and Cooper, Maurice Z. *A Follow-up Study of World War II Prisoners of War*, VA Medical Monograph, Sept. 21, 1954.

Colby, Elbridge. *Army Talk: A Familiar Dictionary of Soldier Speech* (Princeton, N.J., 1942).

Cooke, Elliot D. *All But Me and Thee: Psychiatry at the Foxhole Level* (Washington, D.C., 1946).

Cotterell, Anthony. *An Apple for the Sergeant* (London, n.d.).

Coughlin, Gene. *Assistant Hero* (New York, 1945).

Craf, John R. *Army Selectee's Handbook* (Palo Alto, Calif., 1943).

Crocker, Benjamin C. *Out of Uniform* (New York, 1945).

Curtis, John. *Pour l'amour d'une française* (Paris, 1958).

Curtiss, Mina, ed. *Letters Home* (Boston, 1944).

d'Aquino, Maria Luisa'. *Quel Giorno Trent' Anni Fa* (Naples, 1975).

Dickey, Charles Whitfield. *Here We Go Again* (New York, 1951).

Doward, Jan S. *Battleground* (Nashville, Tenn., 1968).

Draper, Theodore. *The 84th Infantry Division in the Battle of Germany, Nov. 1944–May 1945* (New York, 1946).

Drea, Edward J. *Defending the Driniumor: Covering Force Operations in New Guinea, 1944*, Leavenworth Papers No. 9 (Fort Leavenworth, Kansas, 1984).

Earle, Capt. George F. *History of the 87th Mountain Infantry* (n.p., 1945).

Eichelberger, Robert L. *Our Jungle Road to Tokyo* (New York, 1950).

Elting, Col. John R.; Cragg, Sgt. Major Dan; and Deal, Sgt. 1st Class Ernst. *A Dictionary of Soldier Talk* (New York, 1984).

Eustis, Morton. *War Letters of Morton Eustis to His Mother, Feb. 7, 1941 to Aug. 10, 1944* (New York, 1945).

Falk, Stanley L. *Bataan: The March of Death* (New York, 1983).

Farnum, Sayward H. *"The Five by Five": A History of the 555th Antiaircraft Artillery Automatic Weapons Battalion (Mobile)* (Boston, 1946).

Faubus, Orval. *In This Faraway Land* (Conway, Ark., 1971).

Fine, Leonore, and Remington, Jesse A. *The Corps of Engineers: Construction in the United States (United States Army in World War II).* (Washington, D.C., 1972).

Flynn, George Q. *Lewis B. Hershey, Mr. Selective Service* (Chapel Hill and London, 1985).

Foy, David A. *For You the War Is Over: American Prisoners of War in Germany* (New York, 1985).

French, Herbert. *My Yankee Paris* (New York, 1945).

Friedrich, Carl J., et al. *American Experiences in Military Government in World War II* (New York, 1948).

Fry, James C. *Combat Soldier* (Washington, D.C., 1968).

Gach, Gene. *In the Army Now* (New York, 1942).

Gaige, Corporal (Richard T.). *Me and the Army* (New York, 1943).

Bibliography

Giles, Henry E. *The G.I. Journal of Sergeant Giles*, edited and condensed by Janice Holt Giles, (Boston, 1965).

Gimbel, John. *A German Community under American Occupation: Marburg, 1945–1952* (Stanford, Calif., 1961).

Ginzberg, Eli; Anderson, James K.; Ginsburg, Sol W., M.D.; and Herma, John L. *The Lost Divisions* (New York, 1955).

———; Herma, John L.; and Ginsburg, Sol W., M.D. *Psychiatry and Military Manpower: A Reappraisal of the Experience in World War II* (New York, 1953).

Goldberg, Samuel. *Army Training of Illiterates in World War II* (Contributions to Education, Teachers College, Columbia University, No. 966).

Gray, Jesse Glenn. *The Warriors: Reflections on Men in Battle* (New York, 1967).

Greenfield, Kent Roberts; Palmer, Robert R.; and Wiley, Bell I. *The Organization of Ground Combat Troops (United States Army in World War II)* (Washington, D.C., 1947).

Grinker, Lt. Col. Roy R., M.C., and Spiegel, Capt. John P. *War Neuroses in North Africa: The Tunisian Campaign* (New York, 1943).

Gushwa, Robert L. *The Best and Worst Times: The United States Army Chaplaincy, 1920–1945*, Vol. IV (Washington, D.C., 1977).

Gustafson, Walter. *My Time in the Army: The Diary of a World War II Soldier* (Chicago, 1968).

Havighurst, Robert J., et al. *The American Veteran Back Home: A Study of Veterans' Adjustment* (New York, 1951).

Hillel, Marc. *Vie et moeurs des GI's en Europe 1942–1947* (Paris, 1981).

Hogan, John J. *I Am Not Alone: From the Letters of Combat Infantryman John J. Hogan, Killed at Okinawa*, edited by John J. Hogan's Friends (Washington, D.C., 1947).

Ingraham, Larry H. *The Boys in the Barracks: Observations on American Military Life* (Philadelphia, 1984).

Irgang, Frank. *Etched in Purple* (Caldwell, Idaho, 1949).

Jones, James. *WWII* (New York, 1975).

Jünger, Ernst. *Jahre der Okkupation* (Stuttgart, 1958).

Kahn, E. J., Jr. *G.I. Jungle: An American Soldier in Australia and New Guinea* (New York, 1943).

———. *McNair, Educator of an Army* (Washington, D.C., 1945).

Katz, Lt. Samuel I, and Miller, W.O. J.G. Jordan Y. *We Bought the Eiffel Tower: The Story of the General Purchasing Agent, European Theater 16th May 1942–1st September 1945* (n.p., n.d.).

Kenderdine, Maj. John D. *Your Year in the Army: What Every New Soldier Should Know* (New York, 1940).

Kerr, E. Bartlett. *Surrender and Survival: The Experience of American POWS in the Pacific 1941–1945* (New York, 1985).

Kertzer, Morris H. *With an H on my Dog Tag* (New York, 1947).

King, Spencer B. *Selective Service in North Carolina in World War II* (Chapel Hill, N.C., 1949).

Bibliography

Kleber, Col. Victor. *Selective Service in Illinois 1940–1947* (n.p., n.d.).

Koehler, Franz A. *Special Rations for the Armed Forces* (QMC Historical Studies Series II, No. 6) (Washington, D.C., 1958).

Kreidberg, Marvin A. *History of Military Mobilization in the United States Army, 1775–1945* (Westport, Conn., 1975).

Krueger, Gen. Walter. *From Down Under to Nippon: The Story of the Sixth Army in World War II* (Washington, D.C., n.d.).

Kuby, Erich. *Mein Krieg: Aufzeichnungen aus 2129 Tagen* (Munich, 1975).

Lambiase, Sergio, and Nazzaro, G. Battista. *Napoli 1940–1945* (Milan, 1978).

Leduc, Georges. *Occupation Résistance Liberation de Lagny-sur-Marne et environs 39/45* (n.p., 1970).

Leigh, Lt. Col. Randolph. *48 Million Tons to Eisenhower: The Role of the SOS in the Defeat of Germany* (Washington, D.C., 1945).

Leinbaugh, Harold P., and Campbell, John D. *The Men of Company K* (New York, 1985).

Lewis, Norman. *Naples, '44* (New York, 1978).

Longmate, Norman. *The G.I.s: The Americans in Britain 1942–1945* (New York, 1975).

Luvaas, Jay, ed. *Dear Miss Em: General Eichelberger's War in the Pacific, 1942–1945* (Westport, Conn., 1972).

MacDonald, Charles B. *A Time for Trumpets: The Untold Story of the Battle of the Bulge* (New York, 1985).

———. *Company Commander* (Washington, D.C., 1947).

McDonough, James R. *Platoon Leader* (Novato, Calif., 1985).

McWane, Fred W., Jr. *Memoirs* (Lynchburg, Va., 1951).

Maginnis, John. *Military Government Journal Normandy to Berlin* (Amherst, Mass., 1971).

Marsden, M. H. E. *Khaki Is More than a Color* (Garden City, N.Y., 1943).

Marshall, George O., Jr. *My World War II: The Home Letters of George O. Marshall, Jr., U.S. Army, 1943–45* (Athens, Ga., 1983).

Marshall, S. L. A. *Men against Fire* (Washington, D.C., 1947).

Mauldin, Bill. *The Brass Ring* (New York, 1971).

———. *Up Front* (New York, 1945).

Maule, Harry E., ed. *A Book of War Letters* (New York, 1943).

Mazure, Félix. *Deux lycéens chez les fantômes de Patton* (Paris, 1946).

Medical Department, U.S. Army. *The Blood Program in World War II* (Washington, D.C., 1964).

———. *Internal Medicine in World War II*, Vol. II: *Infectious Diseases* (Washington, D.C., 1963).

———. *Internal Medicine in World War II*, Vol. III: *Infectious Diseases and General Medicine* (Washington, D.C., 1968).

———. *Medical Statistics in World War II* (Washington, D.C., 1975).

———. *Neuropsychiatry in World War II*, Vol. II: *Overseas Theaters* (Washington, D.C., 1973).

———. *Surgery in World War II: The Physiological Effects of Wounds* (Washington, D.C., 1952).

Bibliography

————. *Wound Ballistics* (Washington, D.C., 1962).

Menninger, William C. *Psychiatry in a Troubled World: Yesterday's War and Today's Challenge* (New York, 1948).

Miller, Arthur. *Situation Normal . . .* (New York, 1944).

Montgomery of Alamein, Field Marshal the Viscount. *Memoirs* (New York, 1959).

Moorehead, Alan. *The March to Tunis: The North African War, 1940–1943* (New York, 1965).

Morin, Raul. *Among the Valiant Mexican-Americans in World War II and Korea* (Los Angeles, 1963).

"Old Sarge." *How To Get Along in the Army* (New York, 1942).

O'Leary, Sgt. Edward J. *Semi-Private, Or How to Be a Soldier in Ten Easy Lessons* (New York, 1943).

Palmer, Robert R.; Wiley, Bell I.; and Keast, William R. *The Procurement and Training of Ground Combat Troops (United States Army in World War II)* (Washington, D.C., 1948).

Peckham, Howard H., and Snyder, Shirley A., eds. *Letters from Fighting Hoosiers* (Vol. II of *Indiana in World War II*) (Bloomington, Indiana, 1948).

Perry, John Curtis. *Beneath the Eagle's Wings: Americans in Occupied Japan* (New York, 1980).

Potts, E. Daniel, and Potts, Annette. *Yanks Down Under 1941–45: The American Impact on Australia* (New York, 1985).

Power, J. A. *You're in the Army Now!* (New York, 1940).

Pyle, Ernie. *Brave Men* (Westport, Conn., 1974).

————. *Here Is Your War* (New York, 1979).

Randall, Howard M. *Dirt and Doughfeet: Combat Experiences of a Rifle Platoon Leader* (New York, 1955).

Randolph, John. *Marsmen in Burma* (Houston, Texas, 1946).

Risch, Erna. *The Quartermaster Corps: Organization, Supply and Services (United States Army in World War II)*, Vol. I (Washington. D.C., 1953).

Robinson, Sgt. Don, and Mauldin, Sgt. Bill. *News of the Forty-fifth* (Norman, Okla., 1944).

Rontch, Yitzak E., ed. *Jewish Youth at War: Letters from American Soldiers* (New York, 1945).

Ross, William F., and Romanus, Charles F. *The Quartermaster Corps: Operations in the War against Germany (United States Army in World War II).* (Washington, D.C., 1965).

Rossetti, Louis E. *APO 451* (New York, 1969).

Ruppenthal, Roland G. *Logistical Support of the Armies (United States Army in World War II)*, 2 vols. (Washington, D.C., 1953, 1959).

Schrader, LTC Charles R. *Amicicide: The Problem of Friendly Fire in Modern War* (Combat Studies Institute Research Survey No. 1) (Fort Leavenworth, Kans., 1982).

Simpson, Harold B. *Audie Murphy, American Soldier* (Hillsboro, Texas, 1975).

Bibliography

Springs, Holmes B. *Selective Service in South Carolina: An Historical Report* (Columbia, S.C., 1948).

Stanton, Shelby L. *Order of Battle U.S. Army, World War II* (Novato, Calif., 1984).

Stauffer, Alvin P. *The Quartermaster Corps: Operations in the War against Japan (United States Army in World War II)* (Washington, D.C., 1956).

Steere, Edward, and Boardman, Thayer M. *Final Disposition of the World War II Dead* (QMC Historical Studies, Series II, no. 6) (Washington, D.C., 1957).

Stein, Ralph, and Brown, Harry. *It's a Cinch, Private Finch!* (New York, 1943).

Stewart, Sidney. *Give Us This Day* (New York, 1956).

Stouffer, Samuel, et al. *The American Soldier* (Vol. I: *Adjustment during Army Life*; Vol. II: *Combat and Its Aftermath*), 2 vols. (Princeton, N.J., 1949).

Stradling, John S. *Johnny* (Salt Lake City, Utah, 1946).

Terkel, Studs. *"The Good War": An Oral History of World War II* (New York, 1984).

Thorpe, Elliott R., BG USA (Ret). *East Wind, Rain: The Intimate Account of an Intelligence Officer in the Pacific 1939-49* (Boston, 1969).

Toole, John A. *Battle Diary* (Missoula, Montana, 1978).

Tumey, Ben. *GIs' Views of World War II: The Diary of a Combat Private* (New York, 1959).

Vaïsse, Maurice, ed. *8 Mai 1945: Victoire en Europe* (Reims, 1985).

Weber, Wayne M. *My War with the U.S. Army* (New York, 1951).

Welker, Robert H. *A Different Drummer: The Odyssey of a Home-Grown Rebel* (Boston, 1958).

Wheeler, Major William Reginald, ed. *The Road to Victory: A History of Hampton Roads Port of Embarkation in World War II*, 2 vols. (Newport News, Va., 1946).

White, Walter. *A Rising Wind* (New York, 1945).

Wolff, Corp. Perry S. *A History of the 334th Infantry, 84th Division* (Mannheim, 1945).

Woolner, Frank. *Spearhead in the West, 1941-45: The Third Armored Division* (Frankfurt am Main, 1945).

Ziemke, Earl F. *The U.S. Army in the Occupation of Germany, 1944-1946* (Washington, D.C., 1975).

Index

Adler, Mortimer J., 5
Africk, Sanford, 148
Air Forces, 21, 30, 35, 38, 46, 86
Alcohol, 92, 152, 153; alcoholism,
26; "blowing off steam," 77–78;
Calvados, 208, 209; in combat,
143; Germany, excesses in, 217,
225; induction drunkenness, 26,
31; liberation army, excesses of,
207–9; overseas habits of G.I.,
123, 207–9; Railey report on
drunkenness, 69–70; returned
veterans having learned to drink,
233
American Medical Association, 14
American Soldier, The (Stouffer
et al.), 71, 84, 129, 133, 138, 139,
153, 233, 237
American Veteran Back Home, The
(Havighurst et al.), 234

Amicicide, 175–76
Aptitude tests, 34–35
Army, 4, 8; air cadet programs, 21;
Air Forces, 21, 30, 35, 38, 46, 86;
aptitude tests, 34–35, 38; combat,
see Combat; diversity of, 60–61;
draft, *see* Draft, the; Ground
Forces, 46, 47–48; induction, *see*
Induction; Interservice rivalry,
19–21; language of, 62–63;
mixture of men, 22–23; negative
view of, 79–85, 238–39; "New
Army," 8, 36; overseas movement
of troops, *see* Overseas movement;
pampering the G.I., 91–95;
PULHES system, 28, 39;
Quartermasters Department, 95–
105; Regulars, 77, 80–81; Service
Forces, 37, 38, 46, 47, 95–109,
127–28; Special Training Program,

Army (*continued*)
21–22, 35, 38–39; training camps,
see Training camps; veterans,
see Veterans
Army Life, 134, 135
Articles of War, 34, 52, 68
Artillery. *See* Weapons
AWOL, 112, 113, 139, 153, 154
Ayres, Lew, 16

Babcock, Myles, 132, 165, 167, 168,
176, 231
Baker, George, 88
Ball, Ed, 157–58, 216
Basic training. *See* Training camps
Bataan Death March, 163, 183
Battle. *See* Combat
Battle of Britain, 3
Battle of the Bulge, 170–71, 183, 229
Beebe, Gilbert, 175
Beery, Wallace, 79
Bernstein, Walter, 100, 136, 160–61
Black market, 201–5
Black soldiers, 25, 35, 175; aptitude
tests, 35; discrimination against, 14,
35, 237–38; draft representation,
11, 14; fights involving, 86–87, 221;
in the liberation, 194, 206–7; Navy
recruitment, 20; Regulars, clashes
with, 81; veterans returning, 234,
237–38
"Boomtowns," 77–78
Bradley, Omar, 145
Breger, Dave, 88
Bridge on the River Kwai, The, 189
British soldiers, 125–26
Buddies, 58, 63, 65, 139–40
Burger, Knox, 226
Burke-Wadsworth bill, 3–4

Casualties: beachhead assaults, 175;
dangerous jobs, 173–74; deaths in
battle, 172–73, 180–82; first aid,
177–78; from friendly fire, 175–76;
medical treatment, 178–80;
"million dollar wound," 176;
missing in action, 182–83; prisoners

of war, 182–90; remains and
personal effects, 180–82; self-
inflicted wounds, 176–77; statistics
of, 173–77; survival chances, 177–
80; telegrams home, 173, 180
Cherokee Indians, 11–12
Chevalier, Maurice, 206
Children: in occupied Europe, 199,
216; liking for G.I.s, 118–19, 199;
"mascots," 199. *See also* Fathers
as soldiers
Cigarettes, 94, 97, 100, 120, 205
Clark, Mark, 141
Clause, Georges, 210
Climate, 149–50, 152, 154–55
Clothing and dress: antagonism to
uniform and dress code, 81–83;
development of, 102–5, 108;
improvement for some, 40; M1
helmet, 104–5, 175; reception
process, 33–34; shoes, 33–34, 103–4;
sloppiness of G.I., 82
Coast Guard, 8
Coca-Cola, 93
Cole, Hugh, 107, 109, 170
College-educated men, 59–60, 80, 84
Combat: areas of operation, 127–28;
artillery, fear of, 135–36; automatic
response to, 136; battle lines, 127–
28, 151; bonding of men in, 139–40;
caste system in, 130; death in
battle, 172–73; 180–82; definition
of, 128–29; delusions in, 144;
discipline at front line, 130–31;
enemy opinions of American
soldiers, 169–71; enjoyment of,
137–38; fear in, 134–38; food in
combat zone, 132; humor in, 143–
44; isolation at the front, 132;
leadership, effects of, 140–43;
material conditions in combat
zone, 131–32; morale and fighting
spirit in, 133–40, 142–46; motivation in, 138–43; numbness and
breakdown, 144–48; prayer in, 138–
39; rank distinctions in, 129–31;
replacements, 146; rotation system,

146; rumors in combat zone, 132–33; sleep in combat zone, 132; snipers, 160, 167–68; types of soldiers involved, 128–30, 136–38; supply lines, 127–28; sustenance in, 138–40, 143–44; training methods, effects of, 49–50; trauma of, described, 147–48; treatment for exhaustion, 146–47; waiting, stress of, 150. *See also* Battle of the Bulge; Casualties; European war; Liberation; Pacific war

Communications Zone, 128

Conquest. *See* Germany, conquest of; Japan, conquest of

Conscientious objectors, 12, 16

Cotterell, Anthony, 125, 126

C ration, 99–100, 101, 132

Criminals, 18–19, 30

Dances, 5, 119

D'Aquino, Maria Luisa, 195

"Dear John" letters, 75–76

Deaths: in battle, 172–73, 180–82; in traffic accidents, 123. *See also* Casualties

DeBakey, Michael, 175

Dietrich, Marlene, 202

DiMaggio, Joe, 15

Discharge: plan, 223–24; waiting for, 225–26

Discrimination: in the draft, 11, 14–16; in induction and placement, 35–36

Diseases: in European population, 196; in Pacific war, 153–55; in prison camps, 188. *See also* Venereal disease

Division identity, 87

Dodd, Howell, 158

"Dogface Dictionary," 83

Dog tags, 182, 239

Dos Passos, John, 5, 6

Draft, the: actors, 15, 16; athletes, 15; black representation, 11; Burke-Wadsworth bill, 3–4; conscientious objectors, 12, 16; criminal records

of draftees, 18–19; defense plant workers, 14–15; deferments, 12–16; disadvantages and flaws, 10, 22; discrimination, 11, 14–16; educational standards, 18; effectiveness, 20–21, 22–23; ethnic representation, 11–12, 18; extremes of draftees, 23; farm workers, 15; fatherhood and deferment, 13, 21, 22; favoritism of boards, 11; "greetings" from draft board, 24–25; interservice disputes, 19–21; legislation, 3–4; letters to draft board, 13–14; local draft boards, 9–16; lottery system, 9; married men, 13; medical and dental standards, 15–18; minority representation, 11–12; numbers of draftees, 4; occupational deferments, 14–16; Pearl Harbor, effects of, 9; penalties for violations, 8; physical standards, 15–18; popular reaction, 4–9; protests, 4, 7, 8; registration, 6–8; of "troublemakers," 12; used in strikebreaking, 14–15. *See also* Induction; Selective Service Act

Draftaway (dance step), 5

Draftie (comic strip), 5

D ration, 100, 102

Eichelberger, Robert, 101, 131, 146, 200, 219

84th Infantry Division reunion, 229–30, 237, 239–41

Eisenhower, Dwight D., 82, 127, 200, 216, 218

European war: Ardennes, 170–71; artillery of Germans, 152; attitudes to and exchanges with Germans, 155–62; Battle of the Bulge, 170–71, 183; climate and terrain, 152–53; discharge, waiting for, 224–26; fighting and killing Germans, 159–62; friendly fire casualties, 175–76; German opinion of American soldiers, 169–71; map of combat zone, 127–28; prisoners of war,

European war *(continued)*
184–85, 187, 188, 189, 190; SS
troops, 161; surrender protocol,
160–62; truces and fraternization
with Germans, 157–59; weapons of
Germans, 152, 156, 160. *See also*
Germany, conquest of; Liberation,
the
Eustis, Morton, 142–43

Fathers, as soldiers, 13, 21, 22, 223,
224
Faubus, Orval, 82, 108, 125–26, 130,
146, 160, 161, 177–78, 180, 194,
208, 224, 238, 239
FBI, 8, 30, 71
Fear, 64, 113, 134–38, 145–48
Feather merchants, 78
Flamethrower, 174
Food: in the Army, 98–102; Euro-
pean shortages, 196, 197–98, 203;
in prison camp, 187–88
Foot inspections, 33–34
French, Herbert, 129
Friendly fire casualties, 175–76
Furloughs: "furlough syndrome,"
74–75, 232–33; induction furlough,
31; preembarkation furlough,
111–12

Gallup polls, 6, 11
"Gangplank fever," 113
Gas masks, 106–7
Geneva Convention, 164, 184, 185,
186, 188
Germany, conquest of: fear of
populace, 213–14; French
compared with Germans, 217;
nonfraternization orders, 211–13,
215–16; rape and pillage, 217–18;
relaxation in relations with
Germans, 214–18; women in
Germany, 216–17. *See also*
European war
G.I., origin and use of term, 87–88
Giles, Henry, 80

Ginzberg, Eli, 138, 145
"God Bless America," 190, 240
Goodman, Benny, 16
Grable, Betty, 49
Greenberg, Hank, 15

Harper's Magazine, 5
Harvard Educational Review, 236
Havighurst, Robert J., 234
Helmets, 104–5, 175
Hemingway, Ernest, 5
Hershey, Lewis B., 9, 10, 11, 13, 14,
20, 28–29, 30, 37
Hogan, John, 139–40
Holleyman, Percival H., 190
Hollywood, 52, 79, 89, 93, 189
Homosexuality, 29, 64
Hopi Indians, 7

Illiteracy, 18
*Index and Specifications for Occupa-
tional Specialists (AR 615–20)*,
37–38
Indians (American), 7, 11–12
Induction: adaptation to Army, 39–
41; aptitude tests, 34–35; Articles
of War, reading of, 34; assign-
ments, 36–39; clothing issue, 33–34,
40; combat soldier classification,
39; criminals detected during, 30;
dental health of inductees, 26;
departure ceremonies, 31; drunkenness, 26, 31; fingerprinting, 30; foot
inspections, 33–34; furlough for
inductees, 31; general service
category, 27–28; "greetings" from
draft board, 24–25; homosexuality,
29; malingering, 26–27; occupational assignment process, 36–39;
physical examination, 25–28, 32;
psychiatric examinations, 28–30;
reception centers, 31–41; rejection,
effects of, 28; "shortarm" examination, 32; injections given, 34; swearing in, 30–31
Infantry Journal, 134

Jackson, Stonewall, 229
Japan, conquest of: devastation in Japan, 220–21; discharge, waiting for, 225, 226; distance from populace, 219–21; economic effects, 221; racial confrontations, 221; relaxation in relations with Japanese, 221–22; women in Japan, 220. *See also* Pacific war
Japanese-Americans, 20, 35–36
Jeeps, 107, 180
Jehovah's Witnesses, 12
Johnson, Lyndon, 43
Jones, James, 138, 143–44, 145, 172, 178
Jünger, Ernst, 213–14

Kanin, Garson, 73–74
Kasten, Walter A., 213
Keitel, Wilhelm, 185
Kenderine, John, 24
K ration, 100, 132
Krueger, Walter, 33–34, 82
Kuby, Erich, 84

Ladies' Home Journal, 232
Lambiase, Sergio, 203, 204
Language: barracks speech, 62–63; civilians, derogatory terms for, 78; differences abroad, 122; G.I., origin and use of term, 87–88; profanity, 62–63, 76–77, 122; on sexuality, 76–77
Lear, Ben, 67
Leduc, Georges, 193–94
Letters: censorship of, 71, 73–74, 118, 141; combat zone, lack of mail in, 132; "Dear John," 75–76; death in action, news of, 180; "Green Banana," 75–76; "greetings" from draft board, 24–25; last letters home, 173; morale importance of, 71, 73–74, 75–76, 229; obsessions with, 73; Presidential letter, 114–15; to prisoners of war, 185, 188; shipboard letters, 118; training camp, letters home from, 53–54

Liberation: aid to populations, 198; alcoholic excesses, 207–9; audience to combat, 193; black market activities, 201–5; cast-offs of G.I.s, 199–200; celebration, 193–94; culture shocks, 206–9; devastation in Europe, 195–98; discharge, waiting for, 222–26; displaced persons joining Army, 198–99; employment to locals, 198–99, 203–4; food shortages, 196, 197–98, 203; in Italy, 194–95; in Lagny-sur-Marne, 192–94; "mascots," 199; in Mayenne, 192; in Naples, 202–5; in Paris, 207; purchasing limitations on G.I., 195–97; Reims, view from, 209–10; souvenirs of war, traffic in, 202; theft of supplies, 200–201, 205; tourist G.I.s, 195–96; welcome wearing out, 206–10
Life magazine, 68–69
Lincoln, Abraham, 229
Logistics, 91–98
Luce, Clare Boothe, 223

MacArthur, Douglas, 141, 150, 219
MacDonald, Charles, 171
MacLeish, Archibald, 5
MacLemore, Henry, 94
McNair, Leslie J., 46, 71, 92, 176
Maginnis, John, 208, 209
Mailer, Norman, 164
Manhattan Project, 10
Marching, 55, 82–83, 125
March to Tunis, The (Moorehead), 94
Marines, 8, 9, 79–80, 86
Marriage, 92; "Dear John" letters, 75–76; as deferments from draft, 12–13; impulsive, 74; strains of separation, 75–76
Marshall, George C., 16, 35, 38, 43, 44, 46, 55, 67, 68, 71, 79, 82, 92, 104, 180, 202, 225
Marshall, S. L. A., 133, 134–35, 137, 142, 174
Matchett, H. J., 134

Mauldin, Bill, 8, 33, 34, 80, 82, 88
Mazure brothers, 191–92, 199
Meadows, Maureen, 126
Medical conditions: battlefield
    treatment, 178–80; draft standards,
    15–18; foot inspections, 33–34;
    induction examinations, 25–30, 32;
    in prison camps, 188; venereal
    disease, 17–18, 32. *See also* Diseases
Medical Statistics in World War II,
    174
Men Against Fire (Marshall), 133
Menninger, William C., 145
Mexican-Americans, 12
Military Police (MPs), 85–86, 113,
    114, 153
Miller, Arthur, 40, 56, 58, 72, 85, 89,
    144, 160
M1 rifle, 106
Montgomery, Bernard L., 93
Moore, "Cy," 8
Moorehead, Alan, 94, 108
Morale: Air Forces, resentment of,
    86; Army, negative view of, 79–85;
    "blowing off steam," 77–78;
    civilians, resentment of, 78; in
    combat conditions, 133–40, 142–46;
    confidence of G.I. abroad, 124–26;
    crisis of 1941, 67–71; "Dear John"
    letters, 75–76; demanding nature
    of G.I., 97; division identity, 87;
    dress code antagonism, 81–83;
    "furlough syndrome," 74–75; letters
    to and from home, 71, 73–74, 75–
    76; maladjustment, 79; marital
    strains, 75–76; Morale Division,
    92–93; MPs, resentment toward, 85–
    86; North-South antagonisms, 60–61,
    81, 86–87; nostalgia effects, 74;
    opinion surveys of, 71, 133; over-
    seas movement, regarding, 112–13;
    in Pacific war, 155; patriotism, 89,
    90; phone calls home, 72; positive
    motivation of G.I., 88–89; Presi-
    dential letter, 114–15; Railey report
    on, 69–71; rank, resentment of,
    83–85; Regulars, clashes with, 80–
81; rivalries, 86–87; rotation system,
    146; rumors and gossip affecting,
    61–62, 132–33, 166–68, 213; salute,
    84–85; self-image of G.I., 87–88;
    sexuality, *see* Sexuality; on troop-
    ships, 116. *See also* Psychological
    conditions
Murphy, Audie, 136–37

Naked and the Dead, The (Mailer),
    164–65
Naples, Italy, 202–5
National Guard, 8, 67, 68–69, 71, 80
Navy, 8, 9, 21, 25, 79; favored status
    of, 19–21; recruiting practices of,
    19–21
Nazzaro, G. Battista, 203, 204
New Republic, 235
New York Times, The, 69, 88
Nimitz, Chester, 150
Nisei, 20, 35–36
Nuremberg trials, 185

Obscenity, 62–63
Occupation. *See* Germany, conquest
    of; Japan, conquest of
Officer Candidate School, 35
"Old Sarge," 24, 30
Overseas movement: aboard ship,
    115–18; behavior of G.I. abroad,
    121–26; children and G.I.s, 118–19;
    confidence of G.I., 124–26; cultural
    impact of G.I., 119, 121–24;
    economic impact of G.I., 119–21;
    embarkation, 114–15; furlough
    before, 111–12; girls overseas, 119;
    instructions to G.I., 121–22;
    Liberty Ship, 116–17; loud Ameri-
    cans, 123–24; morale regarding,
    112–13, 116; ports of embarkation,
    113–14; preparation for, 111–15;
    problems abroad, 122–24; on "the
    Queens," 115, 116; reception
    abroad, 118–26; reckless driving
    abroad, 123; replacements prior
    to, 113; screening prior to, 112–13;

sexual contacts, 121, 122; sinkings of troopships, 117–18; souvenirs for sale, 120

Pacific war: attitudes toward Japanese, 163–68, 170; Bataan Death March, 163, 183; burial of enemy dead, 181; climate and terrain, 154–55; cultural isolation in, 153; diseases in, 153–55; friendly fire casualties, 176; Japanese opinions of American soldiers, 169–70; morale in, 155; night fighting, 168; prisoners of war, 185–90; racial feelings, 163, 167; "superiority" of Japanese, 167–68; surrender protocol, 162–63, 163–66. *See also* Japan, conquest of

Pacifists, 7, 8
Paratroopers, 51, 87
Paris, 207
Patriotism, 89, 90
Patton, George S., 35, 82, 105, 107, 111, 128, 141, 145–46, 158, 181, 191, 216, 225
Paul Hamilton (ship), 117–18
Peace Mobilization Society, 4
Pearl Harbor, 9, 46, 79, 110, 111, 163
Pendleton, Nat, 79
Pepper, Claude, 4
Perry, John Curtis, 222
Pershing, John J., 28
Peters, Don, 182
Pocket Guide to Germany, 212, 213
Polish-Americans, 11
Prisoners of war, 182–90
Profanity. *See* Language
Prostitution, 77–78, 122, 203
Protests, 4, 7, 8
Psychological conditions: artillery shelling, 136; breakdowns from battle, 145–48; combat, 133–40, 142, 143–48; induction exams, psychiatric, 28–30; infidelities of women left behind, 75–76; nostalgia effects, 74; overseas movement, regarding, 112–13; psychopaths in battle, 138;

self-confidence, 124–26; training camps, strain of, 63–64; treatment for combat exhaustion, 146–48; veterans returning, 231–34; waiting for combat, stress of, 150. *See also* Morale

PX system, 57–58, 93–94
Pyle, Ernie, 82, 94, 96, 130, 133, 139, 144, 157, 180, 195

Quartermasters Department, 95–105
Queen Elizabeth (ship), 115, 116
Queen Mary (ship), 115, 116

Radio men, 174
Railey, Hilton H., 69–71, 78, 81, 82, 83, 89
Railsplitters' reunion, 229–30, 237, 239–41
R-Day, 6
Reader's Digest, 6
Reckord, Milton, 70
Red Cross, 94, 114, 161–62, 184, 185, 186, 187
Reims headquarters, 127, 209–10
Religion, 138–39, 140
Robinett, Paul S., 48
Roche, John, 157, 201
Rommel, Erwin J., 109
Roosevelt, Eleanor, 45, 132
Roosevelt, Franklin, 4, 6, 19, 68, 114–15, 124
Rossetti, Louis, 139, 195, 198, 199, 201–2, 208, 213, 225

Sad Sack, 61, 88, 236
Salaries, 94–95, 119–20
Saturday Evening Post, 232
Selective Service. *See* Draft, the
Selective Service Act, 4, 8
Seminole Indians, 7
Service Forces, 37, 38, 46, 47, 95–109, 127–28
Sexuality, 29, 32–33, 67, 153; attractiveness of G.I. abroad, 122; "blowing off steam," 77–78; "Boomtown" pursuits, 77–78; French

Sexuality (*continued*)
customs, shock of, 207; Germany, in
occupation of, 212, 213, 216, 217,
218; graphic "bull sessions," 76–77;
infidelity of women left behind,
fears regarding, 75–76; in Japan,
during occupation, 220; prostitution, 77–78, 122, 203; vulgarity,
76–77, 209

Shapiro, Sam, 116
Sinatra, Frank, 16
Slaughterhouse Five (Vonnegut), 188
Smith, M. B., 236
Special Services Overseas Unit, 93–94
Stars and Stripes, 82, 132, 213, 224,
225, 232
Stewart, Jimmy, 15–16
Stilwell, Joseph, 82
Stimson, Henry, 19, 35, 71
Stouffer, Samuel, 71, 84, 129, 138
Strikes, labor, 14–15
Sulzberger, A. H., 69
Surrender: prisoners of war, 182–90;
protocol, European war, 160–62;
protocol, Pacific war, 162–63, 163–
66; Reims headquarters, 127. *See
also* Germany, conquest of; Japan,
conquest of
Survey of Aging Veterans (Veterans
Administration), 230, 234–35

Tanks. *See* Weapons
Task Force South Pacific, 110
Thorpe, Elliott, 141, 154, 222
Tokyo Rose, 166
Toole, John, 80
Training camps: buddies, 58, 63, 65;
camps and forts, 42–44; casualties
in training, 51–52, 64; close order
drills, 56; college men, 59–60;
combat experience, effects of, 49–
50; construction of, 43–44; films,
use of, 49; gossip and folklore,
61–62; hasty beginnings, 45–46;
language of, 62–63; letters home,
53–54; likes and dislikes, 56;
marches and obstacle courses, 55;

North-South antagonisms, 60–61;
obscenity, use of, 62–63; overseas
training, 49; psychological problems, 63–64; realistic training,
50–52, 56; recreation, 57–58; rigors
of, 53–55; schedule of, 52–54; social-
ization process, 58–64; specialty
training, 47, 48, 49; standard cycle
of, 47–49; structure and appearance of, 45; subjects covered, 51–52;
"types" in barracks life, 61
Transportation, 107–8; wounded,
evacuation of, 179–80. *See also*
Overseas movement

Uniform. *See* Clothing
Union Theological Seminary, 7, 8
USO, 78

Venereal disease, 17–18, 32, 132, 153–
54, 203
Veterans: animosity to Army, 238–
39; black soldiers, 234, 237–38;
broadening effect of experience,
235–37; G.I. Bill, 234; government
programs for, 233, 234; interna-
tionalism produced in, 236–37; job
concerns of, 231, 234; medals and
decorations, 238; minority group
advancement among, 234; nostalgia
shared, 237, 239–40; problems on
return, 230–34, 237–39; psychological state of, 231–34; rank
surviving among, 240; reabsorption,
ease of, 233–35; returns to Europe
and Pacific, 237; reunion of
Railsplitters, 229–30, 237, 239–41;
U.S., appreciation for, 235–36
Vonnegut, Kurt, 188

Weapons, 105–7; artillery and tanks,
107, 108, 109; German weaponry,
152, 156, 160; improvisation in,
108; M1 rifle, 106
Welker, Robert, 74–75, 80, 129
West Point (ship), 115
"What the Soldier Thinks," 71

Williams, Hosea, 237–38
World War I, 24, 28, 33, 48, 88, 89, 106, 114, 150–51, 206, 207
Wounded soldiers. *See* Casualties

Yank, 46, 80, 83, 85, 86, 87–88, 92, 93, 98, 99, 103, 116, 119, 120, 122, 123–

24, 132, 163, 164, 213, 216, 217, 219, 220, 222, 224, 225, 226, 231, 232, 236

Yoohoo Affair, 67
York, Alvin, 10

Zanuck, Darryl, 52